Teach Yourself®

Perfect your French

Jean-Claude Arrag

For UK order enquiries: please contact Bookpoint Ltd, 130 Milton Park, Abingdon, Oxon OX14 4SB. *Telephone*: +44 (0) 1235 827720. *Fax*: +44 (0) 1235 400454. Lines are open 09.00–17.00, Monday to Saturday, with a 24-hour message answering service. Details about our titles and how to order are available at www.teachyourself.com

For USA order enquiries: please contact McGraw-Hill Customer Services, PO Box 545, Blacklick, OH 43004-0545, USA. *Telephone*: 1-800-722-4726. *Fax*: 1-614-755-5645.

For Canada order enquiries: please contact McGraw-Hill Ryerson Ltd, 300 Water St, Whitby, Ontario L1N 9B6, Canada. *Telephone*: 905 430 5000. *Fax*: 905 430 5020.

Long renowned as the authoritative source for self-guided learning – with more than 50 million copies sold worldwide – the *Teach Yourself* series includes over 500 titles in the fields of languages, crafts, hobbies, business, computing and education.

British Library Cataloguing in Publication Data: a catalogue record for this title is available from the British Library.

Library of Congress Catalog Card Number: on file.

Previously published in UK 2004 as *Teach Yourself Improve your French* by Hodder Education, part of Hachette UK, 338 Euston Road, London NW1 3BH and in US by The McGraw-Hill Companies, Inc.

This edition published 2011.

Typeset by MPS Limited, a Macmillan Company.

Printed and bound in Great Britain for Hodder Education, an Hachette UK Company, 338 Euston Road, London NW1 3BH, by CPI Group (UK) Ltd, Croydon, CR0 4YY

Impression number 10 9 8 7 6 5 4
Year 2017

To Lesley, Marc, Claudine, Élise and Poppy.

Acknowledgements

I should like to express my gratitude to all my family, who gave me their full help and support during the preparation of this book, to my friends who did not take offence at my monastic refusals to accept their dinner invitations, to my colleagues who granted me some free time when I needed it most, and to my native Lot-et-Garonne, just for being there to inspire me.

Abbreviations and symbols

See also the beginning of the French–English vocabulary section for abbreviations used in the vocabulary list.

masc./m.	masculine	d.o.	direct object
fem./f.	feminine	i.o.	indirect object
adj.	adjective	s.	subject
adv.	adverb	fam.	familiar
v.	verb	pol.	polite
prep.	preposition	lit.	literally
past part./p.p.	past participle	i/o	instead of
sing.	singular	🔊	recorded material
plur./pl.	plural		

Contents

Practise what you have learned with dozens of interactive exercises online at www.teachyourselfextra.com.

Meet the author

I was born in south-west France. After completing my secondary education, I went on to study English language, philology and German for a **Licence** (*BA*) at Bordeaux University. I then spent two years in English grammar schools as a French Assistant, before going back to France to do my military service. On completion of my national service duties, I returned to England, where I took up a post as Head of French in a Secondary School. I then went on to become Lecturer and later Senior Lecturer in French at what is now Huddersfield University.

In addition to teaching French full-time and at evening classes at all levels from beginners to postgraduates, I have also taught English to international students, done technical interpreting and translations for local companies, and have written dramatic material for a BBC French Language series and for the Open University.

As a result of this experience I have developed this course, which is written for readers with some knowledge of French. As your learning develops, I will help you to become more adventurous and to make your learning experience increasingly rewarding. You will gradually be able to deal confidently with a wider array of structures and situations, and I shall guide you in your progress. You will develop your ability to communicate with native speakers, to understand what they say and to respond in French in a meaningful way. Prioritizing does not mean overlooking other important elements of communication. These will not be forgotten, but I will introduce them to you when you are ready.

Depending on your level of French, you will be able to decide where you want to resume your learning experience instead of covering material you are already confident with.

In this course, you will find all you need to develop your skills to a level where you can enjoy talking and understanding what is said. The teaching notes throughout Units 1–10 provide comprehensive instructions on how to use the course to full advantage. Happy learning and **bonne chance**!

Only got a minute?

The French are immensely proud of their nationality, their language and their culture. They are ready to be critical of themselves (but do not always take kindly to someone criticizing them!). Any attempt by a foreigner to speak their own language will be greatly appreciated and will help create positive feelings, which will lead to closer links. What in your mind appears as a feeble effort to express yourself in French will be met by encouraging comments such as: '**Ah, vous parlez bien français!**' ('*Oh, you speak good French!*'), or '**Vous avez un très bon accent!**' ('*You have a very good accent!*'). This may even lead to: '**Venez prendre un petit apéritif avec nous**' ('*Come and have a little aperitif with us*'). Note, however, that the word **petit** is a term of affection and in no way reflects the size of the drink! When French people have warmed to you, they may well ask you for a meal: '**Venez manger à la maison!**' ('*Come and have a meal at our house!*'). Lifelong friendships have been known to develop from such modest beginnings! Don't be surprised or offended, however, if your new French friends are keen to show you that they know a little English.

You should also bear in mind that French spoken with an English accent is perceived as 'sexy', but then the same is said in England about a French accent!

5 Only got five minutes?

As a learner of French, one useful thing for you to note is that a very large number of words of Latin origin can be found in both English and French with similar meanings. If, as is now claimed, it is true that at least a third of English words are of Latin origin, this will give you an enormous advantage when it comes to developing your vocabulary. To convince yourself of this you only need to leaf through a good English dictionary, where you will usually find the origin of the word at the end of each definition. Historically, the dual influence of Old English and Latin has often led to doublets, that is to say words from different origins having the same or very similar meaning; for instance: freedom and liberty, feud and hostility, foe and enemy, guilt and culpability, halt and stop, ownership and possession, weapons and arms, etc. Knowledge of the existence of these Latin-based words in English will make the acquisition of new French vocabulary quite easy. Although it is true that Latin-based words usually belong to a more elevated language register, they are nevertheless frequently used and (with some exceptions) you can try them out in French with a high degree of confidence.

There are also numerous commonly used expressions and sayings which have been borrowed from French: for a start, the mottos of the Royal Coat of Arms and the Most Noble Order of the Garter: **'Dieu et mon droit'** ('*God and my right*'), **'Honni soit qui mal y pense'** ('*Evil unto him who evil thinks*'), as well as a host of others: **coup de grâce, double entendre, je ne sais quoi, laissez-faire, tête à tête, bon vivant/bon viveur, bon voyage**, etc.

An additional advantage of the co-existence of Latin-based vocabulary in the two languages is that, with certain categories of nouns, you can predict the gender of the French equivalent, for example:

Most abstract nouns (i.e. referring to concepts rather than concrete things) ending in *-ty* have a French equivalent in **-té.** All are feminine: **autorité, beauté, nationalité, opportunité, réalité, virilité**, etc.

Most nouns in *-tion* and *-(s)sion* have a French equivalent: **abstention, condition, détermination, émotion, préparation, réaction, solution, tentation, admission, confession, passion, aversion**, etc. All are feminine.

Most English nouns ending in *-ism* have a French equivalent in **-isme**, and all are masculine: **altruisme, fascisme, réalisme, socialisme, tourisme, vandalisme**, etc.

This means that when making up a sentence containing these words, you will know what the form of the adjective should be, since you have learnt that French adjectives, unlike English ones, become masculine, feminine, singular or plural according to the gender and number of the noun they relate to: if you wish to mention *the French nationality* or *a great emotion*, you will say: **la nationalité française** (and not le nationalité français), and **une grande émotion** (and not **un grand émotion**). So, you could start thinking about how many of these words you know and jotting them down!

Language learning is in part akin to detective work. You must keep your eyes peeled and your ears open, compare what you already know and what you are hearing, make up your own theories about what you have learnt, and experiment. This is the key to effective and rewarding learning!

10 Only got ten minutes?

French has for many centuries been the favoured language of the educated classes of Europe. In the 17th and 18th centuries, the nobility of most European courts (Prussia, Austria, Russia ...) used French as its lingua franca (a language systematically used to communicate between persons not sharing a mother tongue). France was internationally recognized as the centre of artistic, literary and cultural excellence. The 17th century was marked by the personality and work of **René Descartes**, scientist and philosopher, author of the famous statement: '**Je pense donc je suis**' ('*I think therefore I am*'). Despite having given way to English as the new international language, French, which played a key role in **le Siècle des Lumières** (the Age of Enlightenment that was the 18th century), is still spoken in over 50 countries by more than 270 million people. In the eyes of many, France remains a country much admired. It was no accident, for example, that writers from all over the world congregated in Paris at the end of the Second World War to debate the merits of various literary movements or philosophical doctrines (in particular the existentialism of **Jean-Paul Sartre** and **Simone de Beauvoir**) in the cafés of **Saint Germain-des-Prés.**

Historically, the key factor for the development of French was its adoption as the official language, set out by the **Ordinance of Villers-Cotterêts** (1539), which decreed that from that date, all administrative and legal documents were to be written in French and not in Latin as had been the norm until then. This measure forced people in key posts to use exclusively the now official language. This, however, did not mean that from that time onwards everybody in France spoke French. There were a number of regional languages, patois and dialects which made communication and commercial activities difficult between people from different geographical areas. The stated aim of that measure, which was endorsed by successive national governments, was to eradicate regional differences and to create one national language. To ensure the effectiveness of the

Ordinance, the French Academy, **l'Académie Française**, was created in 1635. It was a learned body composed of respected intellectuals and members of different professions. Its work was to be devoted to the preservation of the purity of the French language. It was then decided that, because Paris was the official seat of administrative and political power, the national language would be based on **la langue d'oïl** (**oïl** meaning *yes* and pronounced like the English 'hoi' in 'hoi polloi') used in the north of France. At that time, poets and writers also devoted themselves to the enrichment of the French language. Two of the most famous names of that period are those of **Pierre de Ronsard** and **Joachim du Bellay**, both members of a group of poets called **La Pléiade**, whose literary manifesto '**Défense et illustration de la langue française**' was written by **du Bellay**. In their work, they introduced large numbers of words and expressions to instil new energy into the language.

The **Académie** still exists today, and its 40 members, **les Immortels** (*the Immortals*), work tirelessly for the production, review and updating of the **Dictionnaire de l'Académie Française** and the weeding out of words or expressions inappropriate to the purity of the language. Nowadays, one of the constant headaches of the **Académie** is the proliferation of Anglicisms and Americanisms, particularly in the fields of IT, business, science and technology. The government has tried (without much success) to stem the flow of these expressions, collectively referred to as **le Franglais**, by introducing legislation forbidding the use of English words in official documents, but the versatility and flexibility of English, coupled with the technological innovations of the Anglo-Saxon world, means that words to describe new processes are coined much more easily than in French and 'exported' throughout the world. Sometimes, however, the meaning of those Franglais words is only distantly related to the original: **le footing** is *jogging*, **le catch** is *wrestling*, **le starter** is *the choke*, whereas **un jogging** is *a jogging suit*, and **un relook(ing)** is *a makeover*. As for **le ball-trap**, an English speaker may be hard-pressed to guess that it means *clay pigeon shooting*! A useful pointer: all Franglais words are masculine, unless they refer to a woman e.g. **la call-girl, la script-girl ...**

In a further effort to control the influence of English, the government has recently imposed quotas on the percentage of American and English pop songs broadcast by the French media!

The covert reason for the imposition of **la langue d'oïl** as the official language in the 17th century was political. People in **Occitanie,** the area south of the Massif Central, spoke **la langue d'oc** (from the particle **oc** also meaning *yes*). This was seen as a threat to the king's power. So, after having remained throughout the Middle Ages a centre of cultural enlightenment and commercial excellence, **l'Occitanie** was devastated in the 13th century by a Crusade called by Pope Innocent III and King Louis VIII of France. Allegedly, the aim of the Crusade was to put an end to the **Cathar** (or Albigensian) **Heresy.** Innocent III was reported to have told the crusaders: '**Tuez les tous, Dieu reconnaîtra les siens**' ('*Kill them all, God will recognize his own*'). As a consequence, the **Occitan** area was brought to its knees and mercilessly plundered. Hosts of people were massacred and all the confiscated territories were claimed by the king.

Despite this, **Occitan** continued to be spoken in the South and is still thriving to this day. It is said to be used by approximately 8 million people, not only among the older generations, but also among young people, eager to rediscover the beauty of the language, its writers, its poets, and its history. This has been aided by European directives fostering the revival of regional languages and by the efforts of dedicated individuals who run summer schools in **Occitan** (**Escòlas Occitanas d'Estiu**). Furthermore, other regional languages (**Breton, Alsacien, Catalan, Basque ...**) which, after the 1539 **Ordinance,** were relegated to the rank of dialects or patois, have regained respectability: French universities now offer them for study at graduate and postgraduate levels.

The determination of successive governments' policies to eradicate all but the official language led to great efforts to stop children from using regional languages at schools. This practice was continued until the 1950s and the author of this book, who spoke **Occitan** as his second language, was frequently punished for using it in the playground.

French regional variations

Because the meaning of words like *accent*, *patois*, *dialect* and *slang* is not always very clear, it can lead to confusion in the minds of learners. Let's try to clarify them:

Accent: This is the way Standard French is pronounced in a given area. The standard grammar and word order are (more or less) respected, but the words are said in a way characteristic of the region considered. Consequently, an accent marks the speaker as a member of a geographical or social group. The educated Parisian accent is accepted as the norm and used by presenters on radio and television. The southern accent is characterized by strongly articulated vowels, including the -e which sounds similar to the vowel in Standard English 'fir'. People from other areas of France often make reference to the 'cheery' and 'sunny' quality of the southern accent!

Patois: This way of speaking does not always follow the grammar or pronunciation rules of the standard language. In France, patois are generally used by ageing members of a rural community. They vary from area to area and are not always understandable by Standard French speakers. The economic development and the rural exodus (movement of people to big cities between the 1950s and the mid-1970s) have dealt them a serious blow and led to a decline in the number of such speakers. Using patois is definitely seen as 'uncool' by younger generations.

Dialect: The traditional meaning refers to a way of speaking characteristic of a small regional area. Each dialect has its own grammar, pronunciation and vocabulary. Formerly, they used to create a strong sense of identity within a given community. As society progressed, dialects began to be considered by speakers of Standard French as unrefined, and young people refused to use them, believing it made them sound like uneducated peasants. Schools also frowned upon dialects being used in the playground. As a consequence, regional dialects have slowly been disappearing and are now, like patois, mostly spoken by ageing members of the population in rural areas. There is, however, another meaning to the word: it refers to vocabulary and expressions linked with certain types of professional activity: technicians, engineers, students, doctors, soldiers, etc. Unlike regional dialects, these are still thriving. There are also urban dialects spoken by certain minorities wanting to assert their identity. The dividing line between these and slang is often blurred (see below).

Slang (**l'argot**) is a form of speech which wilfully disregards the basic rules of the language. According to some linguists, slang, which they see as a secret code originally developed by members of the criminal underworld, was and is still used to create a sense of belonging within a tight-knit group and to exclude those who do not belong to that group. This is the case of **verlan** (*backslang*), mostly spoken by young people from a working-class, urban background. Words are created by switching the order of syllables as in: **chébran** (for **branché** – *trendy*), **bléca** (for **câblé** – *in the know*), **un ripou** (for **un pourri** – *a 'bent copper'*), or in more cryptic forms like **keuf** (for **flic** – *policeman*) or **meuf** (for **femme** – *woman*). The constant invention of new vocabulary makes it difficult for speakers of Standard French to understand **verlan**.

Sometimes **argot** is also used to refer to a way of speaking which, while preserving the basic characteristics of the standard language, uses a vocabulary specific to a social or professional group (school slang, military slang, etc.). In this latter sense, it is similar to the second meaning of the word 'dialect'.

Some of the variations encountered in France are not dialects but proper languages. This is the case of **Breton**, the language spoken in Brittany, which is Celtic in origin.

Alsacien, spoken in Alsace, has more in common with High German than with French. **Occitan**, mentioned above, and **Catalan,** spoken in France and Spain on the Mediterranean side of the Pyrenees, are also Latin-based languages which are both closer to

Spanish than French. If you visit those areas, you may well hear them in small and medium-sized southern towns on market days.

The list of regional languages would not be complete without mention of **Basque**, spoken on the Atlantic side of the Pyrenees in both France and Spain. The origins of the Basque language are still shrouded in mystery. The Basque people are fiercely 'nationalistic': they want to be independent from both France and Spain and some are prepared to use violence to achieve that aim.

Introduction

Learning a language: a few tips

A great deal of intellectual material has been produced on the art of language learning and, as a result, a good many potential learners have been put off by words like *grammar, tenses, moods,* etc. To make things worse, language experts have stated that 'some of us have a natural ability to learn languages and others have not'. Although there may be a certain amount of truth in such a statement, many modern linguists now believe that, since we have been able to learn our native language successfully without being conscious of categories such as *nouns, adverbs, prepositions,* or of such skills as phonetics or phonology (the study of speech sounds and systems), there is no reason why we should not be able to use such innate skills again, given the right circumstances and frame of mind.

One of the factors that hinders the progress of language learners is their self-consciousness. Two important things should be pointed out to them: the first is that young children, when learning their language, do not worry unduly over the fact that they may sound 'funny' or inaccurate: they will say and repeat any words they come across because they are fascinated by sounds and want to test their ability to reproduce what they hear. Their accuracy improves with age, but they are not afraid to 'have a go'. This desire to experiment is not just confined to sounds. It also covers words, phrases and sentences.

On the basis of what has been heard previously, the child's brain will formulate his or her own 'theories', without even being conscious of what the process involves. Not yet aware of the fact that all 'doing words' (verbs) do not behave in the same way, he/she will say 'I seed' for 'I saw' or 'he singed' for 'he sang'. This is because the child's brain is latching onto a pattern and trying to make sense of the incoming information on the basis of what he/she knows already. Mistakes – if any – will be corrected on the strength of new information, before going into the long-term memory store.

Another reason for many people's lack of success in language learning is the fear of appearing or sounding stupid. It is fairly common to hear learners say 'I don't like speaking a foreign language, because I feel silly when I do'. They should be reassured: in the same way as many British people like a French accent, an English accent is perceived by most French people as appealing and – dare we say it – even sexy.

So our advice is:

- do not be afraid to make mistakes; and
- do not feel silly because you can't (to begin with at least) speak French 'like a native'.

Another very important thing to realize is that communicating usually involves trying to transmit a message. The most important thing we know about such a message is that it must make sense. So, the need to say something absolutely perfectly is not essential for being understood. The person receiving the message will try to make sense of it, using all the means at his or her disposal to do so. You do the same in your own language: should a French person say to you what sounds like 'I came across on a big sheep', you will immediately reject what you have actually heard, and replace it with what makes sense according to what you know, 'I came across on a big ship'.

When learning a language, train your brain to act as a detective: keep your eyes and ears open at all times (on the bus, the train, in the street ...). That way, you will learn an amazing amount from listening not only to adults, but also to children – even young ones. Words, phrases, shop signs, adverts, etc. will give you plenty of food for thought and very often there will be clues to guide you towards the meaning. Do not hesitate to formulate your own theories about the things you learn. Keep saying to yourself 'I wonder if ...'. As suggested earlier, look for clues, practise whatever you have discovered or learnt, and try out your theories on native speakers. If what you say is not correct, you will generally be put right later. When in the company of French people, encourage them to correct you if what you say is wrong. Humility pays off!

Do not try to run before you can walk, but be positive: build up your confidence first, and remember that you can do a great deal of learning on your own and that most of the time you can reformulate complicated ideas in a simpler way – this is a good exercise. Another very effective way of making quick progress is to practise conversations or dialogues in advance, by imagining what is likely to happen when you go into a shop, a bank, etc. Prepare what you are going to say (greetings, questions, apologies, etc.). Try to anticipate other people's statements, responses or questions. This should be fairly easy, provided you know what you want. Rehearse what you would say in the privacy of your own mind, and when the time comes, the words you prepared will roll off your tongue!

Finally, make sure you have access to a good bilingual dictionary and reference grammar. We give some help, with appendices and a French–English vocabulary at the back of this book, but we cannot hope to provide the depth and detail that you really need to get the most out of your language studies. Once you have completed the course you can practise what you have learned with dozens of interactive exercises online at www.teachyourselfextra.com.

We hope you find this book both enjoyable and profitable.

Bon courage!

1

L'Hexagone

In this unit you will learn (or revise)

- ***Some basic facts about the geography and the economy of france***
- ***How to say 'some' ('several' and 'a certain amount')***
- ***How to give information about a person***
- ***How to use* encore *and* toujours *with the present tense***
- ***How to translate 'for' and 'since' in relation to the present***
- ***How french verbs are organized and identified (moods and groups)***
- ***How to recognize and form the present tense of the three groups***
- ***About france's administrative divisions***
- ***How to locate the french regions***
- ***How to recognize which area something (or somebody) comes from***

L'Hexagone

It seems strange that France should sometimes be referred to as **l'Hexagone**. If, however, we look at the map on the next page, the reason becomes clear: drawing straight lines to join the extreme points of the country gives an almost perfect six-sided geometrical figure (a hexagon).

France is about 19 times smaller than the United States. It is over twice as large as Great Britain. As a result of it stretching inland for 1,000 kilometres, it has a variety of distinctive features (landscapes, climate, rivers ...) some of which will be briefly presented in this unit, through text, dialogues and maps.

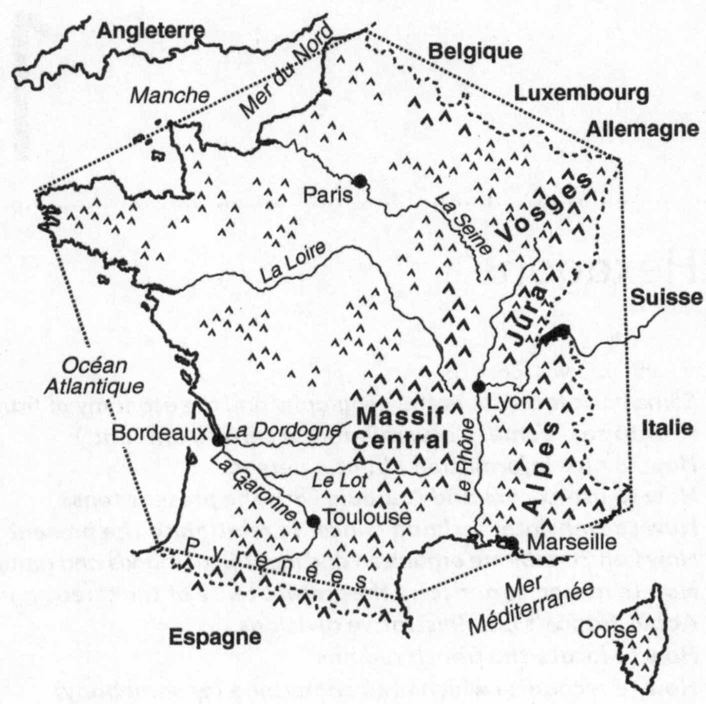

L'Hexagone: fleuves et relief.

> **Insight**
>
> French nouns are divided into two categories: masculine and feminine. It is important for you to know the gender of a noun, because this affects the form of any adjective relating to it. Compare: **un beau pays** (*a beautiful country*) and **une belle ville** (*a beautiful town*). Fortunately, there are rules to help you work out the gender of many nouns.

Reading 1

First, read the following passage at least once. If you feel confident enough, don't look at the vocabulary at this stage. Then, having checked the notes that follow the text, read it again at least once before completing the exercises.

La France – généralités

La France a une superficie de 550.000 kilomètres carrés. Elle est le premier pays d'Europe pour la grandeur de son territoire. Elle est protégée par une variété de frontières naturelles. Des mers d'abord: la Mer du Nord, la Manche au nord-ouest, l'Océan Atlantique à l'ouest, la mer Méditerranée au sud. Ensuite, des montagnes: les Pyrénées au sud-ouest, les Alpes au sud-est, les Vosges à l'est. Enfin, un fleuve, le Rhin, qui la sépare de l'Allemagne. La seule frontière ouverte, la plus vulnérable aux invasions successives qui ont marqué l'histoire de l'Hexagone, est celle qui est située au nord et qui le sépare de la Belgique.

La France partage le reste de ses frontières avec les pays suivants: l'Espagne, l'Italie, la Suisse, l'Allemagne, le Luxembourg et la Belgique.

Grâce à la diversité des sols et du climat, elle possède des paysages très variés: on y trouve de grandes plaines comme en Beauce, des régions de collines comme en Normandie, des montagnes très vieilles comme le Massif Central et les Vosges, ou plus jeunes comme les Pyrénées, le Jura ou les Alpes, qui sont toutes idéales pour l'élevage, les forêts et, bien sûr, le tourisme.

Du fait de sa superbe position géographique, l'Hexagone est plus avantagé que ses voisins au point de vue économique et climatique, ce qui fait parfois l'envie des autres pays d'Europe. En France, il y a des climats pour tous les goûts: du climat maritime, doux et humide, que l'on trouve en Normandie, en Bretagne et avec quelques légères modifications dans la région parisienne, au climat continental de montagne, à l'est, avec ses hivers froids et ses étés chauds, sans oublier le climat méditerranéen, chaud et ensoleillé et très apprécié par les touristes étrangers, les artistes et les vedettes de cinéma.

QUICK VOCAB

la superficie *area/surface (expressed in square metres or square kilometres). This word is only used to refer to large areas.*
la grandeur *size (also greatness)*
le nord *north. The other* **points cardinaux** *are:* **le sud** *(south),* **l'est** *(east) and* **l'ouest** *(west). All are masculine.*
le massif montagneux *mountain range*
partager *to share*
le pays *country (e.g. France, Spain, etc.); the country as opposed to the town is* **la campagne**. **Le paysage** *covers the various meanings of the English word landscape.*
privilégié *privileged. Sometimes advantaged.*
grâce à *thanks to*
le sol *soil/ground*
la colline *hill*
l'élevage *(masc.) rearing (of animals, not children!)*
du point de vue de … *from the point of view of …*
le goût *taste. The expression* **il y en a pour tous les goûts** *means that France can cater for every taste.*
sans oublier … *not forgetting …*
ensoleillé *sunny (but only about the weather)*

Insight

In French, names of countries ending in -e are feminine, with the exception of **le Cambodge, le Mexique, le Mozambique, le Zimbabwe.** Whatever their ending, all the other countries are masculine: **le Guatémala, le Honduras, le Maroc**, etc.

Comprehension 1

Having read the passage above, try to answer the following questions in English. Please note that, in an attempt to make the work less mechanical, we have not put the questions in sequence!

1 Why are other European countries sometimes said to be envious of France?
2 Why has France often been invaded from the north?
3 Which seas or oceans form France's natural boundaries?
4 What European country is separated from France by the Pyrenees?

5 What is the type of landscape generally found in Normandy?
6 France shares common boundaries with six European countries. Which ones?
7 How many broad types of climate are there in France?

Activity 1

True or false? Check the statements below and say whether, according to the information given in the text, they are true or false. If false, give the correct answer.

1 France is the largest country in Europe.
2 France is protected on all sides by 'natural barriers'.
3 French landscapes are very diverse.
4 The area known as La Beauce is very hilly.
5 In geological terms, the Massif Central and the Alps are 'young mountains'.
6 Some French mountains are ideal for tourism and cattle raising.

Activity 2

There follows a list (**A** to **E**) of the five main types of climate to be found in France. With the help of the information provided so far in the unit and your own knowledge, match each type of climate with the number (1 to 5) which best describes it. If, for instance, you feel that type **A** matches the description 2 (which it doesn't!), then you should write your answer as **A2**.

A Le climat continental (est).
B Le climat océanique (sud-ouest).
C Le climat maritime (ouest).
D Le climat méditerranéen (sud).
E Le climat parisien (région parisienne).

1 Des hivers doux;
Des étés secs et ensoleillés;
Un vent du nord parfois très violent (le mistral);
Des averses en automne et au printemps.

2 Des hivers doux;
Des étés frais;
Des pluies fines mais très fréquentes.

3 Des hivers froids et neigeux;
De fortes précipitations au printemps et en automne;
Des étés chauds avec des orages parfois violents.

4 Des hivers doux et humides;
Des étés agréables;
Des pluies fréquentes (environ 160 jours par an).

5 Des hivers frais;
Des printemps et des automnes doux et ensoleillés;
Des étés chauds;
Des orages fréquents en été et en automne.

Note: the vocabulary should be fairly easy to understand or to guess, but if you have any problems, check in the vocabulary section at the back of the book.

Activity 3
The following nouns appear (in sequence) in the reading passage:

1 invasions; **2** diversité; **3** paysage; **4** tourisme; **5** position

For each, try to formulate the rule which would enable you to avoid gender agreement mistakes, e.g. **variété** is feminine, like all abstract nouns ending in **-té**.

Reading 2

The following passage introduces some aspects of the French economy. Read it carefully in preparation for the activities that follow.

L'économie de la France

En général, les sols sont riches, ce qui explique le succès des activités agricoles: culture des céréales, des fruits, des légumes, et surtout de la vigne qui est un véritable trésor économique. La France produit en moyenne entre 60 et 75 millions d'hectolitres de vin par an, mais une partie seulement de ce vin est de qualité supérieure. Le reste est appelé vin de table ou vin de consommation courante.

L'agriculture sous ses formes les plus productives représente encore une activité économique importante que l'on nomme l'agroalimentaire et qui rapporte des milliards d'euros au gouvernement français. Cependant, malgré ces avantages naturels, la concurrence des importations venues du reste de l'Union Européenne et des pays à bas niveau de vie menace l'existence de bon nombre de petites fermes françaises non-spécialisées dans la culture intensive.

Si la France est riche au niveau des sols et des cultures, elle l'est moins, par contre, au niveau des ressources naturelles. En général, elle est pauvre en minéraux et en pétrole et elle doit acheter ces produits à l'étranger, ce qui déséquilibre la balance des paiements. Le charbon et le fer, qui autrefois ont fait la richesse des régions du nord, de l'est et du Massif Central, viennent aujourd'hui de l'extérieur.

La France doit importer la majorité du pétrole qu'elle consomme. Cependant, elle est riche en uranium, ce qui explique peut-être que la majorité de l'électricité française est d'origine nucléaire!

QUICK VOCAB

en moyenne *on average*
rapporter *to bring in (money). Also to bring back.*
la concurrence *(business) competition.* **La compétition** *is competition in sport.*
des minéraux *(masc. plur.) minerals (resources)*
la balance des paiements *the balance of trade/payments*
le charbon et le fer *coal and steel (as minerals and as industries)*
consommer *to consume (a product or a service). The consumer is* **le consommateur/la consommatrice.**

Comprehension 2

Give as full an answer to the following questions as the text will allow:

1 What are the advantages for France of having rich soils?
2 What information does the text give about wine production?
3 What is **l'agroalimentaire** and what is its role in the French economy?
4 What are the factors which adversely affect French agriculture today?
5 Give two reasons which may explain why France is relying so heavily on nuclear power for its electricity production.

Insight

In French, before a word beginning with a vowel, the definite articles **le** and **la** (*the*) lose their own vowel. Compare: **le gouvernement** (*the government*) and **l'élevage** (*cattle rearing*), both masculine; or **la culture** (*culture*) and **l'agriculture** (*agriculture*), both feminine.

With words beginning with mute (*silent*) **h**, the vowel is also dropped: **l'hiver** (*winter* – masculine) and **l'heure** (*the hour* – feminine).

Activity 4

How would you translate the following into French? Use appropriate expressions taken from the text.

1 France is rich and superbly situated in Europe, which explains its economic success.
2 Agriculture is still very important for the national economy.
3 The country is forced to import a good many products from abroad.
4 The soil and the climate are excellent.
5 Wine brings billions of euros to the French economy.
6 Foreign imports threaten the balance of payments and the existence of a good many small farms.

1 How to say 'some' (an unspecified number)

The word des (meaning *some/several*, and often not translated in English), appears in French as **de** or even **d'**, as shown in the examples below:

1 Dans le sud, nous avons *des* étés chauds.	*In the south, we have (some) hot summers.*
2 En Normandie, il y a *de* beaux printemps.	*In Normandy, there are (some) beautiful springs.*
3 Dans l'ouest, il y a *d'*excellents automnes.	*In the west, there are (some) excellent autumns.*
4 En hiver, il y a *de* très violents orages.	*In winter, there are (some) very violent thunderstorms.*

Can you work out the reason for those changes?

The answer is as follows:

1 If des is immediately followed by a noun (as in Example 1), it will keep its full form.
2 If des is immediately followed by an adjective which does not begin with a vowel, as in Example 2, it will change to **de**.
3 If des is immediately followed by an adjective which begins with a vowel (as in Example 3), it will be abbreviated to **d'**.
4 If des is immediately followed by an adverb, like **très** in Example 4, it will either be **de** or **d'**, depending on the absence or presence of a vowel at the start of the next word.

Activity 5

In the sentences that follow, fill the blanks with **des**, **de**, or **d'**, as appropriate.

1 J'ai _____ énormes problèmes.
2 La France produit _____ grandes quantités de vin.
3 Il y a _____ vieilles montagnes dans la région.
4 Vous avez _____ excellents amis.
5 Dans le sud, il y a _____ touristes anglais.

2 How to say 'some' meaning a part or portion of a whole

Sometimes we need to express the fact that we are referring to a part or portion of a whole. In such cases, the words needed are called partitive articles. They are **du, de la, de l'** and **des**. The form required depends on the gender of the noun which follows immediately and also on the first letter of that word.

In the masculine singular, if a consonant follows, it is **du** that must be used; in the feminine singular, it is **de la**, except if the word which follows begins with a vowel, in which case it is **de l'**. In the plural, des is used for both the masculine and the feminine:

Du pain, s'il vous plaît.	*(Give me) some bread please! (masc. sing.)*
Vous voulez de la bière?	*Do you want some beer? (fem. sing.)*
Il a de l'argent.	*He has (some) money. (masc. sing.)*
Tu veux des confitures?	*Do you want some jam? (fem. plur.)*

Activity 6

The activity which follows is part of your self-assessment (see the self-assessment record form). Award yourself five marks for each correct answer, then enter your score on the self-assessment record form.

In the sentences below, say which form of the partitive is required.

Vous désirez (**1**) fromage ou (**2**) dessert?
Pour cette expédition, il faut (**3**) courage et (**4**) énergie.
Il a (**5**) patience!
Tu veux encore (**6**) café?
Ils mangent (**7**) chocolat sans arrêt.
Vous buvez (**8**) vin ou (**9**) eau?
Dans ce travail, il faut (**10**) attention.

Language learning tip 1

In French, the names of seasons, points of the compass and months are all masculine.

Insight

In French, to indicate that an action happened in the past, you use **être** (*to be*) with verbs of movement including **naître** (*to be born*) and **mourir** (*to die*), and **avoir** (*to have*) with other verbs: **elle est née** (*she was born*), **elle est allée** (*she went*), **elle a rencontré John** (*she met John*), **elle a trouvé un poste** (*she found a post/job*).

Reading 3

We are now going to meet Marc Swift, who will appear at regular intervals throughout the units. He is a friendly, outgoing young Englishman who loves all things French. For reasons which are explained in the text below, he is a Francophile and travels to l'Hexagone regularly, on business or for pleasure.

If you have the recording, listen to the passage at least twice, and read it a couple of times before embarking on the exercises.

CD1, TR 1, 01:44

Marc Swift est un jeune Anglais de trente-trois ans qui habite à Londres. Son père, John, est britannique. Sa mère, Claudine, est française. Elle est née à Poitiers, le chef-lieu du département de la Vienne. En septembre 1963, Claudine est allée faire un séjour en Angleterre dans le cadre de ses études supérieures. Elle préparait une Licence d'anglais, et elle a passé une année dans une école secondaire à Richmond, près de Londres, comme assistante de français. Elle a rencontré John pour la première fois dans un club londonien le 22 novembre 1963, jour de son vingt-troisième anniversaire et de la mort du président Kennedy. Ils se sont tout de suite plu, et ils se sont mariés deux ans après, le 14 juillet 1966, autre date fatidique! Claudine a ensuite trouvé un poste de professeur dans un établissement secondaire de la banlieue londonienne, et elle est restée en Angleterre, au grand désespoir de ses parents. John est employé de banque. Marc, leur fils unique, est né le 25 février 1970. Après ses études secondaires, il est allé à l'université pour préparer un BA de marketing et de français. Depuis six ans, il travaille dans une grande entreprise britannique spécialisée dans les équipements de sport et de loisir. Il est complètement bilingue. La France le passionne. Sa curiosité n'a pas de bornes et il ne rate jamais une occasion de parfaire sa connaissance de la langue et de la culture françaises.

QUICK VOCAB

une Licence *here: a higher education degree (= BA or BSc). Beware: except in sport, a licence is normally* **un permis**.
un(e) assistant(e) *a (foreign language) assistant*
Londres *London (the adjective is* **londonien***)*
ils se sont plu *they liked each other.* **Se plaire** *is a pronominal (reflexive) verb (she liked him and he liked her). You might have expected* **plus***, because in reflexive verbs the past participle agrees with the subject. But the construction here is indirect, so agreement is not needed.*
tout de suite *immediately or at once*
une date fatidique *a fateful date*
il est fils unique *he is an only son. The feminine would be:* **elle est fille unique**. *Note the absence of the article* **un** *or* **une***!*
sa curiosité n'a pas de bornes *his curiosity knows no bounds*
parfaire *to perfect*
rater une occasion *to miss an opportunity*
pour affaires *on business*

Le 14 juillet, autre date fatidique *another fateful date* indeed, since it is the anniversary of the French Revolution of 1789!

au grand désespoir de ses parents *to her parents' great dismay* In those days, French parents did not easily forgive their offspring for going to live abroad. Very few French people leave France permanently to go and live abroad.

Activity 7

True or false? On the basis of the information given in the reading section, say if the following statements are true or false. If false, give the correct answer.

1 Marc's parents are British.
2 There was nothing memorable about John and Claudine's first meeting.
3 Claudine and John are both teachers.
4 Marc is now at university where he is studying marketing and French.
5 He is an only child.
6 He is almost bilingual.
7 His curiosity about the French language and culture is insatiable.

Language learning tip 2

Did you notice anything unusual about the names of months and dates in French?

- Names of months begin with a small letter, not a capital: **janvier, février, mars …**
- Except for the first day of the month (**le premier**), which takes an ordinal number, all the other days are indicated by the cardinal number: **le deux juin, le trois juillet, le quatre août, le trente septembre, le trente et un décembre …**

Note: **du premier janvier au trente et un décembre:** all the year round.

Insight

In formal French, there are two main ways of formulating questions:

– either with an inversion: **êtes-vous/avez-vous ...?** (*are you/ have you ...?*)

– or by using **est-ce que**, without an inversion: **Est-ce que vous êtes/vous avez ...?**

In familiar French, however, you can use the statement form and simply raise your voice at the end: **'Vous êtes anglais?'** ('*Are you English?*'), **'Vous habitez (à) Paris?'** ('*Do you live in Paris?*').

Dialogue

Marc has just arrived in the cafeteria of one of the big and very busy railway stations in Paris where he is going to catch a train. He is looking for a seat and manages to find one at a small table, opposite a customer who also appears to be waiting for a train. Talkative and friendly as ever, Marc, who is in Paris on business, is about to introduce himself to the stranger.

If you have the recording of the dialogue, listen to it a couple of times to take in the information it contains and to get acquainted with the southern accent of the stranger.

CD1, TR 1, 07:14

Marc Pardon, la place est libre, s'il vous plaît?
Pierre Oui. ... Une seconde, j'enlève ma serviette.
Marc Merci. ... Permettez-moi de me présenter – Marc Swift.
Pierre Enchanté, Pierre Castel. Vous êtes anglais?
Marc Oui.
Pierre Eh bien, félicitations, votre français est excellent!
Marc Merci. ... Vous habitez Paris?

Pierre Non, je suis ici pour affaires. Je vis dans le sud-ouest, à Villeneuve-sur-Lot, une petite ville entre Bordeaux et Toulouse.

Marc Je vois que vous avez l'accent! … Vous êtes originaire du sud-ouest?

Pierre Moi, oui, mais mes parents sont nés dans le nord. Mon père est natif de Lille, et ma mère de Charleville.

Marc Ah, le pays noir!

Pierre Oui. … Ils sont partis dans le sud-ouest deux ans avant ma naissance.

Marc À cause du climat?

Pierre Non, pas vraiment! Mon père était enseignant et il a été muté dans le sud-ouest.

Marc Vous avez encore de la famille dans le nord?

Pierre Très peu. … Quelques cousins … Mes grands-parents sont décédés.

Marc Et vous avez toujours vos parents?

Pierre Oui. Ils sont maintenant à la retraite, et le climat du sud-ouest leur réussit: ils se portent très bien!

Marc Et vous avez quel âge?

Pierre Trente-six ans.

Marc Qu'est-ce que vous faites comme métier?

Pierre Je suis libraire, et vous?

Marc Je suis dans le marketing des équipements sportifs et de loisir.

Pierre Et le travail marche bien?

Marc Pas mal, mais la conjoncture n'est pas très bonne en ce moment.

Pierre Je sais. Pour nous non plus.

Marc Est-ce qu'il y a beaucoup d'industries dans votre région?

Pierre Non, peu en fait, sauf dans les grandes villes. Elle était traditionnellement agricole, mais depuis la fin de la Deuxième Guerre mondiale, les activités agricoles ont diminué.

Marc Pourquoi?

Pierre Parce que la concurrence étrangère est devenue très forte et que les jeunes ne veulent pas rester à la campagne. Ils préfèrent aller vivre à la ville, avoir des horaires fixes, un bon salaire, des loisirs, des vacances assurées …

Marc	Certains doivent le regretter!
Pierre	C'est sûr, mais quand ils prennent leur retraite ils reviennent au pays. … Ah, voilà mon train. Merci de votre compagnie. … Si vous passez par Villeneuve, venez me voir, mais donnez-moi un coup de fil avant, je suis souvent en déplacement. Voilà ma carte …
Marc	Merci, c'est très gentil à vous, je n'y manquerai pas. Bon voyage!

Insight

In familiar French, the subject pronoun **on** which usually means *one* is used instead of **nous** with the verb in the 3rd person singular. So, the sentence **'Nous sommes contents'** (*'We are pleased'*) becomes **'On est contents'** but note the agreement of the adjective!

QUICK VOCAB

la place est libre? *is this seat/place free (unoccupied)?*
la serviette *here: briefcase, but it can also mean towel, serviette, or napkin, so beware!*
permettez-moi de … *please allow me to …*
habiter *to live, but in the sense of to dwell (or inhabit a place).* **Vivre** *has a broader meaning, which incorporates lifestyle, habits, etc.*
vous avez l'accent *you have a regional accent. Here, a southern accent, which is easily recognizable and well liked by people from other areas. It is said to be evocative of sunshine and blue skies!*
être originaire du *to be a native of/originally from*
le pays noir *the black country (because of coal and heavy industries). In fact, nowadays, most of the coal mines have closed down. Recently, however, the whole of the area has been given a new lease of life, thanks to the Channel Tunnel* **(le Tunnel sous la Manche)**.
la naissance *birth. Note that in French the present perfect is used instead of the past. I was born:* **je suis né**.
Mes grands-parents sont décédés. *My grandparents (have) passed away.*
être enseignant *to be in the teaching profession. The word covers all types of teaching from primary school to university.*

être muté *to be posted to another area/town*
là-bas *down there. It can also mean over there.*
la famille *In French this means not only parents and children, but also other relatives (cousins, uncles, aunts, nephews, etc.).*
à la retraite *retired. In France, the age of retirement is currently 60 for both men and women.*
le climat leur réussit *they thrive on the climate (lit. the climate is a success for them)*
le/la libraire *bookseller. The shop is called* **une librairie***: a 'false friend';* **une bibliothèque** *is a library.*
marcher *normally to walk. Here, to go well (of an activity/a business or a machine).*
la concurrence *competition (e.g. in business). Another 'false friend'. In sport, the word* **la compétition** *is used.*
c'est sûr! *that's for sure! For emphasis, people often use:* **c'est sûr et certain!**
la carte *Here: business card, but it can also mean postcard, playing card or map.*
un coup de fil *a phone call (usually quick). A familiar expression.*
en déplacement *away on business (lit. in displacement)*
je n'y manquerai pas *I will do it without fail*

3 *Encore* and *toujours*

Occasionally, these two seem to create some confusion in learners' minds. Encore normally means *still* and serves to indicate the continuation of an action:

Je travaille encore dans une banque. *I'm still working in a bank.*

It can also be used with the meaning of *again*, to express incredulity or irritation:

Il est encore malade! *He's ill again!*

Note: pas encore means *not yet*:

Le dîner est prêt? Non, pas encore! *Is (the) dinner ready? Not yet.*

Toujours can mean:

1 always

Ils arrivent toujours en retard.	*They always arrive late.*

2 still (in expressions of time)

Vous travaillez toujours à Paris?	*Do you still work/Are you still working in Paris?*

A little practice will soon clarify the difference.

Activity 8
In the dialogue, there are a couple of sentences with **toujours** and encore. Can you:

1 Spot them?
2 Give their meaning?

Activity 9
How would you translate the following? (Note that some sentences may have two meanings!)

1 Vos parents sont encore dans le nord?
2 Il est toujours au café!
3 Le facteur sonne toujours deux fois. (Title of a well-known thriller by the author James M. Cain.)
4 Il est encore en retard.
5 Elle habite toujours à Bordeaux?

Insight

In French, you do not need to use **un/une** (*a*) before the name of a profession, unless you qualify it with an adjective. Compare: *'I am a bookseller'* and **'Je suis libraire'** or *'My father was a teacher'* and **'Mon père était enseignant'**.

But note: **'Mon père était *un* excellent enseignant'** (*'My father was an excellent teacher'*).

4 Saying 'since when' or 'for how long' you have been doing something

In everyday conversation, we are often called upon to say that *we have been doing something* for a certain period or from a particular point in time. In English this is expressed by using the past continuous tense: *we have been doing*. In French, it's simpler: all you need to do is to use the *present tense* and add a word or an expression to indicate the duration of the 'activity'.

The start of the 'activity' can be indicated by a time, a date or a specific event.

Ils habitent ici depuis cinq ans.	*They have been living here for five years.*
Ils habitent ici depuis le premier juillet.	*They have been living here since 1 July.*
Ils habitent ici depuis la guerre.	*They have been living here since the war.*

Notes: In the case of the first example only, you may replace **depuis** by **il y a ... que ...**:

Il y a cinq ans qu'ils habitent ici.	*They have been living here for five years.*

In casual conversation, you may express the same idea a little more informally:

Ça fait cinq ans qu'ils habitent ici.	*They have been living here for five years (lit. that makes five years ...).*

Language learning tip 3

The phrase **ça fait** ... can also be used to ask for or to confirm a price:

Ça fait combien?	*How much is that* (lit. ... *does that make)?*
Ça fait 12 euros.	*That's* (lit. *that makes) 12 euros.*

If you want to say that you did something for a certain period in the past, but that you no longer do it, you could use **pendant** (*during/for*):

J'ai habité ici (pendant) dix ans.	*I lived here for ten years.*
J'ai habité ici pendant la guerre.	*I lived here during the war.*

Activity 10

Imagine that you wish to give about yourself the information suggested in the six sentences below in French. What would you say? (There may be more than one way to express some of the statements. In such cases, give the alternatives too.)

1 State that you have been in the area where you now live since birth.
2 Say to someone you've just met outside Notre Dame that you have been in France for two weeks.
3 Say you have been in the café for ten minutes.
4 Say that you have been 'coming' to France for ten years.
5 Indicate how long you have been doing your present job (three years).
6 State that, for six years, you lived in a flat (**un appartement**), but now you live in a small house in the country.

Insight

The subject pronoun **je** (*I*) contracts to **j'** when the verb that follows begins with a vowel or with mute **h: je ai** (*I have*) becomes **j'ai,** and **je habite** (*I live/dwell*) becomes **j'habite.**

Note, however: **je hais** (*I hate*). Here, the **h** is said to be aspirated.

5 Moods, tenses and verb groups

As you know from earlier language studies, French tenses are organized according to a number of moods, each containing several tenses. Each mood is used to convey a certain meaning and should be seen as an important element in language communication. These moods are:

1 The infinitive (or non-working form of the verb). It is the form in which you will find the verb in the dictionary. It is very useful for building certain tenses, as we will see in Unit 9. It is also used on its own to convey orders or strong advice.

2 The indicative, used to express the reality of an action in the past, the present or the future.

3 The conditional, which normally serves to indicate that, if certain conditions were met, an action could/might take place (now or later) or could/might have taken place at some time in the past.

4 The imperative, used without subject pronouns, to give commands, orders or strong advice.

5 The subjunctive, generally used to express doubt, fear, obligation, desire, etc. The subjunctive is distinct from the indicative in that it does not deal with reality, but rather with supposition or conjecture.

Activity 11

Examine the English sentences below. For each one, use one of the numbers 1 to 5 above, to indicate which mood you would need to express the meaning in French.

a Call the hospital, he is injured.
b We know he is injured.
c We fear he may be injured.
d We would be sad if he was/were injured.
e In case of allergy consult your doctor.

5.1 How to recognize which group a verb belongs to

As you will remember, French verbs are organized into three main categories called *conjugations*, on the basis of the endings of their infinitives. They are not, as in English, identified by the presence of the particle 'to' as an infinitive marker. French uses not only the endings (**-er**, **-ir**, **-re**) to classify its verbs, but another two clues to make sure that no confusion occurs. These clues are:

1 The present participle, the equivalent of the *-ing* form of English verbs: *speaking*, *finishing*, *leaving*, etc.
2 The past participle, equivalent to the final section in the verb phrases in *we have eaten*, or *she has finished*. This form is used – as in English – to form compound tenses and, in particular, the perfect (**le passé composé**).

The distinguishing features arising from the **-er**, **-ir**, **-re** endings and the present and past participles are combined to produce the table below, which allows us to recognize the three French verb groups. Do not try to take in everything at once. We will go over the key points again as we progress.

Verb group	*Infinitive endings*	*Present participle ending*	*Past participle ending*
1st group	-er	-ant	-é
to speak	parl**er**	parl**ant**	parl**é**
2nd group	-ir	-issant	-i
to finish	fin**ir**	fin**issant**	fin**i**
3rd group	-ir	-ant	-i
to leave/go	part**ir**	part**ant**	part**i**
or:	-ir	-ant	-u
to come	ven**ir**	ven**ant**	ven**u**
irregulars:			
to die	mour**ir**	mour**ant**	**mort**
to offer	offr**ir**	offr**ant**	off**ert**
or:	-re	-ant	-u
to sell	vend**re**	vend**ant**	vend**u**
irregulars:			
to be	êt**re**	ét**ant**	ét**é**
to do/make	fai**re**	fais**ant**	fai**t**
or:	-oir	-ant	-u
to want	voul**oir**	voul**ant**	voul**u**
irregulars:			
to see	v**oir**	vo**yant**	v**u**
to know	sav**oir**	sa**chant**	s**u**

5.2 The present tense endings of the three groups

The table below shows the endings you need to add to the root/stem of verbs of each group to form their present tense.

Insight

Although the first, second and third person singular and the third person plural endings of most **-er** verbs may be spelt differently, they are pronounced in the same way: **je travaille, tu travailles, il/elle travaille, ils/elles travaillent** all sound exactly the same. This is also the case for the first three persons of 2nd and 3rd group verbs.

1st group		*2nd group*		*3rd group*	
-er + -ant		*-ir + -issant*		*-ir/-oir/-re + -ant*	
je	-e	je	-is	je	-s
tu	-es	tu	-is	tu	-s
il/elle/on	-e	il/elle/on	-it	il/elle/on	-t
nous	-ons	nous	-issons	nous	-ons
vous	-ez	vous	-issez	vous	-ez
ils/elles	-ent	ils/elles	-issent	ils/elles	-ent

Remember: to form the present indicative, you must remove the infinitive marker (-er, -ir, -re), before adding the appropriate ending(s) shown above.

It is also helpful to bear in mind that, except for the 2nd group, verbs do not always behave as logically as they should. The infuriating thing is that it is the most frequently used verbs that are among the most troublesome!

Here are some examples:

all*er* *to go*: je vais, tu vas, il/elle/on va, nous allons, vous allez, ils/elles vont.
avo*ir* *to have*: j'ai, tu as, il/elle/on a, nous avons, vous avez, ils/elles ont.

êt**re** *to be*: je suis, tu es, il/elle/on est, nous sommes, vous êtes, ils/elles sont.
fai*re to do/make*: je fais, tu fais, il/elle/on fait, nous faisons, vous faites, ils/elles font.
pouv*oir to be able to*: je peux, tu peux, il/elle/on peut, nous pouvons, vous pouvez, ils/elles peuvent.
recev*oir to receive*: je reçois, tu reçois, il/elle/on reçoit, nous recevons, vous recevez, ils/elles reçoivent.
voul*oir to want*: je veux, tu veux, il/elle/on veut, nous voulons, vous voulez, ils/elles veulent.

Language learning tip 4

In French, **on** has two distinct meanings:

1 In formal French, it is used to convey the neutral form *one/someone* when you do not know the gender of the person(s) you are referring to. It uses the same endings as **il** or **elle**:

On frappe! (*Somebody is knocking on the door!*). It could be one (or more) male(s) or female(s).

2 In familiar French, **on** is frequently used to replace **nous:**

On va à la gare. = Nous allons à la gare. (*We go/are going to the (train) station.)*

Activity 12

In the text below, replace the infinitives by the correct form of the present tense.

Quand nous (aller) en France pour nos vacances, nous (choisir *2nd gr.*) une région tranquille, où on (pouvoir) se reposer. Nous n'(aimer) pas les plages où il y (avoir) beaucoup de monde. Personnellement, je (préférer) la campagne, mais ma partenaire (adorer) la mer. Elle (vouloir) se baigner tous les jours. Elle (passer) des heures au soleil. Je lui (dire) que c'(être) dangereux, mais elle se (moquer) de moi.

Activity 13

For each of the verbs listed below, give the *present participle* and the *past participle* forms. This exercise will help you to recognize and form French compound tenses in the forthcoming units.

Example: aller – allant, allé.

1 choisir; **2** pouvoir; **3** avoir; **4** vouloir; **5** dire

Activity 14

The phrases below have been taken from the dialogue in Unit 1. For each one can you:

a indicate which of the three groups (1st, 2nd or 3rd) the underlined verb belongs to;
b give the past participle of each.

1 vous êtes; **2** je vis; **3** ils sont partis; **4** le travail marche bien?; **5** les jeunes ne veulent pas rester; **6** ils prennent leur retraite; **7** ils reviennent

---

The administrative divisions of France

The map on the following page shows the 22 administrative regions of l'**Hexagone.**

The second map shows the administrative subdivisions of the 22 regions, called **départements**. There are 95 of them. The first 89 are organized alphabetically from **Ain** (01) to **Yonne** (89). Number 90 is **Le Territoire de Belfort**, near the German Border.

A few decades ago, the sprawling **département de la Seine** (75), which included Paris, was divided into smaller areas (numbered from 91 to 95), to alleviate administrative pressure on the capital itself.

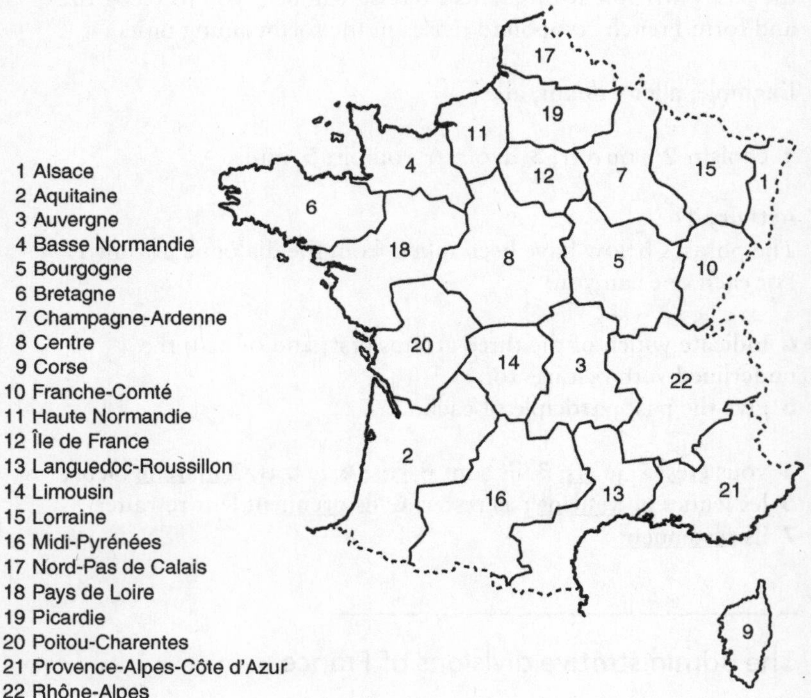

La France: les régions.

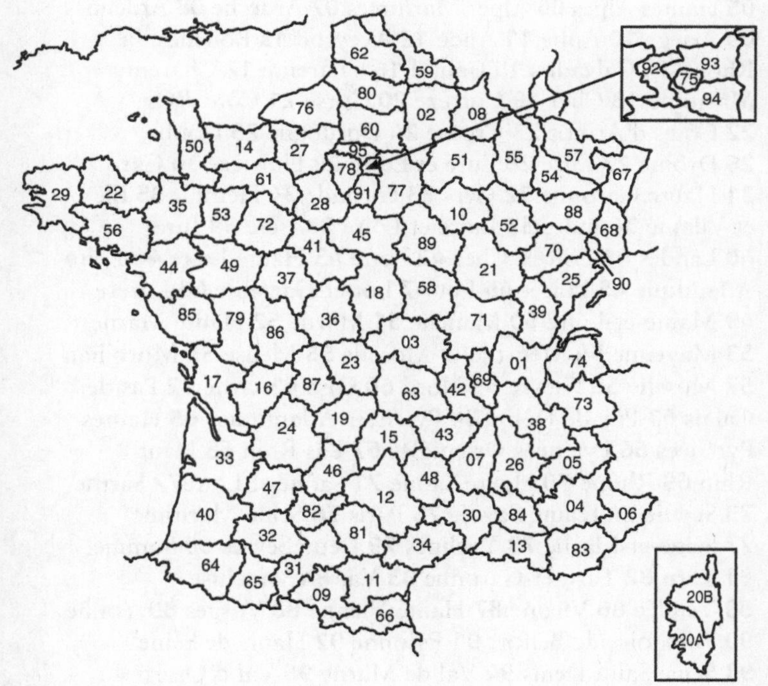

La France: les départements.

Liste alphabétique des départements français

01 Ain **02** Aisne **03** Allier **04** Alpes de Haute Provence **05** Hautes Alpes **06** Alpes Maritimes **07** Ardèche **08** Ardennes **09** Ariège **10** Aube **11** Aude **12** Aveyron **13** Bouches du Rhône **14** Calvados **15** Cantal **16** Charente **17** Charente Maritime **18** Cher **19** Corrèze **20** Corse **21** Côte d'Or **22** Côtes d'Armor **23** Creuse **24** Dordogne **25** Doubs **26** Drôme **27** Eure **28** Eure et Loire **29** Finistère **30** Gard **31** Haute Garonne **32** Gers **33** Gironde **34** Hérault **35** Ille et Vilaine **36** Indre **37** Indre et Loire **38** Isère **39** Jura **40** Landes **41** Loir-et-Cher **42** Loire **43** Haute Loire **44** Loire Atlantique **45** Loiret **46** Lot **47** Lot-et-Garonne **48** Lozère **49** Maine-et-Loire **50** Manche **51** Marne **52** Haute Marne **53** Mayenne **54** Meurthe-et-Moselle **55** Meuse **56** Morbihan **57** Moselle **58** Nièvre **59** Nord **60** Oise **61** Orne **62** Pas de Calais **63** Puy de Dôme **64** Pyrénées Atlantiques **65** Hautes Pyrénées **66** Pyrénées Orientales **67** Bas Rhin **68** Haut Rhin **69** Rhône **70** Haute Saône **71** Saône et Loire**72** Sarthe **73** Savoie **74** Haute Savoie **75** Paris **76** Seine Maritime **77** Seine-et-Marne **78** Yvelines **79** Deux Sèvres **80** Somme **81** Tarn **82** Tarn-et-Garonne **83** Var **84** Vaucluse **85** Vendée **86** Vienne **87** Haute Vienne **88** Vosges **89** Yonne **90** Territoire de Belfort **91** Essonne **92** Hauts de Seine **93** Seine Saint Denis **94** Val de Marne **95** Val d'Oise.

The list of **départements** is useful for two reasons:

1 It appears in the postcode, which precedes the name of the town, city, or village. The code begins with the number corresponding to the alphabetical order of the **département**. This is then followed by up to three digits starting from 000 (for the head town of the **département**) to 999 (theoretically for the smallest village of the area). So, the code for the city of Paris is 75 000, and the code for the small town of Villeneuve-sur-Lot, which will figure in various units of the book, is 47 300 (the third largest town in the Lot-et-Garonne **département**. The higher the number, the smaller the place. These numbers are used to specify the postcode (**le code postal**) of each town or village.

2 The second reason is that the **département's** number may be shown on the number plate of motor vehicles to indicate their place of registration.Before 2009, if the owner of a vehicle (or the vehicle itself) moved permanently to another **département**, the vehicle had to be re-registered in the new area and a new registration document (**la carte grise**, lit. *the grey card*) applied for. The advantage of this system was that at any time it was possible to know in which **département** a car was registered. This method was discontinued in 2009. In the new system, vehicle registration numbers comprise two letters, three figures and two letters (e.g. AA 123 AB), which will remain the same throughout the life of the vehicle. Vehicle owners have the option of adding their **département** number to a small panel on the right-hand side of their number plate, but this is not compulsory.

In addition to the above, France still possesses some overseas **départements** and territories known as les **DOM-TOM**.

Les DOM-TOM (Départements et Territoires d'Outre-Mer)

These Overseas Departments and Territories are the remnants of the French colonial empire. Their links with metropolitan France are still strong, and the influence of the mother country is clearly visible in their language, culture and customs. The two appellations **DOM** and **TOM** highlight a different relationship with metropolitan France.

1 The **DOM** (**Départements d'Outre-Mer**) have the same status as any other French metropolitan **département**. They are: the Antilles (Guadeloupe and Martinique), situated in the Atlantic Ocean, off the north-eastern coast of South America; Réunion, south-east of

Madagascar in the Indian Ocean; St Pierre et Miquelon, off the eastern coast of North America; French Guyana, on the coast of South America, north of Brazil.

2 The **TOM** (**Territoires d'Outre-Mer**) have a more flexible status than the **DOM** and enjoy a greater degree of autonomy. They are: New Caledonia, an island in the Pacific Ocean off the eastern coast of Australia; French Polynesia, composed of a large number of small islands situated below the Equator in the Pacific Ocean; the islands of Wallis and Futuna, which lie west of French Polynesia; the island of Mayotte in the Indian Ocean, north of Madagascar.

Vive la France! *Long live France!* This statement always ends official messages made by the President of the Republic.

En France, tout finit par des chansons. *In France, everything ends up with songs.* This optimistic statement has (unfortunately) not always been borne out by the facts!

Insight

All French vowels are tense: when pronouncing them, the tongue and jaw do not change position and the sound is not altered. Compare the French word **nos** (*our*) in which the **o** sound remains steady, and the standard English pronunciation of *no* in which the mouth closes during the pronunciation of the *o*.

TEST YOURSELF

1. Why is France often referred to as l'Hexagone?
2. Why is it useful to create categories of nouns based on such endings as **-sion, -té, -age, -isme, -tion**?
3. English uses ordinal numbers: first, second, third ... when referring to days of the month. Is it the same in French?
4. What are the two meanings of the words **du, de la, des**?
5. Each of the following words **encore** and **toujours** has two meanings. What are they?
6. What are the two possible meanings of **depuis**?
7. What is the main administrative difference between **DOM** and **TOM**?
8. What are the two possible meanings of the subject pronoun **on**?
9. What differences in meaning are expressed by the conditional mood and the imperative mood?
10. What is the key difference between the meanings expressed by the indicative mood and the subjunctive mood?

2

Mythes et réalités

In this unit you will learn

- ***How to make telephone calls***
- ***How to distinguish between the different meanings and uses of the present tense***
- ***How to use prepositions***
- ***How to say 'to', 'at', 'in', 'from' with names of places***
- ***How and when to use the* tu *and* vous *forms***
- ***How and when to use prepositional (disjunctive) pronouns:* moi, toi, *etc.***
- ***How to express various degrees of agreement and disagreement***

In this unit, we will meet French people discussing their idea of 'Frenchness', and we will explore some of the myths, realities and preconceptions associated with France and the French.

The French, perhaps more than most other people in the world, are the subject of numerous preconceptions and stereotypes: hospitable, connoisseurs of good food and good wine, excitable, romantic, good lovers, unfaithful in marriage, a trifle devious, unwilling to join queues and clubs, unruly, prone to bouts of revolutionary fever, daredevils on the road, to name but a few!

Those preconceptions have, to a large extent, come from travellers' tales, literature, films, the media, etc. To our knowledge, no definitive research has been published to support the credibility of some of those ideas and it is therefore difficult to disentangle myth from reality. However, such a reputation can occasionally constitute a heavy psychological burden, particularly with the young, who feel they should live up to the image that foreigners have of them!

Insight

The following expressions will serve you well in your dealings with French people: **bonjour** (*hello when meeting them*), **au revoir** (*goodbye when leaving*), **pardon** (*pardon/forgive me*), **s'il vous plaît** (*please*), **merci beaucoup/merci bien** (*thank you very much*). In very familiar speech, you can use **salut!** for both *hello* and *goodbye*.

Dialogue 1

Marc Swift, currently on business in south-western France, is now in Poitiers, the head town of the **département de la Vienne** (see map in Unit 1), where his mother Claudine was born. Some of her old friends, Élise and Daniel Dufrêne, still live in the area with their daughter Audrey, who is a student at the University of Poitiers. Marc has decided to telephone the family to ask if he can drop in to see them for a couple of hours.

If you have access to the recording, listen to it a couple of times, without looking at the transcript, to get the gist of what is said and to get acquainted with **l'accent du Midi** (= **du sud**). You may also, if you wish, read the exchange out loud before you begin the exercises relating to it.

CD1, TR 2, 01:50

Marc	Allô … Je voudrais parler à Monsieur Daniel Dufrêne, s'il vous plaît.
Young female	Une seconde, [1]je vous le passe. (*Calling her father*) Papa! Le téléphone pour toi!
Daniel	Allô, ici Daniel Dufrêne. [2]J'écoute.

(Contd)

Marc Bonjour, Monsieur Dufrêne. Marc Swift à l'appareil.

Daniel Marc! Quelle surprise! [3]Où es-tu en ce moment?

Marc [4]Je suis à Poitiers depuis deux jours pour affaires, alors je vous passe un coup de fil.

Daniel C'est sympa! Tu [5]restes ici pour quelques jours?

Marc Non, jusqu'à demain matin seulement, mais si ça ne vous dérangeait pas, je pourrais passer pour vous dire un petit bonjour.

Daniel Mais bien sûr! [6]Tu es à l'hôtel?

Marc Oui, au Métropole, en face de la gare.

Daniel Et [7]tu es libre ce soir?

Marc [8]J'ai un client à voir cet après-midi à trois heures, mais je devrais avoir fini vers quatre heures au plus tard.

Daniel Bon, écoute, je passe te chercher à cinq heures et demie. [9]On prend un petit apéritif ensemble, et tu [10]restes dîner avec nous!

Marc C'est très gentil, mais je ne veux pas vous déranger.

Daniel Mais pas du tout! Élise est montée à Paris pour une réunion de travail. Elle [11]rentre dans deux jours, mais Audrey et moi nous allons te préparer un petit quelque chose à manger .... [12]Tu peux passer la nuit chez nous si tu veux!

Marc Euh, c'est très gentil, mais [13]je reprends le TGV pour Paris demain matin à six heures.

Daniel Bon, alors je te ramènerai à ton hôtel après le dîner. Ça va?

Marc D'accord. Merci et à bientôt!

Daniel Au revoir, Marc!

QUICK VOCAB

passer un coup de fil à quelqu'un *to give somebody a phone call/a 'buzz'*

c'est sympa! *it's nice/kind of you. It is short for* **c'est sympathique** *and is used in familiar French.*

le TGV (Train à Grande Vitesse) *A very fast train capable of reaching speeds of over 300 kilometres per hour. The French are very proud of it. The TGV network now links all the main cities, but you must book in advance if you want to travel on it.*

libre *free (of commitments).* **C'est libre?** *is also used to enquire if a place or seat is vacant. The opposite would then be* **C'est occupé?**

au plus tard *at the (very) latest*

monter à Paris *to go (up) to Paris. The expression 'going up to the capital' is often used by people from the South of France and may have something to do with the geographical position of Paris on the map.*

une réunion *a meeting*

un petit quelque chose *a little something (to eat or drink). Be warned: sometimes this little something may turn out to be quite substantial!*

ça *this/that. A neutral form used in spoken French as a replacement for the more formal* **ceci** *or* **cela** *to refer to something the gender of which is unclear.*

Comprehension 1

Use the information contained in Dialogue 1 to answer the questions below. Your answers should be as full and accurate as the information allows.

1 What was the reason for Marc's telephone call?
2 What do we learn about the purpose and duration of his stay in Poitiers?
3 Where is he at the moment, and what is his work schedule for the day?
4 What do we learn about Daniel's wife?
5 What are the suggestions made by Daniel which Marc agrees to?
6 What offer made by Daniel does Marc turn down and why?
7 Are Daniel and Audrey going to take Marc to a restaurant? Explain.

Insight

To translate '*I have been here for two days*' (or similar sentences), the French use the present tense: **'Je suis ici depuis deux jours'**. Note that depuis can sometimes mean *since* as well as *for*, for example: **'Elle habite à Bordeaux depuis 1980'** ('*She's lived in Bordeaux since 1980*').

Activity 1

With the help of the vocabulary and expressions that appear in Dialogue 1, translate the following sentences into French.

1 I have been here on business for six days.
2 I don't want to disturb you.
3 I am staying here until tomorrow afternoon at four o'clock.
4 I am free this evening.
5 I should telephone at about half past five at the latest.
6 It's very kind, but ...
7 Listen, I am coming to fetch you at the hotel.

1 The various uses of the present indicative

The conversation between Marc and Daniel contains several examples of the present indicative. It is important for you to remember that the use of this tense is different in the two languages. Unlike the corresponding English tense, the present indicative, in French, can have a wider range of meanings, particularly in conversation.

It can be used to describe:

a what happens regularly:

Je monte à Paris tous les mois.	*I go to Paris every month.*

b what is happening at this very moment:

En ce moment, je travaille à Toulouse.	*At the moment, I'm working in Toulouse.*

c what has been happening up to now and is likely to continue for a while:

J'habite à Lyon depuis trois mois.	*I've been living in Lyons for three months.*

d what is just about to happen:

Le train arrive dans deux minutes!	*The train will be arriving in two minutes!*

e what will be happening at some time in the not too distant future:

Il va en Angleterre le mois prochain.	*He's (He will be) going to England next month.*

Activity 2

In Dialogue 1, there are 13 expressions marked with a superscript number. Match each one (except number 1, which is given below as an example) with the option (indicated by one of the letters **a, b, c, d** or **e** above), which you feel is the appropriate one, and explain your choice. If the time gap is very short, you should use **d** rather than e.

Example: 1 Je vous le passe = **d:** the action is just about to happen.

2 Prepositions

As you know, prepositions are words or groups of words which are used to express a relationship (of space, time, purpose ...) between related parts of a sentence called subject and object noun phrases. These noun phrases may include a variety of components (determiner, adjective(s) and noun (Example 1)), or may simply be made up of pronouns (Example 2).

1 Les touristes japonais | attendent | devant | le vieux château.
subject noun phrase — verb phrase — preposition — object noun phrase

The Japanese tourists are waiting in front of the old castle.

2 Ils | sont arrivés | après | nous. *They arrived after us.*
s.n.p — v.p. — prep. — o. n. p.

Insight

Prepositions are normally used with nouns or pronouns, but **à, de, pour** and **sans** can also be used with verbs: **'Il vient <u>pour dire</u> bonjour'** (*'He's coming to say hello'*); **'Il commence <u>à pleuvoir</u>'** ('It's starting to rain'); **'Elle part <u>sans dire</u> au revoir'** (*'She's leaving without saying goodbye'*).

2.1 Frequently used prepositions

Prepositions are extremely useful words. Below are some of the most frequently used ones. For a more exhaustive list, you should consult your grammar book.

à	*at/to/in*	**derrière**	*behind*
à cause de	*because of*	**devant**	*before (space)*
à côté de	*beside/next to*	**en**	*in*
à partir de	*from*	**en face de**	*opposite*
après	*after*	**entre**	*between*
au-dessous de	*below*	**par**	*by/through*
au-dessus de	*above*	**parmi**	*among*
autour de	*around*	**pendant**	*during*
avant	*before (time)*	**pour**	*for*
avec	*with*	**sans**	*without*
contre	*against*	**sous**	*under*
de	*of/from*	**sur**	*on*

2.2 Special cases

1 As you can see from the above list, the preposition de (*of/from*) may be used on its own, or to end longer prepositional phrases. In both cases, de will be reduced to **d'** if the word which follows begins with a vowel or a mute **h**. For an explanation of this latter point, see Appendix 6:

Nous venons juste *de* fermer le magasin.	*We have just closed the shop.*
Nous venons juste *d'*ouvrir le magasin.	*We have just opened the shop.*

2 As you will remember, the prepositions **à** (*at/to*) and **de** combine with the definite articles **le** (masculine singular) and **les** (masculine and feminine plural), as shown in the table below, if the word that immediately follows them begins with a consonant:

Preposition	*Masculine sing. + le*	*Feminine sing. + la*	*Masculine/ Feminine plur. + les*
à	au	à la	aux
de	du	de la	des

Les employés vont *au* travail. *The employees (masc.) go/are going to work.*
Nous allons *à l'*aéroport. *We go/are going to the airport.*
J'ai reçu une lettre *du* directeur. *I (have) received a letter from the director.*
Il a reçu une lettre *de* l'usine. *He (has) received a letter from the factory.*

Beware: These combinations do not happen if **le** or **les** are pronouns and not articles.

Ils ont réussi à le persuader. *They (have) succeeded in persuading him.*
Nous venons de les voir. *We have just seen them.*

3 A small number of prepositions can be used either with noun phrases or with verb phrases. They are: **à, de, pour** and **sans**:

Il commence *à* pleuvoir. *It is beginning to rain.*
Ils viennent *de* partir *sans* dire au revoir. *They have just gone without saying goodbye.*

Note, however, that **par** can also be followed by a verb, but only in the two expressions **commencer par** and **finir par**:

Elle a commencé par refuser notre offre, mais elle a fini par accepter.	*She began by refusing our offer, but she ended up by accepting.*

Insight

In English, the United States (of America) or USA can either be singular or plural. The French equivalent is always plural: '**Les États-Unis/les USA sont très puissants**' ('*The United States/the USA is/are very powerful*').

2.3 Prepositions with place names

When you wish to state that you are going to – or staying in – a country, a town, a region, you should use the appropriate preposition as shown below:

1 If you are going to or staying in a country which is feminine in gender, that is to say ends in **-e** (with the exception of **le Mexique** (*Mexico*) and **le Mozambique**), you should use **en**:

Ils vont *en* France.	*They go (are going) to France.*
Nous habitons *en* Angleterre.	*We live (are living) in England.*
Elle est *en* Suisse.	*She is in Switzerland.*

The same applies in the case of regions:

Il a une maison en Bretagne et une autre en Provence.	*He has a house in Brittany and another in Provence.*

If you want to express the idea of *coming from* a country or region which is feminine in gender, you must use **de** or **d'** as appropriate (if a vowel follows):

Nous revenons *de* France.	*We are coming back from France.*
Ils arrivent *d'*Irlande.	*They are arriving from Ireland.*

2 If you want to say that you are going to or staying in a 'masculine' country (i.e. ending in a consonant, or a vowel other than -e), the preposition à is needed:

Nous irons *au* Portugal pour affaires.	*We will go to Portugal on business.*
Moi, je préfère aller *au* Maroc!	*I (personally) prefer going to Morocco!*
Il est *au* Guatémala en ce moment.	*He is in Guatemala at the moment.*

Note: If you want to say that you are going to or staying in a French region which is singular, but not feminine (does not end in -e), dans le should be used.

Outside France most regions are deemed to be masculine: **le Montana, le Maine, le Lancashire, le Yorkshire**, etc. One exception in Britain is **la Cornouaille** (*Cornwall*).

3 If you want to express the idea of coming from a country or region which is masculine in gender, you should use **du** or **d'** as appropriate:

Elle a reçu une lettre *du* Honduras.	*She (has) received a letter from Honduras.*

4 If you are going to or staying in a country whose name is masculine/feminine plural, the preposition needed is **aux** (combination of à + les):

Je vais *aux* Seychelles.	*I am going to the Seychelles.*
Ils sont *aux* États-Unis.	*They are in the United States.*

5 If you want to express the idea of coming from a country or region which is plural (masculine or feminine), you should use **des**:

Nous revenons *des* USA.	*We are returning from the United States.*
L'ouragan vient *des* Açores.	*The hurricane comes from the Azores.*

With the name of a town, the preposition à is used in most cases:

Ils sont *à* Bordeaux et je suis *à* New York.	*They are in Bordeaux and I am in New York.*

The only exception is when the name of the town contains the definite article le/la. In this case, the preposition will be au or à la:

Ils sont arrivés *au* Touquet (*Le Touquet = town in France*).	*They (have) arrived in Le Touquet.*
La conférence se tiendra *à la* Haye (*La Haye = town in Holland*).	*The meeting will be held in The Hague.*

Activity 3

Insert the correct preposition meaning *to* or *at/in* in the following sentences.

1 Je vais __________ Paris pour quelques jours.
2 Le directeur est __________ Sénégal.
3 La Haye est __________ Hollande.
4 Tu viens __________ Londres?
5 Le Touquet est __________ France.
6 Il y a eu une révolution __________ Chili.
7 Le président ira en visite __________ Émirats Arabes Unis.

Activity 4

Are the following correct? If they are not, make the appropriate amendments.

1 Voici une lettre du France.
2 Tu viens de l'Honduras?
3 Le Sultan de la Maroc est en visite au Paris.
4 Huit jours en Égypte? C'est formidable!
5 La réunion sera à Hollande.
6 Nous allons passer trois semaines en Argentine.
7 J'arrive juste d'Espagne.

8 Il y a des problèmes en Pakistan.
9 Elle doit aller au Russie à la fin du mois.
10 Ils habitent au Suisse depuis dix ans.

Activity 5

Having re-read Dialogue 1 between Daniel and Marc, make two lists: A and B. In list A, you should give all the examples of prepositions followed by nouns or pronouns. There should be 27 of them. In list B, you should only include examples of prepositions followed by a verb.

Activity 6

In Dialogue 1, there are five expressions that will be useful to you if you need to make a phone call in French. Make a list of them as they occur. (There is no need for you to include the names of the people.)

3 How (and when) to use *tu* or *vous* when speaking to one person

You will have noticed that in the telephone conversation between Marc and Daniel, the former uses the polite form **vous** and the latter uses **tu** or corresponding forms (**ton, te, etc.**). In the early stages of their studies, many learners of French are puzzled by the fact that, when addressing one person, they have to choose between **tu** (familiar form) and **vous** (polite form), and to try and match the various adjectives or pronouns associated with each of these two forms. As a consequence, they often start using one mode and, in mid-sentence, switch to the other mode:

***Tu as perdu votre portefeuille?**	*Have you (fam.) lost your (formal) wallet?*
***Vous avez ta carte de crédit?**	*Have you (formal) got your (fam.) credit card?*

Please note that, in linguistic terms, the asterisk (*) indicates that the expression or sentence is **not** grammatically acceptable.

The first example (see previous page) should be either: ***tu* as perdu *ton* portefeuille?** (fam.), or ***vous* avez perdu *votre* portefeuille?** (formal). The second should be either: ***tu* as *ta* carte de crédit?** (fam.), or ***vous* avez *votre* carte de crédit?** (formal).

This distinction between the familiar and formal way of addressing one person has all but disappeared in Standard English, but it can still be used in special circumstances (the Lord's Prayer), or in regional forms of speech (Yorkshire) to mark familiarity. In modern French, however, these two ways of addressing one person still exist and have to be distinguished. The rules are in fact quite simple:

- The **tu** form and the other adjectives (*your*) or pronouns (*yours*) associated with it are used between relatives or close friends, but not normally with strangers. There are, however, a few exceptions:

  1 Members of a close-knit group, students for instance, use the **tu** form, even though they may not know each other; in this case, the **tu** form creates a bond between members of the group.

  2 The **tu** form can be used with a complete stranger as a mark of contempt or disrespect. Parisian taxi drivers use this quite often with unruly pedestrians!

- The **vous** form is used in all other cases. It should *not* be seen as a sign of stand-offishness, but as a *mark of respect*. People who have worked together for years in the same office are quite likely to use the polite form with each other, particularly if they belong to the over-forties generation.

In Dialogue 1, it is perfectly logical for Daniel to use **tu**. He is a good deal older than Marc and has probably known him for years. Marc, on the other hand, is much younger, is no blood relation and may see Daniel infrequently, so he will use **vous** as a mark of respect.

Language learning tip 1

The best thing for you to remember about the use of **tu** or **vous** is to take your cue from French native speakers of your age group: if they address you as **tu**, you may do the same with them. Otherwise, use **vous**, just to be on the safe side!

Activity 7

Imagine that you have to answer a phone call in French. Translate your side of the conversation. You should try to make good use of the expressions we have met earlier in the unit.

Caller	Allô, je voudrais parler à Monsieur Smith, s'il vous plaît.
You	*Speaking! What can I do for you?*
Caller	Robert Dupont à l'appareil.
You	*I am sorry, but …*
Caller	Nous nous sommes rencontrés à Paris, il y a quelques semaines. Vous m'avez donné votre carte de visite.
You	*Oh, yes, it was at a business meeting. What a surprise!*
Caller	Vous m'aviez dit de vous donner un coup de fil si j'étais de passage dans la région.
You	*That's true. Where are you at the moment?*
Caller	Je suis en ville.
You	*In a hotel?*
Caller	Non, à la gare. Mon train part dans trois heures. Je ne voudrais pas vous déranger, mais si vous êtes libre, je vous invite à prendre un apéritif.
You	*That's very kind, and I am free at the moment. Listen, I'll get the car and I will be there in five minutes!*
Caller	Excellent! Je vous attends au café, en face de la gare.

Activity 8

Having re-read the first telephone conversation in Unit 2, Dialogue 1, write down the five polite expressions used by Marc and for each, give the English equivalent.

4 Prepositional pronouns

In French, if a preposition is followed by a pronoun, this pronoun must belong to a special set called prepositional pronouns. You will find the list of these pronouns in the middle column of the table below.

Subject pronoun	*Prepositional pronoun*	*English equivalent*
je	moi	*me/myself*
tu (fam.)	toi	*you/yourself (fam.)*
il/elle	lui/elle	*him(self)/her(self)/ it(self)*
on	soi	*oneself*
nous	nous	*us/ourselves*
vous (polite sing./ plur.)	vous	*you/yourselves (pol./ plur.)*
ils/elles	eux/elles	*them/themselves*

Chacun pour *soi*. — *Every man for himself (lit. everyone for oneself).*

Nous partons avec *eux*. — *We are leaving with them (masc. plur.).*

Restez derrière *moi*. — *Stay behind me.*

Vous êtes pour *moi* ou contre *moi*? — *Are you for me or against me?*

Je suis arrivé avant *toi*. — *I arrived before you (fam.).*

Activity 9

In sentences 1–9, replace the word in brackets with the appropriate French prepositional pronoun, paying close attention to the subject noun phrase.

1 Ils sont partis avec (*Marc*).
2 Tu vas garder ce secret pour (*yourself*).
3 Partez, je rentrerai sans (*you*).
4 Elle est arrivée avant (*John and Claudine*).
5 Il n'est pas d'accord avec (*his wife*).
6 Vous devez toujours avoir votre passeport sur (*you*).
7 Ces étudiantes ont toute la vie devant (*them*).
8 On doit toujours regarder devant (*oneself*).
9 J'ai acheté des fleurs pour (*your mother*).

Activity 10

Translate the sentences above into English.

4.1 A question of emphasis

In English, it is possible to indicate the fact that someone did something, rather than someone else, by pronouncing the appropriate word with more power.

In French, the stress system is different from English (see Appendix 6), so a different method needs to be used to achieve a similar effect. This is done with the help of an emphatic pronoun. The good news is that the emphatic pronouns are the same as the prepositional pronouns we have just studied:

C'est *moi* (*not* je) qui ai appelé la police.	*It is* **I** *(and no one else) who called the police.*
C'est *lui* (*not* il) qui a mangé le gâteau.	*It is* **he** *(and not* **I** *or* **you***) who ate the cake.*

If it is necessary to stress the fact that someone wants to claim sole responsibility for an action, or to be clearly distinguished from anyone else, the appropriate emphatic pronoun can be used before the subject pronoun:

***Vous*, vous aimez le champagne.**	**You** *like champagne (by contrast with someone else).*
***Toi*, tu peux partir, mais *moi*, je reste!**	**You** *(fam.) can go, but* **I** *am staying!*

Note that, on their own, the French emphatic pronouns are sufficient to give the idea of distinctiveness, and that English expressions like *as for (me)*, *personally*, *speaking for (myself)* ... do not have to be translated.

Insight

Deciding whether to use **tu** (*you* – familiar) or **vous** (*you* – polite) when addressing a person is easy: use **tu** with a close friend or a youngster, and **vous** with someone you want to show respect to. Compare: '**Tu es libre?**' ('*Are you free?*' – familiar) and '**Vous êtes libre?**' ('*Are you free?*' – respectful). **Vous** can also be used to address several people.

Dialogue 2

As promised, Daniel has gone to fetch Marc at the hotel. They are now having a pre-dinner drink and a chat in Daniel's back garden. They are joined by Daniel's daughter Audrey, who is a student at the local university. From the outset, it is clear that she has a lively personality and a penchant for arguing!

CD1, TR 2, 05:58

Daniel Alors, si je comprends bien, ta mère veut revenir au pays?
Marc Oui. La France lui manque un peu, je crois.
Audrey C'est normal: c'est le plus beau pays du monde!
Marc Vous ne pensez pas que vous ...
Audrey Tu peux me dire tu!
Marc D'accord. Tu ne penses pas que tu exagères un peu?
Daniel Audrey n'a pas tout-à-fait tort. Nous, les Français, nous avons beaucoup de chance: le climat, les paysages, la nourriture, enfin tout ce qu'il faut pour être heureux!
Marc En Angleterre aussi, il y a de beaux coins!
Audrey Peut-être, mais il pleut toujours chez vous!
Marc Je suis désolé, mais c'est un mythe! Il fait un temps superbe à Londres en ce moment.
Audrey L'exception qui confirme la règle! De toute façon, la preuve est là: il y a des tas d'étrangers qui viennent s'installer chez nous, soit pour travailler, soit pour prendre leur retraite.

Marc C'est vrai, mais chez nous, on dit que les Français sont xénophobes.

Audrey Désolée, je ne suis pas du tout d'accord! Autrefois, peut-être, mais de nos jours, non. Grâce à l'Europe, on est devenus plus ouverts et plus tolérants. Bien sûr, il y a toujours des exceptions et des partis politiques extrémistes comme le Front National, qui encouragent ces sentiments …

Daniel De toute façon, il faut être logique: si quelqu'un vient chez nous et refuse de faire des efforts pour s'intégrer, pour parler la langue, alors il est mal vu, c'est sûr! C'est une question de respect de la culture! Moi je connais pas mal d'Anglais qui vivent ici. Ils ont fait un réel effort pour s'intégrer et ils sont très bien acceptés.

Audrey Il faut dire aussi que pour la technologie, la mode, la nourriture la France a été – et est encore – à la pointe du progrès: le Minitel, le TGV, Concorde et j'en passe!

Daniel Cocorico, ma fille!

Marc Je te demande pardon, Audrey, mais Concorde était un projet franco-britannique! Et pour la mode, je ne suis pas tout à fait d'accord non plus! L'Angleterre a des grands couturiers. On dit que les Françaises sont très chic, mais la dernière fois que je suis venu à Paris, je n'ai pas eu cette impression!

Audrey Tu n'étais pas dans le bon quartier!

Marc Mm … peut-être! Et, tu penses que la France mérite toujours sa réputation de pays du bien-vivre?

Audrey Absolument! D'ailleurs, tous les grands cuisiniers sont français!

Marc Désolé de te contredire, mais en Angleterre il y a maintenant d'excellents chefs cuisiniers qui présentent des programmes à la télé pour encourager les gens, surtout les hommes, à faire la cuisine.

Audrey C'est une bonne chose, surtout de nos jours où les femmes travaillent à l'extérieur, pas vrai, papa?

Daniel Je suis tout à fait d'accord sur ce point!

Audrey (*to Marc*) Papa est un amour: il cuisine, il fait le ménage pendant que maman se promène!

Marc	À propos d'amour, tout le monde dit que les Français sont les meilleurs amants du monde. C'est traumatisant pour les autres!
Audrey	Mais c'est absolument vrai!
Daniel	Dis donc, tu es un peu jeune pour juger, toi!
Audrey	Pff!
Daniel	Non, je crois qu'il faut être modeste sur ce point. Je ne suis pas sûr que nous méritions encore cette réputation, qui est très subjective et vient en partie de la littérature. Mais le fait est que nous savons, à l'occasion, être romantiques et les étrangères craquent quand elles entendent un accent français!
Audrey	De toute façon, comme on disait en 68, il vaut mieux faire l'amour que la guerre!
Marc	Sans aucun doute. À propos de guerre, les Britanniques ont l'impression que les Français sont prêts à se révolter pour un oui ou pour un non.
Daniel	C'est un peu vrai! Nous sommes moins flegmatiques que les Britanniques. À mon avis, c'est le climat!
Audrey	Pff, n'importe quoi!
Marc	En tout cas, les manifestations d'agriculteurs, les barrages sur la route des vacances, les sit-in dans les écoles et les universités, on n'a pas ça chez nous!
Audrey	C'est l'héritage de 1789. C'est dans les gènes!
Daniel	Bon, assez discuté! Si on passait à table?
Audrey	Bonne idée. J'ai une faim de loup!

Insight

Although the **tu** form is reserved for use with close friends and relatives, it is often heard between strangers who are part of a close-knit community (e.g. students), even though they may never have met before. Taxi drivers also use it as an insult when addressing other road users!

manquer *to miss, but beware:* **je manque quelque chose** *(I fail to catch/hit something).* **Quelque chose or quelqu'un me manque** *(I miss something or somebody).*

avoir tort *to be wrong.* **Avoir raison** *(to be right).*

la chance *luck, but beware: although it is usually a false friend, it can also mean chance or opportunity e.g.* **la dernière chance** *(the last chance).*

le mythe *myth. The opposite is usually* **la réalité.**

le/la xénophobe *person who hates foreigners or strangers*

le Front National *National Front. Its equivalent in Britain is now called the BNP (British National Party).*

pas mal de ... *a good many ...*

le Minitel *In its time (1980), an advanced system of access to data linked to the telephone and launched by France Télécom. Now largely overtaken by recent developments in IT.*

le Concorde *The famous supersonic aircraft built jointly by the British and the French. It first went into service in 1976 and was 'retired' at the end of 2003.*

et j'en passe! *to name but a few (lit. and I pass on a few)*

cocorico *cock-a-doodle-doo. Apart from its normal meaning, it is used humorously to refer to the (sometimes) excessive national pride of French people. Remember that the Gallic cockerel is one of the national symbols of France.*

pour un oui ... pour un non *at the slightest excuse/at the drop of a hat*

1789 *The date of the French Revolution which led to the beheading of the then King and Queen of France.*

avoir une faim de loup *to be ravenous (lit. to have a wolf's hunger)*

QUICK VOCAB

Comprehension 2

1 What expression, frequently used by Marc, indicates that he feels more British than French?

2 What made Marc have doubts about the reputation of French women for elegance and sophistication?

3 According to Daniel, what should foreigners do to be fully accepted in France?
4 What according to Audrey have been the advantages of France joining the European Union?
5 How does Marc counter Audrey's claim about the best cooks in the world being French?
6 What is the famous slogan of the 1960s quoted by Audrey?
7 What is Daniel's reaction to the suggestion that French men are said to be the best lovers?
8 According to Daniel, what happens when foreign women hear a man speaking with a French accent?
9 What examples does Marc give to show that the French are more hot-blooded than the British?

Activity 11

In the conversation between Marc, Daniel and Audrey, there are useful phrases to express various shades of agreement and disagreement. In this activity, match the meanings of the two columns. For example, if you feel that the English phrase A matches the French number 1 (which it does not!), write A1 as your answer.

A *I totally agree.*
B *I don't agree at all.*
C *That's for sure.*
D *I'm sorry.*
E *Sorry to disagree with you.*
F *It must be said that …*
G *There's some truth in it/this.*
H *I'm not sure.*
I *She's not entirely wrong.*
J *It's absolutely true.*
K *I didn't have that feeling.*
L *We have talked (about it) enough.*
M *I beg your pardon.*

1 Elle n'a pas tout a fait tort.
2 Je suis désolé.
3 Je suis tout a fait d'accord.
4 Je ne suis pas sûr.
5 Je ne suis pas du tout d'accord.
6 C'est sûr.
7 Il faut dire que …
8 Je te demande pardon.
9 Je n'ai pas eu cette impression.
10 Désolé de te contredire.
11 C'est absolument vrai.
12 C'est un peu vrai.
13 Assez discuté.

Insight

In the plural, the article **des** is used before a noun to translate 'some'/'an unspecified number of ...'. If, however, an adjective is placed between **des** and the noun, **des** will change to **de** (or **d'** if a vowel or a mute **h** follows).

Compare: **'Il y a <u>des</u> exceptions'** (*'There are some exceptions'*) and: **'Il y a <u>de</u> rares exceptions'** (*'There are some rare exceptions'*).

Reading

The following editorial exemplifies the feelings of national pride which most French people harbour towards all things French. Read it several times before completing the exercises which follow it.

Ne m'appelez plus jamais Concorde!

C'est avec une grande tristesse que les Français ont accueilli la nouvelle de la mise à la retraite du plus célèbre des avions de transport de passagers du monde. Né dans les ateliers aéronautiques de Toulouse, d'une étroite collaboration entre les avionneurs français et britanniques, d'où son nom, il a été pendant toute sa vie active un fleuron de la technologie française. Il a, en son temps, fait beaucoup d'envieux: les Russes en ont même fabriqué une copie, ironiquement baptisée Concordski! Mais tout a une fin. Comme son cousin le France, qui avait sillonné les mers pendant plusieurs décennies, il a fini dans un musée après un peu moins de trente ans de bons et loyaux services. Plus qu'un avion, Concorde était un symbole du génie français, des capacités technologiques de nos ingénieurs et techniciens.

Il était capable de voler à Mach 2 et d'assurer la liaison entre Paris et New York en un peu moins de trois heures et demie. Un rêve pour les hommes d'affaires pressés, qui pouvaient voyager sans fatigue dans le plus grand confort et arriver frais et dispos à leur destination. Il faut dire que le billet n'était pas à la portée de toutes les bourses, puisque l'aller-retour Paris–New York coûtait près de 10.000 euros!

Bien sûr, il a eu des problèmes, notre Concorde: d'abord un coût de développement qui avait considérablement dépassé le budget initial, ensuite, le faible nombre de passagers qu'il pouvait transporter comparé aux jumbo jets. Enfin, les normes strictes imposées par les autorités américaines concernant la pollution et le bruit. Mais c'est probablement le triste accident survenu en 2000 qui a signé son arrêt de mort: on ne badine pas avec la sécurité du public! Pourtant, une chose est certaine: sa silhouette restera pour toujours gravée dans nos mémoires, et qui sait? Il inspirera peut-être à Michel Sardou une autre de ses chansons!

La Gazette

QUICK VOCAB

un avionneur *an aircraft manufacturer*
un atelier *a workshop*
un fleuron *a jewel (in the crown)*
une étroite collaboration *a close cooperation*
en son temps *in its day*
sillonner les mers *to sail to and fro across/to criss-cross the seas*
la décennie *ten-year period/decade*
assurer la liaison *to link (for a service)*
pressé *(adj.) in a hurry*
frais et dispos *fresh as a daisy*
à la portée de toutes les bourses *affordable by everybody (lit. within the reach of all purses)*
un aller-retour *return ticket*
un arrêt de mort *death warrant*
on ne badine pas avec … *one does not trifle with … (expression based on the title of a 19th century play called:* **On ne badine pas avec l'amour***)*
gravé dans nos mémoires *engraved on our memory*
qui sait? *who knows?*

Michel Sardou *French singer, author of a number of controversial songs, including* **'Ne m'appelez plus jamais France'**, *written as a protest about the scrapping of the famous French liner* **le France**; *hence the title of the editorial.*

Concorde: le grand oiseau blanc (the big white bird).

Comprehension 3

This activity is part of your self-assessment strategy. Award yourself ten marks per correct answer and add this to your total on the self-assessment record form at the end of the book.

Having read the article about Concorde, answer the following questions in English.

1 What triggered the writing of the editorial?
2 What has been the fate of the aircraft?
3 In the article, there is a reference to Russia. Can you clarify what it is about?
4 List the capabilities of the aircraft and the reasons which made it popular with business people.
5 What are the reasons given in the editorial for Concorde's demise?

Activity 12

There are, in the editorial, several statements that could be seen as characteristic of the **cocorico** attitude mentioned earlier in the unit. Can you spot them?

Language learning tip 2

- Generally, the names of planes, ships, lorries are masculine in French: **le Concorde, le Boeing; le France, le Queen Mary, le Titanic; le Ford, le Peugeot …**
- Cars, on the other hand, are always considered feminine: **la Citroën, la Ford, la Peugeot, la Rolls-Royce …** Could this have anything to do with the love affair that exists between the French and their cars?
- If you wish to find out further information and opinions about the retirement of Concorde, try to access http://museedelta.free.fr/index2.htm on the net. If the site is still accessible, you will find some interesting linguistic material!

Tout homme a deux patries: la sienne et puis la France! *Every man has two homelands: his own and France!* This statement obviously predates the political correctness era, to which the French are not overly sensitive.

En France, on n'a pas de pétrole, mais on a des idées! *In France, we have no crude oil reserves, but we have ideas/imagination!*

Insight

French has two auxiliaries to create compound tenses: **avoir** (*to have*) and **être** (*to be*), whereas English has only got one (*to have*).

Verbs of movement (+ **naître** – *to be born* and **mourir** – *to die*) use **être** as their auxiliary. The others use **avoir**. Compare: **il est parti** (*he/it has gone*); **elle a vu** (*she/it has seen*); **ils sont venus** (*they have come*); **vous avez eu** (*you have had*).

TEST YOURSELF

1. What five shades of meaning can the present tense be used to convey?
2. When can **ça** (*this/that*) be used to replace **ceci** or **cela**?
3. Where do the main preconceptions about French people come from?
4. What is the meaning of **le Midi** when it does not refer to 12 p.m.?
5. What are prepositions?
6. When do the combinations **au** (= **à + le**) and **aux** (= **à + les**) not take place?
7. When do the prepositions **à** and **de** change to **au** and **du** before names of towns?
8. What makes **à, de, pour,** and **sans** different from other prepositions?
9. In what circumstances is the familiar form **tu** used as a mark of disrespect or contempt?
10. Which of the two following sentences is wrong: **'Tu as perdu votre passeport'** or **'Vous avez fini votre travail'**?

3

Autrefois et aujourd'hui

In this unit you will learn

- ***How to form and use the imperfect indicative to say how things used to be***
- ***About the role of cafés in French culture***
- ***How to distinguish between simple tenses and compound tenses***
- ***When to use avoir and when to use être to form the perfect***
- ***How to distinguish between the two uses of the perfect in French***
- ***How to distinguish between demonstrative adjectives and pronouns and use them***
- ***How to distinguish between a voiced and a silent* h *and why it is important***
- ***How to use indeterminate pronouns***
- ***Basic information about wine and food***

1 *The imperfect*

As we know, it is essential, when trying to communicate, to situate actions in the proper time zone, otherwise we may confuse our listener(s) or reader(s). It is for that reason that we need different tenses. Basic information about the imperfect indicative is presented below. A detailed description of the meaning of the moods and tenses used in French is given in Appendix 4.

The imperfect, as you will recall from prior language studies, is used in a specific number of cases:

1 To translate *used to*, i.e. to express actions which happened regularly/repeatedly in the past. In English, this idea is given by expressions like *when(ever)*, *every time*, etc.

Quand j'étais (*imperfect*) **jeune, je lisais** (*imperfect*) **beaucoup.**	*When I was young, I used to read a great deal.*

We can safely assume that being young lasted a while, and reading was a regular occurrence during that period!

2 To express that an action (1) was in progress when another one (2) happened:

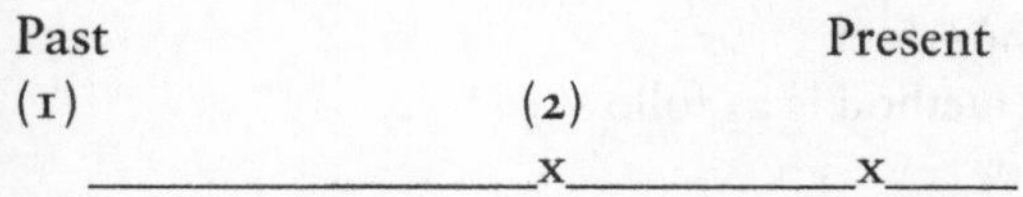

Je lisais quand elle est arrivée.	*I was reading when she arrived.*

This does not automatically mean that action (1) ceased when action (2) took place.

Note: In modern French (particularly in speech), **le passé composé** (*perfect*) is used to express action (2).

3 To describe enduring features characteristic of someone or something in the past:

Elle était grande et brune.	*She was tall and dark-haired (enduring features).*
En été, il faisait très chaud.	*In summer, it (the weather) used to be very hot.*

Beware: The use of the imperfect does not automatically imply that the action which occurred regularly (or lasted a long time) is happening now.

4 To express a condition which holds good for the present, but which could still apply in the future:

Si j'avais (1) le temps, je regarderais (2) le film. — *If I had time (now or later), I would watch the film.*

In this example, the tense referred to as number (2) is a present conditional, which we will be studying in a later unit.

Insight

The adverb **si** (*if*), not to be confused with the particle **si** used to counter negative questions, can express a condition or a doubt: **'Si j'ai le temps, je téléphonerai'** (*'If I have time I will phone'*); **'Je ne sais pas si je téléphonerai'** (*'I don't know if I'll phone'*).

1.1 How to form the imperfect

As you know, the basic method is as follows:

Take the present participle of the verb, i.e. the equivalent of the English *-ing* form – (see the table below), remove the **-ant** ending and add one of the endings indicated in the right-hand column of the table.

A simpler – but less accurate – method is to remove the infinitive marker (-er, -ir, -re), and to replace it with the required ending from the last column of the table below.

Infinitive (and group number)		*Meaning*	*Present participle (-ing equivalent)*	*Stem/ root*	*Endings of the imperfect tense*	
rentrer	(1)	*to return*	rentr**ant**	rentr-	je	-ais
manger	(1)	*to eat*	mange**ant**	mang(e)-	tu	-ais
finir	(2)	*to finish*	finiss**ant**	finiss-	il/elle/on	-ait
partir	(3)	*to leave*	part**ant**	part-	nous	-ions
être	(3)	*to be*	ét**ant**	ét-	vous	-iez
voir	(3)	*to see*	voy**ant**	voy-	ils/elles	-aient

Sometimes, however, these simple recipes do not work. Here are some examples of stems/roots which do not follow the normal pattern:

1 The root used for the imperfect of **avoir** *to have* is **av-** and not **ay-** as you would expect from the present participle **ayant**.

Autrefois, nous *avions* un chien.	*(In the past) we had/used to have dog.*

2 Verbs whose infinitives end in **-ger** like **changer** *to change*, **charger** *to load*, **bouger** *to budge/move,* **nager** *to swim*, **loger** *to lodge*, etc. keep the **e** after **g**, when the next letter is an **a** (or an **o**), but drop that **e** when the next letter is an **i**:

je nageais, but **nous nagions**
tu changeais, but **vous changiez**

The reason for such seeming irregularities is simple and will be explained in due course. It will also be investigated at the end of the book, in Appendix 4.

Important: in English, you can use the simple past for past actions which lasted or were habitual:

Pendant qu'elle cuisinait, nous lisions le journal.	*While she cooked/was cooking we read/used to read the paper.*

Activity 1

This activity is part of your self-assessment schedule. There are 20 verbs to be put into the imperfect. You should award yourself five marks for each correct answer. This total should then be added to your previous scores in the self-assessment record form at the back of the book. There are a possible 100 marks available.

In the passage below, replace each infinitive by the appropriate form of the imperfect.

Quand **j'être** (1) enfant, mes parents **n'avoir** (2) pas de voiture. **J'aller** (3) à l'école à pied avec mes camarades. Les matins d'automne, quand nous **arriver** (4) dans la cour, nous **devoir** (5) ramasser les feuilles mortes qui **tomber** (6) des arbres. Il **faire** (7) froid et nous **courir** (8) pour nous réchauffer. Quand la cloche **sonner** (9), le directeur nous **faire** (10) mettre en rang et il **inspecter** (11) nos mains. Si elles **être** (12) sales, il nous **envoyer** (13) les laver dans l'eau glacée. Nous **avoir** (14) peur de lui et nous le **détester** (15) tous. Quand l'école **finir** (16), nous **sortir** (17) en courant et nous **rentrer** (18) chez nous. C'**être** (19) un plaisir d'oublier l'école! Nous **manger** (20) de bon cœur avant d'aller nous coucher.

Reading 1

On the next page are the opening lines of a well-known poem by the French writer Victor Hugo (1802–85), probably better known for his novel ***Les Misérables*** (1862), which was used as a basis for the musical production of the same name.

The poem depicts the return of the French army led by Napoleon in 1812 after a disastrous attempt to conquer Russia and to capture Moscow. Although romanticized, it gives a powerful impression of the appalling conditions under which the French army retreated. In that campaign, many thousands of soldiers died.

The full poem can be found online by, typing Victor Hugo and the poem title 'L'Expiation into a French search engine such as www.google.fr or http://fr.yahoo.com.

Read the passage twice before listening to the recording of it (if you have it), to get a feel for the sounds and the rhythm of the piece, then complete the activities which follow it.

Insight

The imperfect is used in French to express duration or repetition in the past, or the fact that an action was in progress when another action occurred: **'Il allait souvent au cinéma'** ('*He often used to go to the cinema*'); **'Je travaillais quand elle a téléphoné'** ('*I was working when she phoned*').

🔊 **CD1, TR 3, 00:57**

La Retraite de Russie (1812)

Il neigeait. On était vaincu par sa conquête.
Pour la première fois l'Aigle baissait la tête.
Sombres jours! L'empereur revenait lentement,
Laissant derrière lui brûler Moscou fumant.
Il neigeait. L'âpre hiver fondait en avalanche.
Après la plaine blanche, une autre plaine blanche.
On ne connaissait plus les chefs ni le drapeau.
Hier la Grande Armée, et maintenant troupeau.
On ne distinguait plus les ailes ni le centre.
Il neigeait. Les blessés s'abritaient dans le ventre
Des chevaux morts; au seuil des bivouacs désolés
On voyait des clairons à leur poste gelés,
Restés debout, en selle et muets, blancs de givre,
Collant leurs bouches en pierre aux trompettes de cuivre.
Boulets, mitraille, obus, mêlés aux flocons blancs,
pleuvaient;
Les grenadiers, surpris d'être tremblants,
Marchaient pensifs, la glace à leurs moustaches grises.
Il neigeait. Il neigeait toujours! La froide bise sifflait;
Sur le verglas, dans ces lieux inconnus,
On n'avait pas de pain et l'on allait pieds nus.

QUICK VOCAB

l'Aigle *the Eagle: nickname given to Napoleon because of the embroidered eagles which adorned the imperial flag.*
laissant derrière lui brûler Moscou fumant *The Russians adopted scorched earth tactics and destroyed everything which could be of use to the retreating French army.*
fondre *Usually to melt, but here to swoop like a bird of prey. An echo of the Eagle mentioned in the first line?*
on ne connaissait plus les chefs ni le drapeau *The soldiers no longer followed their leaders or the flag.*
la Grande Armée *The name used to refer to Napoleon's troops.*

(le) troupeau *the herd: a reference to the chaotic state of the army in retreat.*
des clairons *buglers (frozen to death at their post). The word can also refer to the instrument, the bugle.*
le givre/le verglas *here: ice/frost*
boulets, mitraille, ... pleuvaient *cannon balls, a hail of bullets, ... mixed with the snow, rained down (upon the soldiers)*
les grenadiers *grenadiers: the most trusted and faithful soldiers of the Emperor, sometimes affectionately referred to as* **les Grognards** *(the grumblers)*
la froide bise sifflait *in standard French* **la bise** *is an icy winter wind, not to be confused with* **la brise** *(a gentle spring breeze).* **Faire la bise** *is a familiar way of saying to give a kiss.*

Comprehension 1

Write down the line number(s) of the poem which give a clue about the following. Note, however, that the items are not in sequence.

1 The state of deprivation the soldiers were in.
2 The fate that had befallen the buglers.
3 The desperate measures used by the wounded to find shelter.
4 The backdrop to the retreat.
5 The state of disarray of Napoleon's Great Army.
6 The frame of mind Napoleon was in at the time.
7 The relentless violence of the storm and of the enemy.

Activity 2

Translate the following into 'fluid' English:

1 Pour la première fois l'Aigle baissait la tête.
2 L'empereur revenait lentement.
3 On ne distinguait plus les ailes ni le centre.
4 On voyait des clairons à leur poste gelés.
5 Il neigeait. Il neigeait toujours.
6 La froide bise sifflait.

Insight

The adverb **toujours** can mean *still* or *always*. So, **'Il est toujours malade'** could mean *'He is still ill'* or *'He's always ill'*. In Victor Hugo's poem, **toujours** expresses the idea of relentless continuity: **'Il neigeait toujours'** (*'It kept on snowing'*).

Activity 3

If we count as one the five repetitions of **il neigeait**, there are, in the poem, 14 verbs in the imperfect. For this activity, you should make a list of them and, for each, give the infinitive form and the group it belongs to.

Activity 4

There are, in the passage, two present participles and one reflexive verb. Can you find them and write them down? Give the infinitive of the two present participles.

Activity 5

You should now put the verbs contained in the poem into the present tense, as if the retreat were happening now. Do not re-write the whole piece, just list the verbs in the order they occur.

Dialogue 1

Marc Swift, who is developing his network of business contacts for the British company he works for, is seeing some clients in Reims, the main town of the Champagne region (see the map in Unit 3, Reading 2) and the world capital of the wine of the same name. As he has some time to kill before going to a **déjeuner de travail** (*working lunch*) with a prospective customer, and is eager to practise his French, he does, as is his wont, strike up a conversation, this time with the owner of the Café de la Paix, a small establishment in a side street just off the town centre. As you will not fail to notice, the café owner and Marc are well matched: they both like to talk. The dialogue is therefore in two parts.

CD1, TR 3, 03:45

The owner	Alors, qu'est ce que je vous sers?
Marc	Un petit noir, s'il vous plaît. C'est bien calme chez vous ce matin!
The owner	Vous savez, à cette heure-ci c'est normal. Vous êtes de passage?
Marc	Oui, je suis ici pour affaires.
The owner	Vous travaillez dans quelle branche?
Marc	Les équipements de sport et de loisir.
The owner	Ah, c'est une industrie en expansion, pas vrai?
Marc	Par rapport au reste de l'économie, oui. Et vous? Vous tenez ce café depuis longtemps?
The owner	Oui. Je suis venu ici il y a plus de trente ans.
Marc	Comme employé?
The owner	Non, non, comme patron. Voilà votre café!
Marc	Merci. Vous avez commencé votre carrière ici?
The owner	Non, avant de venir à Reims, ma femme et moi nous étions gérants d'un débit de boissons pas loin d'ici dans un petit village de 300 habitants.
Marc	Qu'est-ce qui vous a poussés à venir à Reims?
The owner	Ben, la population du village devenait trop faible pour nous permettre de gagner notre vie.
Marc	Pourquoi ça?
The owner	Eh ben, parce que les jeunes ne voulaient plus rester à la campagne. Ils étaient attirés par la ville, les salaires, les conditions de travail et tout ça. La population diminuait constamment. À la fin, on réussissait juste à joindre les deux bouts. Alors un jourqu'on était venus faire des courses en ville ma femme et moi, on a vu ce café en vente dans une agence immobilière. On a pris notre courage à deux mains, et voilà!
Marc	Et les affaires marchent bien ici?
The owner	Moyennement. Faut pas se plaindre. Heureusement, je fais aussi bureau de tabac.
Marc	Et vous n'avez jamais eu de remords?
The owner	À quel sujet?
Marc	Eh bien, à cause du fait que vous vendez des produits dangereux pour la santé: l'alcool et le tabac!

The owner	Il faut regarder les choses en face: d'abord les gens ne sont pas obligés de consommer ces produits. Ensuite, si je ne les vends pas c'est un autre qui le fera, et en plus, on dit que l'alcool est bon pour la santé!
Marc	Je veux bien vous croire. Et les choses ont bien changé depuis votre arrivée à Reims?
The owner	Oui. Autrefois les gens venaient au bistro pour rencontrer leurs copains et prendre un verre à midi, ou le soir, avant de rentrer à la maison. On bavardait, on jouait à la belote. Le bistro était une institution: il jouait un rôle essentiel dans la société française …

(à suivre)

Insight

Most French nouns form their plural by adding **s: le café** (*the coffee*), **les cafés; la boisson** (*the drink*), **les boissons,** etc. There are, however, many exceptions: **le journal** (*the newspaper*) becomes **les journaux; le travail** (*the work*) becomes **les travaux; le ciel** (*the sky*) becomes **les cieux,** etc.

QUICK VOCAB

tenir *here: to manage (a business or shop)*
le patron (*or* **le propriétaire)** *the owner*
le gérant *the manager (but not the owner)*
un débit de boissons *a bar (drinking establishment)*
ben *or* **eh ben (***fam. for* **eh bien)** *well/well then*
être attiré par … *to be attracted by …*
constamment *constantly*
joindre les deux bouts *to make ends meet*
les affaires marchent (bien) *the business is doing well*
avoir des remords *to suffer remorse/pangs of conscience*
regarder les choses en face *here: to face up to things (lit. to look things in the face)*
les copains *friends/pals*
bavarder *to chat*
un bistro *(fam.) a bar or café*
la belote *popular card game*

Un petit noir: *a (small!) cup of black coffee.* Sometimes the word **serré** (*extra strong*) will be used after it. Although you will sometimes hear a customer ask for **un (café) crème,** many French people prefer to take their coffee without milk.

L'alcool est bon pour la santé: Some doctors have long maintained that alcohol, wine in particular, is good for you (in moderation of course), because it contains health-preserving *trace elements* (**des oligo-éléments**).

Le bistro était une institution. It is true that French cafés have traditionally been places where literary and artistic figures met to discuss music, painting, philosophy, poetry, etc. The most famous is probably the Café de Flore in the St-Germain-des-Prés area of Paris. If you feel you want to know more about it, why not look on the net at http://www.cafe-de-flore.com?

Comprehension 2

The statements below relate to Dialogue 1. Say whether they are true or false. If false, give the correct answer or evidence to justify your choice.

1 The café owner was single when he bought the bar in Reims.
2 The owner is now barely able to make ends meet.
3 In the village where he was before coming to Reims the number of inhabitants was small but stable.
4 In addition to alcohol the owner now sells tobacco and cigarettes.
5 He does feel a little remorseful about the type of products he sells.
6 In the old days people used to stop at the bar for a drink or a game of cards on their way home.
7 The owner claims that alcohol is good for your health.

Activity 6

In Dialogue 1, there are 11 examples of the imperfect tense. List them in the order in which they appear and for each, give the infinitive and the group it belongs to. To refresh your memory on the latter point, refer to the information on verb groups, Unit 1.

Activity 7

How would you say the following in French? Select key expressions from the Dialogue 1 and modify them to complete the task appropriately.

1 It's very quiet in town this morning!
2 What type of work do you do?
3 Compared to the rest of the economy it's an industry which is doing well.
4 Have you been working here long?
5 Before coming to Reims, I worked in a small village.
6 What made you decide to come here?
7 We just about managed to make ends meet.
8 Is business doing well here? Mustn't complain.
9 Sport is good for your health.
10 I am prepared to believe you.

Insight

English makes a distinction in meaning between the perfect tense (1) and the preterite or past definite (2): *I have reserved* (1) is different in meaning from *I reserved* (2).

In modern spoken French, the preterite (2) is rarely used. So people say: **j'ai réservé** for *I have reserved* or *I reserved*.

2 The perfect tense

Before launching into the study of this tense, it may be useful to clarify something which you know very well: in French there are two types of tenses, as follows:

1 Simple tenses. These are formed by adding an ending to the verb's root/stem. An example of this is the imperfect: **je regard*ais*** (*I used to look*), or **il fin*issait*** (*he used to finish*).
2 Compound tenses. These are created by bringing together two elements: an auxiliary and a form of the main verb called the past participle (see Column 4 of the verb table in Unit 1 Section 5.1).

Apart from slight agreement changes, the past participle remains the same whatever the tense. It is the auxiliary whose job it is to express the time zone of the action. The perfect tense, like the present and the imperfect, belongs to the indicative mood, which expresses reality as opposed to supposition, doubt, etc.

You should bear in mind that, in some cases, the perfect is used in French as in English to express an action which is now completed: **j'ai fini** (*I have finished*), **elle est partie** (*she has now gone*), **nous avons mangé** (*we have now eaten*), but this is not always the case: there are some significant differences between the two languages regarding its use.

1 The first one is that, instead of having one auxiliary (helping verb) as is the case in English where *to have* is used systematically, French has two: **avoir** (*to have*) and **être** (*to be*), which are used to form the perfect and all the other compound tenses, along with a past participle, the equivalent of the English forms *finished*, *gone*, *eaten*, etc.

As you may remember from earlier French studies, this is not a question of free choice: so-called verbs of movement (**aller, venir, monter, descendre**, etc.) take **être**, as do reflexive verbs, that is to say verbs indicating that the performer of the action is also the one on which the action falls: **se raser** (*to shave oneself*), **se couper** (*to cut oneself*), **se laver** (*to wash oneself*), etc.

2 The second difference is that, in French, the perfect tense can be used to convey two meanings:

je suis arrivé(e) could mean: (1) *I have arrived* (action completed = *I am now here*), or (2) *I arrived* (earlier).

This is because the tense traditionally used to indicate (2), called **le passé simple** (*simple past*), is now seen as 'too sophisticated' and is therefore avoided in everyday conversation. You may still, however, see it in formal written texts. For a description of this tense, and a more complete list of verbs of movement and reflexives or pronominal ones, you should consult your grammar book.

The agreement rules of past participles with **avoir** and **être** will be explained in Unit 5. In conversation, you need not worry too much about such agreements.

The present tense of the two auxiliaries needed to form the perfect in French is indicated below:

Avoir	*Être*
j'ai	je suis
tu as	tu es
il/elle/on a	il/elle/on est
nous avons	nous sommes
vous avez	vous êtes
ils/elles ont	ils/elles sont

As mentioned before, you are not free to choose which auxiliary to use to make up a given compound tense. The rules are very strict and are as follows:

1 Most verbs use **avoir**:

j'ai mangé	*I have eaten, or I ate (earlier)*
ils ont travaillé	*they have worked, or they worked (earlier)*

2 There are, however, two categories of verbs which do not follow that rule and take **être** as their auxiliary. Can you remember them from your previous studies?

a The first category is that of 'the famous 14' which it is helpful to learn in pairs with opposite meanings:

aller	*to go*	**venir**	*to come*
arriver	*to arrive*	**partir**	*to leave/go*
descendre	*to go down*	**monter**	*to go up*
entrer	*to go in*	**sortir**	*to go out*
naître	*to be born*	**mourir**	*to die*
passer	*to go by*	**retourner**	*to return*
rester	*to stay/remain*	**tomber**	*to fall*

Remember also that if a prefix such as re- (indicating repetition) is used with one of the famous 14, the 'new' verb will also use **être**: ***re*monter** (*to go up again*), ***re*descendre** (*to go down again*), ***re*venir** (*to come back again*), etc.:

Elle est venue hier et elle est repartie ce matin.	*She came yesterday and went back this morning.*

b The second category is that of reflexive verbs (verbs which indicate that the performer of the action is also the person subjected to it), e.g. **se raser** *to shave (oneself)*, **se couper:** *to cut oneself*. These verbs are signalled by the presence of one of the following reflexive pronouns: **me, te, se, nous, vous, se** inserted between the subject and the verb:

Compare

J'ai coupé le pain.	*I (have) cut the bread.*
J'ai rasé le client.	*I shaved (or have shaved) the customer.*

And:

Je *me suis* coupé.	*I (have) cut myself.*
Il s'*est* rasé.	*He (has) shaved (himself).*

Activity 8

Go back to Dialogue 1, and write down all the examples of the perfect you can find.

Activity 9

We have already seen that, in French, **on** can have two distinct meanings:

1 *one/somebody* (in standard French);
2 *we* (in familiar French).

Having found in the text all the examples of the use of **on**, list them according to the two categories we have just mentioned.

Dialogue 2 (*suite*)

We shall now return to the Café de la Paix, where Marc is still in conversation with the owner. Read the passage a couple of times before listening to the recording (if available). There will be some exercises on the material later on.

CD1, TR 3, 07:47

Marc Vous venez de dire que le bistro jouait un rôle essentiel dans la société française. Vous ne pensez pas que c'est un peu exagéré?

The owner Pas du tout! Vous savez sans doute qu'à Paris, les artistes, les écrivains se réunissaient dans les cafés pour échanger leurs idées, discuter de philosophie, etc. J'admets que dans les établissements de province, c'était plus terre-à-terre, mais on discutait des événements de la journée ou de la semaine, de la politique …

Marc De la politique du café du commerce!

The owner Peut-être, mais au moins on communiquait. Quelquefois les clients vous racontaient leurs problèmes. On les écoutait, on leur donnait des conseils. Aujourd'hui, tout ça c'est terminé. La majorité des gens ne vont plus au café. Ils rentrent directement chez eux et s'installent devant la télé. Ils achètent l'alcool au supermarché et ils boivent à domicile. Si vous voulez mon avis, ça, c'est un danger, surtout pour les mineurs: ils ont accès à l'alcool, sans contrôle. Nous, on ne servait pas les mineurs, les moins de 18 ans. Donc il a fallu s'adapter. Maintenant on fait un peu de restauration: ma femme cuisine des trucs simples: sandwichs, steak-frites, ce genre de trucs!

Marc Et ça vous aide?

The owner Pff … un peu! Le problème c'est qu'il y a des tas de petits commerces comme les boulangeries et les pâtisseries, qui font la même chose maintenant. Et puis y a les pizzerias, les McDo et j'en passe! … Entre nous, je suis un peu d'accord avec José Bové.

Marc Avec qui?

The owner José Bové. Vous connaissez pas?

Marc	Euh ... non, ... je suis anglais.
The owner	Vous êtes anglais? Alors là, chapeau hein! J'aurais jamais deviné!
Marc	Merci! Vous disiez, à propos de José Bové?
The owner	C'est un paysan qui a 'démonté' un McDo en 1999. On l'a surnommé 'Robin des Champs' à l'image de votre 'Robin des Bois'! Faut dire qu'il y a pas mal de Français qui sont d'accord avec lui. Avouez que c'est une honte d'avoir des trucs comme ça chez nous, quand on a la meilleure réputation du monde pour la bouffe!
Marc	Vous n'avez pas tort! Je vous dois combien pour le café?

Insight

To express a negative meaning, English uses *not* or *never* e.g. *you do not know*; *I would never have guessed* ... In standard French, the equivalent markers are: **ne pas** or **ne jamais: vous ne connaissez pas** or **je n'aurais jamais deviné.** In familiar French, however, **ne** is dropped: **vous connaissez pas** or **j'aurais jamais deviné.**

QUICK VOCAB

se réunir *to get together/meet*
terre-à-terre *trivial, not intellectually sophisticated*
la politique du café du commerce *A derogatory phrase to describe a low-level intellectual discussion about politics (there is a* **café du commerce** *in virtually every town in France!).*
à domicile *at home*
un mineur *a person below 18 years of age. This noun can also refer to a coal miner.*
il a fallu *(+ infinitive) it has been/was necessary to ...*
la restauration *the serving of food (as a business activity). It can also mean the repair/restoration of buildings.*
un truc *A word frequently used in familiar French to mean a thingy/thingammy. It can also mean a trick.*
démonter *to take to pieces, dismantle. Here, to wreck!*
une honte *a shame. Here it is stronger and means a disgrace.*
la bouffe *good food, nosh, grub*

Le steak-frites (*steak and chips*). A very popular form of food which can be prepared quickly. French people generally prefer their steak **saignant** (*rare*), so if you wish to have it prepared differently, you will have to specify either **à point** (*medium rare*) or **bien cuit** (*well done*). In this latter case, do not be surprised if the person taking your order frowns at you disapprovingly: the French often refer to 'a well-cooked steak' as **une semelle** (*the sole of a shoe*), because they consider that all the flavour of the meat has been destroyed!

Comprehension 3

Having studied Dialogue 2, answer the questions below as fully as you can.

1 In what way did Parisian cafés play a significant role in French society?
2 Show that, on a more modest scale, provincial cafés had their uses too.
3 How does the owner explain the current decline of cafés?
4 What, in his view, is the danger facing the under-18 age group?
5 How have the owner and his wife adapted to the changes?
6 Why is the food side of their business only moderately successful?
7 What is the owner's reaction when Marc tells him he is English?
8 What do we learn about José Bové?

Activity 10

Using expressions from Dialogues 1 and 2, translate the following sentences into French:

1 I admit that we have had to adapt.
2 There are lots of people who go straight home.
3 My wife cooks simple things; it helps us a little.
4 It must be said that a lot of French people agree with José Bové.
5 If you want my opinion, it's dangerous, particularly for the under 18s.
6 In the olden days, customers used to come and have a drink at lunchtime or in the evening.
7 We must face up to things, today all that's over.

3 Demonstratives

You are no doubt familiar with the grammatical word 'demonstratives'. It refers to words or expressions used by the speaker(s) or writer(s) to 'point' at something or somebody, to distinguish them from other similar things or beings.

There are two sorts of demonstratives: adjectives and pronouns. Adjectives are used before the noun phrase and pronouns instead of the noun phrase. Let us take a couple of examples:

this new car
those naughty children

This and *those* are followed by a noun. They are demonstrative adjectives.

In the following sentences, however, *these* and *those* are not followed by a noun phrase, they are used instead of it:

Here are some old books. Have you read these?
I don't like these books; I prefer those.

It is important to remember that because French nouns are split into two gender categories, you will have to choose the correct demonstrative for the situation.

First, let us have a look at demonstrative adjectives:

Gender/ number of the noun	*Demonstrative adjective*	*Particle (used if a more precise location needs to be determined)*	*English meaning*
Masc. sing.	ce (*or* cet) *see next page*	-ci *or* -là	*this* or *that*
Fem. sing.	cette	-ci *or* -là	*this* or *that*
Masc. plur.	ces	-ci *or* -là	*these* or *those*
Fem. plur.	ces	-ci *or* -là	*these* or *those*

The particles -ci and -là mean *here* (closer) and *there* (further away in space or time), but in ordinary French they are not usually added to the demonstrative adjective, unless a clear distinction is essential (*this one here/that one there*).

Je n'aime pas ce disque-ci, je préfère ce disque-là.	*I don't like this record (here), I prefer that record (there).*
Elle a commandé ces livres-ci, mais elle a reçu ces livres-là.	*She ordered these books (here), but she received those books (there).*

It should be noted that the style of the two sentences above can be improved by replacing the second demonstrative adjective with its corresponding pronoun as shown in Unit 3, Section 3.1.

From previous experience you know that for the masculine singular, there are two forms. Can you remember why? Try to find the key to the puzzle by looking carefully at the following sentences:

1 ***Ce* travail est compliqué.**	*This/That work is complicated.*
2 ***Cet* étrange animal est dangereux.**	*This/That strange animal is dangerous.*
3 ***Cet* exercice est facile.**	*This/That exercise is easy.*
4 ***Ce* village est pittoresque.**	*This/That village is picturesque.*
5 ***Cet* article était très intéressant.**	*This/That article was very interesting.*

As you can see from the above examples, **cet** is used when the next word begins with a vowel. This is the case in 2, 3, and 5. So far, so good! There is, however, an additional reason to use **cet** instead of **ce** with a masculine word. It is the case when a mute **h** begins the next word.

Compare:

***cet* horrible garçon**	*this/that horrible boy*
***cet* homme intelligent**	*this/that clever man*

and:

ce hameau abandonné	*this/that abandoned hamlet*
ce haut monument	*this/that high monument*

The problem of how to distinguish between the aspirated **h** and the totally silent mute **h** is addressed in Appendix 6. Read that section carefully before you continue.

Recognizing which **h** is aspirated and which is silent/mute will also help you in these circumstances:

Compare:

l'heure *(fem.)* — *the hour*

and

***la* haine** — *hate/hatred*

or

un *beau* hameau — *a beautiful hamlet*

and

un *bel* hôtel — *a beautiful hotel*

or

un *vieil* homme — *an old man*

and

un *vieux* hachoir — *an old cleaver*

From these few examples, it is clear that the form of the definite article and of some adjectives is affected by the quality of the **h** (aspirated or silent).

Insight

In standard French, the particles **-ci** and **-là** placed after the demonstrative adjectives **ce/cet, cette, ces** indicate the relative closeness or distance of a thing or being e.g. **ce livre-ci** (*this book*); **ce livre-là** (*that book*). In familiar French, **-là** is used in both cases, or the particle is dropped altogether.

Activity 11

In each of the examples below, state which of the demonstrative adjectives is required (do not use the particles -ci and -là). You may wish to consult Appendix 5 at the back of the book.

1 ______ conversations
2 ______ voyage
3 ______ aventure
4 ______ évaluation
5 ______ confusion
6 ______ jogging
7 ______ département
8 ______ cage
9 ______ structure
10 ______ beauté

Activity 12

If you have a French dictionary, open it at the letter **h**, and check which of the following masculine singular words take **ce** and which take **cet**. If you do not have a dictionary, try to guess the answers. Do not copy the words out again. Simply write down your answers against each of the numbers (1 to 10) below.

1 habit (*formal dress*)
2 hublot (*porthole*)
3 harpon (*harpoon/hook*)
4 hâle (*suntan*)
5 hélicoptère (*helicopter*)
6 hôpital (*hospital*)
7 humain (*human being*)
8 hoquet (*hiccup*)
9 hameau (*hamlet*)
10 homard (*lobster*)

Activity 13

In the following sentences, state whether the use of **ce** or **cet** is correct or wrong.

1 Cet héros a gagné la bataille.
2 Je suis très fier de ce honneur.
3 Je trouve cet humour déplorable.
4 Cet haricot n'est pas cuit.
5 Ce horrible travail est fini.
6 Cet haut building est superbe.
7 Cet hiver est très froid.

3.1 Demonstrative pronouns

When the gender of the person or thing 'pointed at' is clear, the corresponding demonstrative pronoun can easily be determined. If, however, the gender is not known or not clear, we have to resort to a neutral form, as shown in the last line of the table.

Gender/number	*Demonstrative pronoun*	*English meaning*
Masc. sing.	celui-ci (*or* -là)	*this one* or *that one*
Fem. sing.	celle-ci (*or* -là)	*this one* or *that one*
Masc. plur.	ceux-ci (*or* -là)	*these* or *those*
Fem. plur.	celles-ci (*or* -là)	*these* or *those*
Neutral form for indeterminate gender/number	ceci (*or* cela, *or* ça *or* c' *in* c'est)	*this* or *that* (when gender not specified or known)

As mentioned above, combining a demonstrative adjective and the corresponding demonstrative pronoun can greatly improve the style of a sentence. If we go back to the examples in Unit 3, Section 3, we can make them more elegant precisely by doing that. So:

Je n'aime pas ce disque-ci, je préfère ce disque-là.	*I don't like this record, I prefer that record.*

becomes:

Je n'aime pas ce disque-ci, je préfère celui-là.	*I don't like this record, I prefer that one.*

and:

Elle a commandé ces livres-ci, mais elle a reçu ces livres-là.	*She ordered these books, but she received those books.*

becomes:

Elle a commandé ces livres-ci, mais elle a reçu ceux-là. *She ordered these books, but she received those.*

Insight

Contrary to what happens with demonstrative adjectives (as mentioned in the previous Insight), the particles **-ci** and **-là** cannot be dropped in the case of demonstrative pronouns. You have to say (and write) **celui-ci, celui-là, celle-ci, celle-là,** etc. in familiar as well as in standard French.

3.2 What does 'indeterminate gender or number' mean?

As you know, the two-gender system operates in French grammar. It is usually easy to determine which applies. Sometimes, however, the idea of gender is unclear. As a consequence, certain words are used to sidestep the issue. Such was the case in **on frappe** *someone is knocking (on the door)*. In this case, **on** could refer to a man or a woman since the gender of the person who is knocking is unknown. It is, as it were, a neutral form. The same can be said of the indeterminate demonstrative pronouns **ceci, cela, ça, c'**:

Il est absent. *Cela* m'inquiète. *He is absent. That worries me. (Here, 'that' refers to 'the fact* that *he is absent'.)*

or:

***C'*est ridicule!** *That's ridiculous!*

compare:

Il ne gagne jamais. *Il* est ridicule! *He never wins. He is ridiculous!*

Il ne gagne jamais. *C'*est ridicule! *He never wins. That is ridiculous!*

Activity 14

In the sentences which follow, check whether the gender and number of the demonstrative pronouns are correct. If they are not, suggest the appropriate correction. The particles -ci and -là should remain as they are.

1 Ces pommes sont vieilles. Je préfère ceux-là.
2 Ce costume-ci est trop petit. Il faut prendre celui-là.
3 Ces fleurs sont belles, mais celles-ci sont superbes.
4 Cette route est mauvaise. Nous allons prendre celui-là.
5 Des deux maisons, je préfère celles-là.
6 Vous désirez un taxi? Prenez celle-ci.
7 Ces voisines-ci sont très gentilles, mais ceux-là sont désagréables.

Reading 2

After leaving the Café de la Paix, Marc decided that, as the son of a Frenchwoman, he should try to brush up on his virtually non-existent knowledge of wines. Before leaving Reims, he went to the tourist office (**l'office du tourisme**) and picked up a few free leaflets and local maps. One leaflet offers some basic advice on oenology (the science of wines), which he intends to read on his way back to England.

In the leaflet there is a map of the main wine-producing regions of France, similar to the one reproduced opposite. With the map there is a beginners' guide on how to marry wines and food.

Look at both carefully and then complete the exercises.

Suggestions pour le mariage des vins et des plats

Ce guide est très élémentaire, mais il donne quelques indications de base sur le mariage des vins et des plats.

En règle générale, les vins les plus légers doivent être servis avant les vins plus généreux ou corsés. N'oubliez pas que, de toute façon, c'est le consommateur qui décide!

1 Avec les huîtres, les poissons et les fruits de mer: **vins blancs secs.**

Alsace, Bergerac, Bordeaux, Bourgogne, Jura, Jurançon, Côtes de Provence, Loire.

2 Avec les viandes rouges et les grillades: **vins rouges généreux.**

Bordeaux, Côtes du Rhône, Loire.

3 Avec les rôtis, le gibier et le fromage: **vins rouges corsés.**

Bordeaux, Bourgogne, Côtes du Rhône, Loire.

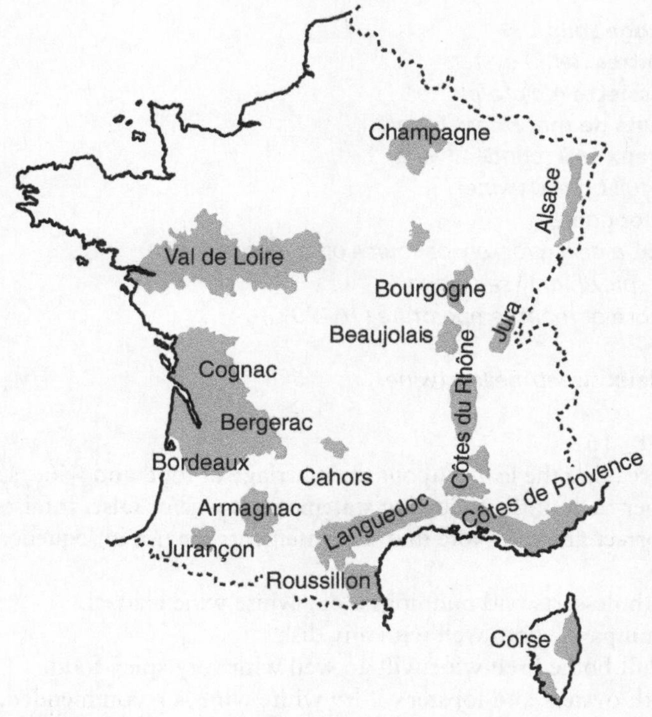

Les grands vignobles français.

4 Avec les plats très épicés: **vins blancs secs ou rosés.**

Blancs secs de Loire, Rosés de Provence.

5 Avec la salade: ne pas servir de vin.

6 Avec les desserts: **vins blancs doux/moelleux.**

Bordeaux, Bergerac, Champagne.

Note: Le champagne est très versatile. On peut le boire en apéritif ou pendant le repas. Il se marie très bien avec tous les plats, mais il doit se boire 'frappé', c'est-à-dire à une température proche de zéro degré C.

QUICK VOCAB

le potage *soup*
les huîtres *(fem.) oysters*
une assiette *a plate/platter*
les fruits de mer *(masc.) seafood*
généreux *well rounded (wine)*
corsé *full-bodied (wine)*
le gibier *game*
un plat *a dish (crockery or course on a menu)*
épicé *spicy/highly seasoned*
chambré *at room temperature (16–20°C)*
sec *dry*
moelleux *sweet/mellow (wine)*

Activity 15

After reading the leaflet about the marriage of food and wine, say whether each of the following statements is true or false. If false, give the correct answer. Note that the statements are not in sequence.

1 With desserts and puddings a dry white wine is ideal.
2 Champagne goes well with any dish.
3 A full-bodied red wine will go well with very spicy food.
4 With oysters and lobsters a dry white wine is recommended.
5 Champagne should be drunk at room temperature.
6 Normally you should always serve stronger wines before lighter ones.
7 With salad, a strong red wine is the best bet.

Activity 16

Marc has decided to invite his parents to dinner when he gets back to England. The menu he is going to cook and serve is as follows:

potage aux champignons
assiette de fruits de mer
canard à l'orange
légumes
salade
plateau de fromages
tarte aux pommes
café

1 Translate the menu into English.
2 Assuming Marc's parents will not be driving home after the meal, suggest what wines he should serve with each dish. Use the map and guide from Reading 2.

Example: If he were to serve game (**du gibier**), you could suggest a full-bodied red from either the Bordeaux or Burgundy areas.

If you want to know more about **José Bové,** who was mentioned in the dialogue between Marc and the café owner, type his name into a french search engine such as www.google.fr or http://fr.yahoo.com.

For further information about wines, why not consult: http://www.guidedugourmet.com/fr

Un verre, ça va! Deux verres, bonjour les dégâts! *One drink – fine, two drinks – trouble!* (lit. *hello, damage!*)

Papa, pense à moi, ne bois pas! *Daddy, think of me, don't drink!*

Both of the above were slogans used a few years ago to raise public awareness about drink-driving problems.

Insight

Teachers of French used to insist that the words **ici** (*here*) and **là** (*there*) had to do with relative closeness or distance, so **'Le sac est ici'** (*'The bag is here'*) indicated proximity, whereas **'Le sac est là'** (*'The bag is there'*) indicated distance. Nowadays, in familiar language, **là** is used in both cases.

TEST YOURSELF

1. What are the four main uses of the imperfect tense?
2. What is the French town of Reims famous for?
3. Why can it be argued that cafés played an important cultural role in French society, particularly in Paris?
4. What is the difference between a simple tense and a compound tense?
5. What auxiliary verbs are used to form the perfect tense in French?
6. What are the rules governing the choice of the auxiliary verb in French?
7. In what circumstances must the masculine singular demonstrative ce be replaced by cet?
8. Which wine would you recommend with salad if a dressing is used?
9. Why is champagne said to be very versatile?
10. What type of wine would you serve with dessert?

4

Les voyages forment la jeunesse

In this unit you will learn
- *About the basics of the French education system*
- *How to say 'to be about to do something', 'to have just done something', and 'to be in the process of doing something'*
- *How to make adjectives agree (the problem of genders)*
- *How to place adjectives and adverbs correctly in the sentence*
- *How to recognize and use non-standard forms in French*
- *How to form and use the possessives*
- *The active and passive voice*

Insight

To express the immediate past (*to have just done…*), use the present of **venir** (*to come*) + **de/d'+** the infinitive of the main verb: **tu viens de finir** (*you have just finished*). For the immediate future (*to be going to do…*), use **aller** (*to go*) + the infinitive of the main verb: **je vais finir**.

The French education system

In this and subsequent units, there will be some passing references to education and qualifications. We therefore hope that the following brief overview of the French educational system will help you make sense of such references.

In the overview which follows, the word 'Cartesian' appears. It is an adjective formed from the name of René Descartes, the

17th-century French philosopher and mathematician, renowned for the intellectual rigour and purity of his approach to the thinking process. Whenever the word is used, there is an implication of logic, rationality and method being applied. Is this another, less obvious example of the **cocorico** mentality?

The system at a glance

In true Cartesian fashion, French education is organized into four sections:

1 Pre-school education, for children aged three to six;
2 Primary education, for children aged six to 11;
3 Secondary education for children aged 11 to 16, which is itself divided into two cycles:

- **a** The first cycle in a **collège** (four to five years of study);
- **b** The second cycle, itself subdivided as follows:
  - ▶ *the short route (two years in a* **LEP – Lycée d'Enseignement Professionnel** *with the possibility of obtaining a professional qualification);*
  - ▶ *the long route (three years of study in a* **Lycée d'Enseignement Général** *with the possibility of obtaining the much-coveted* **baccalauréat,** *roughly equivalent to the English A level (A2), with clear emphasis on academic studies).*

4 Higher education, which is itself subdivided into three separate cycles:

- ▶ *short: two years of study, with strong emphasis on the acquisition of technical/professional skills, and work placement periods. The final qualifications are:* **le BTS (Brevet de Technicien Supérieur)** *or* **le DUT (Diplôme Universitaire de Technologie)***;*
- ▶ *Long: two (or three) years at university with the possibility of obtaining either:*
  - **i une Licence** *(approximately equivalent to a British BA or BSc) after two years;*
  - **ii une Maîtrise** *(similar in value to an MA or MSc) after three years.*
- ▶ *the 'third' cycle, leading to a* **Doctorat** *(PhD) or equivalent qualification.*

In addition to the above, there are very prestigious higher education institutions, often independent of the **Ministère de l'Éducation Nationale** (*Ministry for Education*), which prepare their students for high office and key posts in the civil service, the armed forces, etc. These are known as **les Grandes Écoles.**

Some statistics

Read the following statistics about education in preparation for the next activity.

1 En principe, la scolarité est obligatoire de six à 18 ans en France.
2 Environ 15 pour cent des élèves quittent l'école secondaire sans aucune qualification.
3 Selon des statistiques récentes près de la moitié des élèves quittent l'école à 16 ans pour chercher un emploi.
4 Dans les écoles secondaires, l'emploi du temps des élèves est de 27 heures par semaine en moyenne.
5 Près de la moitié des étudiants qui terminent leurs études dans un LEP vont au lycée pour essayer d'obtenir un baccalauréat technique.
6 Environ 50 pour cent des élèves qui obtiennent le baccalauréat continuent leurs études à l'université.
7 Dans cette dernière catégorie, plus de 60 pour cent abandonnent leurs études à la fin de la première année.

Activity 1

Try to give a translation in English of the above information using full sentences. Bear in mind that a word-for-word rendering is not always the best solution.

1 How to say that you are about to do something or that you have just done something: the immediate future and the immediate past

Frequently in speech or writing, we wish to express actions

1 which are going to happen in the very near future, or
2 which have just happened.

We have seen in Unit 2 that the present tense can be used to express the first of these. We will now investigate new ways of expressing them.

The following timeline may help us visualize things more clearly:

Past	Present	Future
	↓	
	2 × 1	

A In the diagram, Action 1 indicates a point in time which, although in the future, is very close to the present. The tense used to express this notion in French corresponds to the English tense 'to be about to' or 'to be going to'. It is formed by using the present of the verb **aller** (*to go*) and the infinitive of the main verb needed to identify the action.

The present of **aller** is:

je vais	nous allons
tu vas (*fam.*)	vous allez (*formal* sing./plur.)
il/elle/on va	ils/elles vont

Je vais téléphoner.	*I am going to (tele)phone.*
Il va aller au cinéma.	*He is going to go to the cinema.*
Vous allez prendre un café?	*Are you (polite sing./plur.) going to have a coffee?*

B Action 2 on the diagram indicates a point in time which, although in the past, is very close to the present. The tense used for this purpose is called the immediate past. It corresponds to the English 'to have just done something'. It is formed by using the present of the verb **venir** (*to come*) and the infinitive of the main verb preceded by **de** (*from*).

The present of **venir** is as follows:

je viens	nous venons
tu viens (*fam.*)	vous venez *(formal sing./plur.)*
il/elle/on vient	ils/elles viennent

Je viens de voir un film formidable.	*I've just seen/watched a wonderful film (*beware: **formidable** is another false friend!*).*
Elle vient d'avoir un bébé.	*She's just had a baby.*
Ils viennent d'arrêter le coupable.	*They've just arrested the culprit.*

Language learning tip 1

Remember that the present indicative can also be used to indicate an action which is going to take place shortly.

2 How do we say 'to be in the process of doing something'?

Earlier in this unit, we examined how to say 'to have just done' or 'to be just about to do something'. What should we do if we want to translate the English turn of phrase 'to be in the middle' or 'in the process of doing something'?

The answer is quite simple. All you need is the expression être en train de … (nothing to do with the TGV!) and remember:

1 to add an infinitive, not an -ing form, to the expression;
2 to use whichever tense (except the indicative pluperfect) is appropriate to the time zone or the mood you need to situate your action.

Ils *sont en train* de lire le journal.	*They are reading the paper (at this very moment).*
***J'étais en train* d'écrire une carte postale quand tu es arrivé.**	*I was in the middle of writing a postcard when you arrived.*
Si tu viens ce soir à huit heures, nous *serons en train* de dîner.	*If you come tonight at eight, we will be having our dinner.*

Activity 2

In the sentences below, replace the existing verb phrase by the appropriate form of the expression **être en train de.** In order to make your sentence more elegant, you may also need to replace the noun phrase by the appropriate object pronoun (**le, la,** or **les**).

Il a fait son travail? Non, il est en train de le faire!	*Has he done his work? No, he's doing it now!*

Your turn now:

1 Jean-Michel a fini sa traduction?
2 Le professeur avait expliqué le problème quand tu es entré?
3 Les employés sont sortis?
4 Est-ce que Pierre aura visité le château quand nous arriverons?

3 Non-standard forms

When we write, we generally tend to pay more attention to the quality of the language we use than we do in conversation. This may be because, as the French say, we realize that **les paroles s'en vont, mais les écrits restent** (*spoken words disappear, but written words remain*).

In casual (or even not-so-casual) spoken French, the following devices are often used by native speakers to simplify or speed up their speech. Unless the circumstances in which you operate demand a high quality of language, little harm will be done by using these!

1 The standard French negations **ne ... pas** (*not to ...*), **ne ... jamais** (*not to ... ever*), **ne ... rien** (*not to ... anything*), **ne ... personne** (*not to ... anybody*) are simplified by dropping the ne particle in familiar French:

Je ne parle pas.	*I don't speak/I'm not speaking.* (standard)
Je parle pas.	*I don't speak/I'm not speaking.* (familiar)
Il ne sort jamais.	*He never goes out.* (standard)
Il sort jamais.	*He never goes out.* (familiar)
Elle ne gagne rien.	*She wins/earns nothing.* (standard).
Elle gagne rien.	*She wins/earns nothing.* (familiar)

2 In familiar language, the standard French subject pronoun **nous** (*we*) is almost systematically replaced by **on**, with the following verb in the third person singular:

Nous avons vu le film.	*We saw/have seen the film.* (standard)
On a vu le film.	*We saw/have seen the film.* (familiar)

But remember that in standard or formal French, **on** can be used as an equivalent to *someone/somebody*.

3 In familiar language, the standard French expression **ce sont** (*it is* – used with the verb in the third person plural) is replaced by **c'est**, normally used with a third person singular.

Ce sont les enfants qui arrivent.	*It's the children coming.* (standard)
C'est les enfants qui arrivent.	*It's the children coming.* (familiar)

4 Familiar language, instead of using one of the two accepted methods to formulate a question, namely an inversion or the question marker **est-ce que**, simply uses the statement form, but with a rising intonation at the end.

Êtes-vous sûr?	*Are you sure?* (inversion – formal)
Est-ce que vous êtes sûr?	*Are you sure?* (use of the **est-ce que** marker – standard)
Vous êtes sûr?	*Are you sure?* (no inversion, no marker, but the voice goes up – familiar).

In this and future units, look out for such familiar devices and do not be afraid to use them (except in formal situations).

Insight

Non-standard forms can be used freely in familiar French, since in this case substance is relatively more important than grammatical accuracy, but in formal situations try to avoid them, to show your ability to distinguish between correct and casual language.

Dialogue

Jean-Michel is an engineering student who has just passed his **BTS (Brevet de Technicien Supérieur)**. In order to increase his chances of getting a good job he has decided to go to England for a year. As he is leaving the **lycée**, where he has been a student, he meets Monsieur Mercier, one of his former teachers. Listen to the recording of the dialogue twice and read it again another couple of times, in preparation for the work that goes with it.

CD1, TR 4, 00:30

M. Mercier	Bonjour, Jean-Michel. Comment vas-tu?
Jean-Michel	Bonjour, M'sieur Mercier. Ça va!
M. Mercier	Tu viens de finir tes examens. Ça a marché?
Jean-Michel	Pas mal. Merci. Je viens d'avoir mes résultats. J'ai été reçu avec la mention 'Bien'.
M. Mercier	Félicitations. Et maintenant, qu'est-ce que tu vas faire?
Jean-Michel	Je vais aller en Grande-Bretagne.
M. Mercier	Je vois! Tu viens de travailler dur, alors tu vas prendre des vacances.
Jean-Michel	Non, pas du tout! Je vais aller faire un stage là-bas. Je viens juste d'avoir un meeting avec le responsable des échanges européens du lycée. Il vient de me confirmer que j'ai une place. Je vais partir en septembre.
M. Mercier	Mais pourquoi veux-tu aller là-bas? Tu sais bien que les Rosbifs sont francophobes!
Jean-Michel	On le dit, mais je suis sûr que c'est pas vrai! Et de toute façon, je veux mettre toutes les chances de mon côté! Aujourd'hui, l'anglais est indispensable pour un businessman ou un technicien!
M. Mercier	C'est vrai. Mais qu'est ce que tu vas faire au juste?
Jean-Michel	Je vais aller dans une université du nord de l'Angleterre où je vais suivre un cours intensif de six semaines, pour perfectionner mon anglais général et technique et ma connaissance des institutions. Ensuite, je vais passer six mois, de janvier à juin, dans une entreprise britannique. C'est cool!
M. Mercier	Mmm! Et c'est tes parents qui vont financer tes études?

Jean-Michel	Non! Ils ont rien à payer. Je viens d'obtenir une bourse régionale et c'est la Communauté Européenne qui va payer mes frais d'inscription dans le cadre d'un échange SOCRATES, un programme européen, pour encourager la mobilité des jeunes dans la Communauté et pour augmenter leurs chances de trouver un bon emploi à leur retour.
M. Mercier	Oui, je sais. Mais dis-moi, ça va être difficile de trouver un stage en entreprise, non?
Jean-Michel	Pas de problème! C'est les profs de l'université anglaise qui vont s'occuper de ça.
M. Mercier	Et tu vas être payé pendant ton stage?
Jean-Michel	Au début, je vais pas gagner beaucoup, c'est sûr, mais si je fais mes preuves, ça va probablement s'améliorer. De toute façon, j'aurai une autre corde à mon arc!
M. Mercier	Eh bien, alors; bonne chance au pays du fair-play. Tu donneras mes amitiés à Sa Très Gracieuse Majesté, si tu la vois, et j'espère que tu vas nous envoyer une ou deux cartes postales.
Jean-Michel	OK! Au revoir, M. Mercier!
M. Mercier	Bon courage! Au fait, n'oublie pas ton parapluie!

Insight

When it is is followed by a singular noun or pronoun, *it* will be translated in standard French by **c'est: c'est la Communauté** (*it's the Community*). With a plural, **c'est** becomes **ce sont: ce sont les professeurs** (*it's the teachers*), but in familiar language **c'est** is used in both cases: **c'est les profs.** Note also: **c'est nous/vous** (*it's us/you*).

QUICK VOCAB

un BTS (Brevet de Technicien Supérieur) *A technical qualification roughly equivalent to a Higher National Diploma (HND) in Britain.*

Ça a marché? *Did you do well? (lit. did that walk?). The word* **marcher**, *which normally means to walk, can also be used for 'to work well' (of a machine or an activity).*

la mention 'Bien' *A very creditable result which means that the diploma will bear the grade achieved (***bien** *= good pass) as an indication of the quality of the student's work and examination results.*

un stage *here: a period of training in an organization or company, for further learning or hands-on experience.*

les Rosbifs *the roast-beefs: an affectionate nickname given by the French to the British in retaliation for 'frogs'!*

francophobe *who hate(s) the French. The suffix 'phobe' comes from the Greek and means 'who fears or hates'. This has given rise to a large number of words such as* **xénophobe** *which we saw in Unit 2,* **claustrophobe** *(who fears/hates enclosed spaces),* **Europhobe** *(can you guess?), etc.*

travailler dur *to work hard. Here,* **dur** *is an adverb, not an adjective so, in the feminine, it will not change:* **elle travaille dur**.

une bourse régionale *A grant given selectively to promising students by the authorities of an administrative region (see Unit 1), to live and work abroad for a year, as part of their higher education studies.*

dans le cadre d'un échange SOCRATES *within the framework of a SOCRATES exchange scheme. This is a European initiative to encourage higher education students to go and work in another EU member state for a maximum of one year. Under reciprocal arrangements, students' enrolment fees (***les frais d'inscription***) are waived and accommodation can be provided by the host university, though it still has to be paid for.*

les profs *familiar for* **les professeurs** *(teachers)*

si je fais mes preuves *if I prove myself (lit. if I make my proofs)*

J'aurai une autre corde à mon arc *I'll have another string to my bow. Fluency in English is seen as very desirable particularly in business and engineering.*

au pays du fair-play *Despite occasional disagreements with its British neighbour, France still believes that* **le fair-play** *is a true mark of Britishness!*

Sa Très Gracieuse Majesté *Her Most Gracious Majesty (this is an affectionate if light-hearted reference to Her Majesty Queen Elizabeth II).*

bon courage! *good luck/take heart!*

au fait ... *by the way...*

n'oublie pas ton parapluie! *A reference to the fact that, according to many French people, it rains every day in England. Such preconceptions are unfortunately not uncommon, even in this day and age.*

Comprehension 1

Having gone through the dialogue again, answer, in English, the following questions.

1 M. Mercier believes that Jean-Michel is going to England to enjoy a well-earned holiday. Is he right? Explain.
2 How did Jean-Michel perform in the final examinations? How do you know?
3 Why is Jean-Michel sure that he will be going to Britain in September?
4 What will be the structure of Jean-Michel's activities while in England?
5 Will Jean-Michel's parents have to pay for him during his stay in England? Explain.
6 Why is Jean-Michel not worried about finding an industrial placement after his spell at the university?
7 What, according to Jean-Michel, is likely to happen if he proves himself while on placement?

Activity 3

In the dialogue, there are a number of examples of phrases in

1 the immediate past, and
2 the immediate future.

a Make a list of them under each of these two headings.
b Transform all the examples you listed in number 1 into the immediate future, and all those you put in number 2 into the immediate past.

Example: je viens d'avoir mes résultats → je vais avoir mes résultats
tu viens de finir tes examens → tu vas finir tes examens

Activity 4

Using the information given above (Unit 4, Section 3) about non-standard forms, make a list of those used by both Jean-Michel and his teacher.

Activity 5

The dialogue contains a few clues that indicate M. Mercier's feelings towards Britain and the British. Can you spot them and note them down?

Reading

Jean-Michel, who has now been in England for three months, has sent a postcard to Monsieur Mercier. Read it very carefully, since your grammar skills will be tested in the activity that follows.

Cher Monsieur Mercier

Comme promis, voici une petite carte postale pour vous dire que tout marche très bien pour moi. Je vient de finir le stage linguistique à l'université et j'ai commencé mon stage industriel le 14 janvier dans une entreprise de la région.

Pour le moment, le salaire n'est pas formidable, mais le job est intéressant! Si mon manager est content de moi, il va peut-être m'augmenter! Ce week-end, je suis à Blackpool d'où je vous envoi cette carte. Depuis mon arrivée, il a plus deux fois seulement! Le temps n'est pas aussi mauvais qu'on le dis et les gens de la région sont très sympatiques.

Respectueusement

Jean-Michel

Monsieur R. Mercier
Professeur
Lycée Michel Montaigne
90000 Belfort
France

Insight

Thousands of English words, collectively known as **le franglais,** are widely used in France to the despair of the government: **le brain-storming, le cash-flow, le job, le manager, le marketing, le week-end,** etc. All are masculine, except for **la star** (*celebrity*) and names referring to females e.g. **la pin-up.**

Activity 6

In the dialogue as well as on the postcard sent by Jean-Michel, there are a number of English words commonly used in French. Make a note of them. Can you spot something useful about the gender of the English nouns? On this point and others related to the use of Franglais, you should refer to Appendix 2.

Activity 7

Jean-Michel, like many young people of his generation, is not always as grammatically accurate as he could be. Look at the postcard again, and try to find out the errors he made. Correct them, giving an explanation of the mistakes, if you can.

Activity 8

Give your answer to the following questions, bearing in mind the information given in the dialogue and the message on the postcard.

1 There may be several reasons why Jean-Michel sent this postcard to M. Mercier (list three).
2 What point has Jean-Michel reached in his stay (give two clues)?
3 What do we know about his industrial placement (list three things)?
4 In the dialogue M. Mercier mentioned one thing which has, so far at least, turned out not to be true. What was it?
5 What are Jean-Michel's hopes about his job and how does he intend to make them come true?

4 A question of gender

In your earlier French studies, you no doubt wondered why *a table*, *a door*, *a car* (**une table, une porte, une voiture**) should be feminine, and why *a bag*, *a garden*, *a computer* (**un sac, un jardin, un ordinateur**) should be masculine. The reason has nothing to do with the French wishing to put language learners off, but comes from Latin, which had a very strong influence on the development of the French language. Broadly speaking, masculine and neuter Latin nouns became masculine in French, and feminine ones became feminine. Those of you who have studied Latin may find this information helpful. For the rest of us, it is useful to know that there are some practical tips which can help in the determination of the gender of French nouns. A good grammar will list the categories by meaning or ending. A concise section listing the most common rules can be found in Appendix 5. As always, doing some detective work with incoming information and trying to create your own rules will be an excellent exercise.

The reason why it is important for learners to know the gender of nouns is that in French, adjectives agree in gender and number with the noun phrase they qualify.

1 le petit garçon brun	*the small brown-haired boy*
2 la petite fille brune	*the small brown-haired girl*
3 les petits garçons bruns	*the small brown-haired boys*
4 les petites filles brunes	*the small brown-haired girls*

As you can see, the masculine singular adjectives of Example 1 (**petit** and **brun**) change their form in Example 2, where an **-e** ending is added. In Examples 3 and 4, an **-s** is also added to indicate the plural.

In written French, adjective agreements can be a little troublesome. In conversation, the question of agreement is far less important and should not be too much of a concern, except for the truly Cartesian among you!

Insight

Generally, making a gender error when using a French noun is unlikely to create comprehension problems. There are, however, cases when a change in gender determines a change in meaning: **le poste** (*post/job*), **la poste** (*post office*); **le livre** (*book*), **la livre** (*pound*); **le tour** (*turn/tour*), **la tour** (*tower*)...

4.1 Making adjectives agree

The basic rules are as follows:

1 If the adjective ends in a consonant as in Example 1 on the previous page, it will simply add an -e for the feminine, and an -s or -es (as appropriate) for the plural.

But beware:

2 If the adjective ends in -el (but not -al!) in the masculine singular, the feminine will be -elle:

un danger *réel*, une menace *réelle*	*a real danger, a real threat*

3 If the adjective ends in -**on** in the masculine singular, the feminine will be -**onne**:

un *bon* café, une *bonne* bière	*a good coffee, a good beer*

4 If the adjective ends in -ien (not just -in!) in the masculine, the feminine will end in -ienne:

un monument *ancien*, une église *ancienne*	*an ancient monument, an ancient church*

5 If the adjective ends in -if, -ef, -euf in the masculine singular, the f will become v in the feminine:

un feu *vif*, une lumière *vive*	*a bright fire, a bright light*

6 If the adjective ends in -eux in the masculine singular, the **x** will change to s in the feminine:

un homme *curieux*, une femme *curieuse*	*a curious man, a curious woman*

In addition, there are some very common adjectives which undergo changes according to their gender, as shown in the following table.

English	*Masc. sing.*	*Fem. sing.*	*Masc. plur.*	*Fem. plur.*
beautiful	beau (*or* bel + *vowel*)	belle	beaux	belles
new	nouveau (*or* nouvel + *vowel*)	nouvelle	nouveaux	nouvelles
old/ancient	vieux (*or* vieil + *vowel*)	vieille	vieux	vieilles
mad	fou (*or* fol + *vowel*)	folle	fous	folles
soft/gentle	doux	douce	doux	douces
big/fat	gros	grosse	gros	grosses

Remember that the first four adjectives in the table have an alternative form when the word which immediately follows them begins with a vowel or a mute **h** (on this point, see Appendix 6).

Activity 9

This activity is part of your self-assessment. Award yourself five points per (absolutely) correct adjective, and add this to your total in the self-assessment form.

In the sentences that follow, make the adjectives (in brackets) agree as appropriate.

1 Ils ont une (grand) maison dans cette (petit) ville.
2 Les (beaux) jours sont revenus.
3 La (vieux) femme est malade.
4 Les (nouveau) voisins sont (charmant).
5 Sa voix est très (doux).
6 Il a une (gros) voiture (noir).
7 C'est une idée (curieux).

Insight

The position of French adjectives is generally fixed, but if you break the rules, you will still be understood. Note however: **un homme grand** (*a tall man*); **un grand homme** (*a great man*); **ma**

propre maison (*my own house*), **ma maison propre** (*my clean house*). Participles go after the noun: **une occasion perdue** (*a lost opportunity*).

5 Where do we put adjectives and adverbs in the sentence?

5.1 The position of adjectives

In English, adjectives are almost always placed before the noun. In French, some are placed before and some after. In a very small number of cases the position of the adjective can influence the meaning, as in the case of **ancien** (*former/ancient*), or **pauvre** (*wretched/penniless*).

For most adjectives, the placement rules are fairly simple – if not foolproof. If you can remember the following, you should not go far wrong.

1 Adjectives indicating age, size, duration or magnitude go before the noun:

une petite fille	*a small girl*
une longue attente	*a long wait*
une haute montagne	*a high mountain*
une énorme vague	*a huge/an enormous wave*

2 Adjectives denoting colour, permanent features, physical or moral traits, ethnic or geographical origin, religious or political beliefs and historical characteristics will follow the noun:

la voiture noire	*the black car*
un homme fort	*a strong man*
la danseuse espagnole	*the Spanish dancer*
le député socialiste	*the socialist MP*

3 Adjectives derived from verbs will also be placed after the noun:

les voyageurs fatigués	*the tired travellers*
la brigade volante	*the flying squad*

Activity 10

Look at the following sentences and determine whether the position of the adjective is correct or wrong. Beware: a change of position of the adjective may require a slight additional modification.

1 Une femme vieille est venue vous voir.
2 L'américaine voiture est en panne.
3 Le gouvernement socialiste n'est pas populaire.
4 La catholique église est très puissante.
5 C'est une intelligente suggestion.
6 Les touristes anglais aiment le soleil.
7 Vous avez fait une erreur grosse.

Insight

In France as in Britain, the power to legislate is in the hands of two Assemblies:

- **La Chambre des députés**, similar to the Commons in the UK with democratically elected members, **les députés**;
- **Le Sénat** (the higher chamber in the UK), whose representatives are nominated by 'electoral colleges' (groups of prestigious/important citizens).

5.2 The position of adverbs

As you may remember, adverbs are words (or phrases) which modify the meaning of verbs, adjectives or other adverbs. The rules regarding their position in the sentence are as follows:

1 If the verb modified is in a simple (one word) tense, the adverb is placed after it:

ils partiront *vite*	*they will leave quickly*

2 If the verb is in a compound tense (auxiliary + past participle), the adverb is usually placed between those two elements:

Nous avons *souvent* parlé de vous.	*We have often talked about you.*

3 Adverbs modifying an adjective or another adverb are normally placed before them:

Merci, vous êtes *très* aimable!	*Thank you, you are very kind.*
Ralentissez! Vous allez *trop* vite!	*Slow down! You are going too fast!*

Note: although the position of adverbs is reasonably fixed in French, you may notice a few variations particularly in the case of adverbs of time or frequency:

***Longtemps*, il a regardé la mer.** **Il a *longtemps* regardé la mer.**	*He looked at the sea for a long time.*
Je suis *souvent* allé les voir. **Je suis allé les voir *souvent*.**	*I often went to see them.*

Activity 11

Put the adverb (given in brackets) in its rightful place in the following sentences. Remember that there may be more than one possibility!

1 Elle a besoin de moi. (*rarement*)
2 Vous travaillerez dans mon bureau. (*généralement*)
3 Tu as pris des décisions sans me consulter. (*quelquefois*)
4 Les enfants ont grandi. (*beaucoup*)
5 Ils avaient bu. (*un peu*)
6 Nous sommes blessés. (*légèrement*)
7 Il est amoureux de toi. (*follement*)

Insight

Adverbs are used to modify verbs, adjectives and other adverbs. In French their position in the sentence is as follows: after the verb, between the auxiliary and the main verb, before an adjective or another adverb. The position of adverbs of manner, time and frequency is more fluid.

6 The possessives: how to say 'my', 'your', etc.

You know that if, in English, we want to express possession, we use adjectives like *my*, *your*, *his/her*, etc. which we place before a noun phrase. We can also use possessive pronouns to replace a whole noun phrase. In this unit we will study both the possessive adjectives and the corresponding pronouns.

Here are a few examples of sentences with possessive adjectives:

1 *Ton* taxi va arriver bientôt.	*Your taxi will arrive soon.*
2 *Sa* montre est cassée.	*His/Her watch is broken.*
3 *Tes* amies sont ici/là!	*Your friends are here!*
4 *Nos* enfants sont partis.	*Our children have gone/left.*

You will also recall that French, unlike English, makes the agreement according to the gender of the thing/person 'owned' and not according to the 'owner'. This is clearly shown in the examples above:

1 *Your* is **ton**, because **taxi** is masculine;
2 *His/Her* is **sa**, because **montre** is feminine, and not because of the gender of the 'owner'. You must also remember to make the appropriate agreement (hence **cassé<u>e</u>**).
3 *Your* is **tes**, because there are several friends, whose gender is indicated by the feminine (**amies**).
4 *Our* is **nos** (and not **notre**), because there are several children referred to (all male, or male and female).

As a refresher, here is the list of French possessive adjectives.

English		**French**	
One set only	**Masc. sing.**	**Fem. sing.**	**Masc./Fem. plur.**
my	mon	ma	mes
your (fam.)	ton	ta	tes
his/her/its	son	sa	ses
our	notre	notre	nos
your (pol./plur.)	votre	votre	vos
their	leur	leur	leurs

Activity 12

Use the vocabulary and expressions from the dialogue to translate the following sentences into French (use familiar turns of phrase if they appear in the text).

1 My teacher, M. Mercier, is an Anglophobe.
2 I am going on a course (*I am going to follow a course*) to improve my French.
3 Jean-Michel has found an industrial placement in a British firm.
4 They are going to increase their chances of finding a good job.
5 No problem! It's the man in charge of the exchange who's going to deal with that!
6 We are going to take our holidays in September.
7 She's just had a meeting with the technician.
8 The students are going to go and work in Britain within the framework of the European programme.
9 People say that the French are xenophobic, but I'm sure it's not true!

6.1 Possessive pronouns

These, like other pronouns, will serve to lighten the style of our speech or writing. Note that:

a Possessive pronouns incorporate the article (**le, la, les**) appropriate to the noun phrase they are to replace;
b The pronouns **le nôtre, le vôtre,** etc. have a circumflex accent on the **o**, unlike the corresponding possessive adjectives!

English	**French**			
One set only	**Masc. sing.**	**Fem. sing.**	**Masc. plur.**	**Fem. plur.**
mine	le mien	la mienne	les miens	les miennes
yours	le tien	la tienne	les tiens	les tiennes
his/hers	le sien	la sienne	les siens	les siennes
ours	le nôtre	la nôtre	les nôtres	les nôtres
yours	le vôtre	la vôtre	les vôtres	les vôtres
theirs	le leur	la leur	les leurs	les leurs

Activity 13

Are the following pronouns right or wrong? If they are wrong, correct them and state what the problem is:

1 C'est ton automobile? Non, c'est la sienne.
2 Mes amis sont ici. Où sont le tien?
3 Mon passeport est sur la table. Où est la tienne?
4 C'est leur valise? Oui c'est la leur.
5 Ce n'est pas la fille de la voisine, c'est le mien.
6 Je reste dans mon jardin, reste dans le vôtre.
7 Mes difficultés sont grandes. La sienne sont énormes.

Activity 14

This activity is part of your self-assessment. Give yourself ten points for each completely correct answer, and add this to your total in the self-assessment form.

Having looked carefully at the possessive pronouns listed above, replace the gap by what you feel to be the appropriate form. Make full use of the grammatical clues we have seen in this and previous units. Note that, in Sentence 6, **on** means **nous**.

1 Maman, ma montre ne marche pas. Tu me prêtes _______?
2 La maison est belle, mais Jean et moi, nous préférons _______.
3 Je vais renouveler mon passeport. Est-ce que _______ est périmé, papa?
4 Nous avons nos raisons et vous avez _______.
5 C'est ton sac? Oui, c'est _______.
6 On ne va pas manger vos sandwichs, on a pris _______.
7 À ta santé, Jean-Michel! Merci, à _______, Monsieur Mercier!
8 Nous avons nos soucis et nos voisins ont _______.
9 Ta voiture est en panne? Prends _______!
10 Voici votre bureau. Ici, chacun a _______.

Insight

In French, possessive adjectives/pronouns agree in gender and number with the thing(s) or being(s) 'owned' and not, as in

English, with the 'owner' so, instead of saying *my father*, (*my*) *mother and* (*my*) *brothers*, you must say (and write): **mon père, ma mère et mes frères.**

7 Active and passive voices

When we want to express an action, we can generally do so in two ways:

- *The first way is to indicate at the outset the 'performer' of the action:*

1 | La voiture | a heurté | le mur |. *The car (has) struck the wall.*
subject object

- *The second is to state first the person or thing that is/has been subjected to the action:*

2 | Le mur | a été heurté par | la voiture |. *The wall has been/was struck by the car.*
subject agent

The subject of Example 1 becomes the agent in Example 2.

It is clear from Example 2 that the verb needed to change the active form into a passive one is être (*to be*). In the case of compound tenses, the verb used as the auxiliary will be **avoir** (see Examples 2 above and 3 below).

3 Les voleurs *ont été arrêtés* **(par la police).** *The thieves have been/were arrested (by the police).*

In this latter type of sentence, the agent is frequently omitted (hence the brackets), unless it is felt that the subject–agent relationship needs to be stated:

Les voleurs ont été arrêtés par des passants. *The thieves have been/were arrested by passers-by.*

Thieves are not usually arrested by passers-by.

Note: some types of sentences cannot be turned into the passive, in particular:

1 Those which only accept an indirect object (usually introduced by 'to'):

Les riches donnent | aux pauvres |. *The rich give (money)*
indirect object *to the poor.*

2 Those in which the verb is reflexive (since the agent is the same as the subject:

Je me suis coupé. *(J'ai été coupé par moi.) *I (have) cut myself.*

3 Those which use an impersonal verb preceded by **il** (*it*), where that pronoun does not represent anyone or anything in particular:

Il fait beau.	*It (the weather) is nice.*
Il neige.	*It snows/is snowing.*
Il pleut.	*It rains/is raining.*
Il faut ...	*It is necessary ...*
Il importe de ...	*It is important to ...*

Insight

As we have seen, the passive 'voice' is used to indicate that a thing or a being is/has been/will be ... subjected to an action. It is constructed using the auxiliary **être**. Compare: **'Daniel *invite* Marc'** (active) and **'Marc *est invité* par Daniel'** (passive). Some sentences, however, cannot be put into the passive.

Activity 15

The following sentences are in the active form. Change them into passive ones as appropriate. Do not forget to make the agreement if necessary, and to use the correct pronoun in Sentence 7.

1 Les fermiers bloquent la route.
2 Le directeur va fermer l'usine.
3 Les propriétaires ont vendu le magasin.
4 Les parents demandent une réunion.
5 Le vent vient d'arracher les arbres.

6 Le responsable va signer la lettre.
7 La police les a arrêtées.
8 Les autorités ont exigé un visa.

Activity 16

Turn the following passive sentences into the active mood:

1 Le personnel a été licencié par le directeur.
2 La voiture a été volée par un loubard.
3 Elle va être punie par le professeur.
4 Ils ont été avertis par les voisins.
5 La maison a été achetée par des Parisiens.
6 La circulation est bloquée par un gros camion.

Activity 17

Some of the passive sentences below contain grammar errors. Can you spot them, correct them, and explain why the original was wrong?

1 L'argent a été volé.
2 Les visas ont été refusées par les autorités.
3 Ils vont être appelés par le chef du personnel.
4 Les lois sont votés par le Parlement.
5 Elles sont soignés par leur propre docteur.
6 Les gangsters ont été arrêtées par la police.

Language learning tip 2

In French, the adjective **propre** (*own/clean*), which appears in Activity 17, Sentence 5, and a few others such as **ancien** (*former/ancient*), **brave** (*kind/brave*), **cher** (*dearly loved/ expensive*) and **mauvais** (*of poor quality/vicious*), change meaning according to their position in the noun phrase. In the examples given above, the first meaning is the one which applies when the adjective is placed before the noun. For a fuller list, you should consult your grammar book.

Les voyages forment la jeunesse. *Travel broadens the mind.*

Mieux vaut avoir la tête bien faite que bien pleine! *It is better to have a well-made head than a well-filled one!* (A reference to the superiority of independent thinking over rote learning.)

Insight

The adjectives *good*, *better*, *best* are translated in the singular as **bon(ne), meilleur(e), le meilleur/la meilleure,** but remember: French adjectives also agree in number with the noun they relate to: **les meilleurs vins** (*the best wines*). The adverbs **bien, mieux, le mieux** (*well, better, best*) are invariable: **elles travaillent le mieux** (*they work best*).

TEST YOURSELF

1. How is the immediate future formed in French?
2. What is it used for?
3. How is the immediate past constructed?
4. What is its use?
5. When the expression **être en train de** does not refer to rail travel, what is its meaning?
6. In terms of style, what is the significance of removing the first part of the negative expression **ne pas**?
7. What is the difference between adjectives expressing age, duration, colour, size and nationality as regards their position in the sentence? What is the rule for adjectives derived from verbs?
8. The adjectives **beau** (*beautiful*), **nouveau** (*new*), **vieux** (*old*) and **fou** (*mad*) have two masculine singular forms. Can you explain why?
9. What are the rules governing the position of adverbs modifying simple tenses and compound tenses (auxiliary + main verb)?
10. In English, possessive adjectives agree with the owner: 'his car' means 'the car belonging to him'. Is the rule the same in French? Clarify.

5

Si jeunesse savait ...

In this unit you will learn

- ***Essential differences between the various styles and registers used in french***
- ***What verlan (backslang) is, and how to decode it***
- ***How to recognize direct and indirect object complements***
- ***How to make the correct agreement for compound tenses with être and avoir***
- ***How to recognize the different sorts of 'reflexive' verbs***
- ***How to form and use the pluperfect tense***
- ***About may 68 and the rise of young people as consumers***

Language learning tip 1

The title of this unit is the first part of the famous French saying: **Si jeunesse savait, si vieillesse pouvait ...!**, which, roughly translated, means: *If the young had the wisdom, if the old had the strength ...!* Grammatically, the expression contains two verbs in the imperfect. The **si**, which denotes a condition, leads you to expect a verb in the second part of this unfinished sentence in the conditional tense, e.g. **tout le monde serait heureux!** (*everybody would be happy!*).

1 Styles and registers

In general, when we communicate, we tend to adjust our vocabulary (words) and style (grammar) to the situation we are in, and according to the person(s) for whom the message is intended. Sometimes, however, we use specific words and sentences because we know (or think we know!) the impact they will have on the listener(s) or reader(s). On the whole, we take relatively more care about the way we present the written message than we do in conversation.

In the spoken and written language, people tend to distinguish four levels of expression, which relate to the words we choose (*register*) and the sentences we build (*style*).

1 The most elevated form is called **formal** (in French: **formel** or **recherché**). This is characterized by the use of virtually all the grammar rules governing the language, except the most obscure. The person speaking in formal language is giving a few messages about himself/herself: he/she wants to show that he/she has a good level of education, a sense of appropriateness when it comes to choosing words and expressions, and respect for the person(s) he/she is talking to.

2 Standard language (**langage courant**). Since the above level of correctness is sometimes perceived as hypercorrect or 'posh', people tend to use a slightly less formal, more casual way of speaking, which respects many of the rules of correctness, but violates a few lesser known ones.

3 Familiar or informal language (**langage familier**) is the type we use when speaking to people we know well (family, friends, close colleagues ...), or in relaxed, casual circumstances. In this type of expression, what we say (the content of our message) is more important than the way in which we say it (the form). We use this level of language when we have no wish or need to impress others.

4 Slang, vulgar or taboo language (**argot or langage populaire/ vulgaire**) uses words or expressions which are likely to offend or shock. It generally ignores the most basic rules of grammar and will, as a form of rebellion, break many of the conventions of the standard language. Using it is a conscious attempt to create a bond between members of a close-knit group. In this sense, it is designed to act both as a 'code' and a 'social marker'. In addition, slang vocabulary is designed to show disregard for anything intellectual and will often focus on very crude images and taboo words which lower the tone and make fun of the most noble of feelings.

In our own language, we generally know the difference between the above levels. In a foreign language, it is much more difficult to judge precisely which word, expression or turn of phrase to use, and it is also very tempting to show off our knowledge of risqué words.

The best advice we have to offer is for you to learn how to distinguish between those levels. A good dictionary will help you by using a variety of markers. Normally, if a word is unmarked, it means it can be used safely. If it is followed by one asterisk (*), or by the abbreviation **fam.**, this indicates that the word or phrase is familiar, i.e. not in formal/polite use.

Two asterisks (**), or the abbreviation **pop.** (*popular*), indicate a lower level of language. You should use such items with care, as they may shock the sensibilities of certain people who are not used to handling them.

Three asterisks (***), or the abbreviations **arg.** for **argot** (*slang*), **obsc.** (*obscene*) or **vulg.** (*vulgar/taboo*), denote words or phrases likely to offend. Such items are best avoided in polite company. As a rule of thumb, do not use lower registers if you wish to make a positive impression on your listener(s).

Language learning tip 2

When you are with native speakers, make a mental note of the circumstances in which things are said, the ages of the people present, their relationship with each other, etc. You will soon develop a 'sixth sense' about what is acceptable and what is not!

2 Le verlan (backslang)

Verlan is a form of slang said to have originated in French prisons, and in particular in the penitentiary of Toulon on the Mediterranean coast, in the 19th century. The name **verlan** itself comes from the word **(à) l'envers,** which means *the wrong way round*. The technique is usually applied to short (two-syllable) words, the trick being to reverse the order of the syllables. So, Toulon became known as **Lontou.**

A similar – but far less frequent – formation technique can also be found in English: *yob* for boy, *tekmar* for market, etc. **Verlan** faded away for a while but, in the last 15 years or so, it has been revived and has become very common in the speech of young people, particularly in inner city areas.

Although the principle seems easy, there are two main problems associated with the understanding of **verlan.**

1 The first is that the reversal is often applied to slang or familiar words, which you first have to know in order to decode them (see **tarpé** and **keuf** in the table on the next page).
2 The second is that the logic is sometimes a little fuzzy, because some letters or sounds disappear in the process.

Note: The lifespan of many **verlan** expressions is often short. Most of them will never find their way into the dictionary!

The following table contains some very frequently encountered **verlan** words. Study them and try to remember them.

Verlan word	*Origin: slang or familiar French*	*Origin: standard French*	*English meaning*
céfran		français	French (language/ people)
relou		lourd	heavy/oppressive/ unintelligent
meuf		femme	woman
tarpé	pétard	revolver/cigarette de cannabis	handgun/spliff
keuf	flic	policier	policeman
beur		arabe	second/third generation children (originally of North African origin)
ripou		pourri	dishonest policeman ('bent copper')
chébran*/ bléca*	branché/câblé	à la mode	fashionable ('trendy')

*These two expressions were used by the late Président Mitterrand in a television interview in the mid-80s. If he could use them, so can you!

Activity 1

On the basis of what we have learnt about the formation of verlan, can you guess the standard French words which have given rise to the following:

1 téci (*feminine noun*)
2 turevoi (*feminine noun*)
3 zonmai (*feminine noun*)
4 zarbi (*adjective*)
5 ouf (*masculine adj.*)

Remember that in **verlan,** the transposition is sometimes based on the sound, rather than on the spelling!

Dialogue 1

The following dialogue takes place between Gérard Dupuy (GD), who teaches in **terminale** at a **lycée** in Besançon, eastern France, and Olivier Heim (OH), one of his students, who has just sat his **baccalauréat** and is awaiting his results. You can read the same dialogue in Activity 6, with familiar and slang expressions replaced by standard and elevated forms.

If you have the recording, listen first to the dialogue which follows. Otherwise, read it at least twice before beginning the work which has been set.

CD1, TR 5, 01:03

GD Alors, dis-moi, Olivier, ces examens, ça s'est bien passé?

OH Eh ben, vous savez, non, pas vraiment. J'ai un peu les boules!

GD Ah bon? Pourquoi? Tu avais pourtant bien travaillé toute l'année, non? Tes résultats, sans être brillants, avaient été acceptables.

OH Ouais, mais j'sais pas. J'ai paniqué, j'ai eu des trous. Pas moyen de me rappeler des trucs vachement simples. Et puis j'avais fait des impasses sur pas mal de sujets, alors …

GD Mais, nom d'un chien, je vous avais prévenus, toi et tes camarades! Je vous l'avais dit et répété cent fois: 'surtout, ne faites pas d'impasses'!

OH Je sais bien que vous l'aviez dit, mais j'avais pensé que ça marcherait. Et puis vous savez bien que j'avais été malade au deuxième trimestre.

GD Oui, mais ça, c'est pas une excuse!

OH Je sais, mais j'ai pas eu le temps de tout réviser. Manque de pot, je suis tombé sur des trucs que j'avais pas étudiés.

GD Mais tu a bien répondu à certaines questions tout de même?

OH Ouais, mais pas assez en détail. J'ai l'impression que mes résultats vont pas être brillants.

GD C'est la vie! Mais, si tu es recalé, c'est tes parents qui vont être déçus, non?

OH Vachement oui! Mais je suis sûr que j'ai aucune chance.

GD	Alors, que vas-tu faire maintenant?
OH	Bof, j'sais pas. J'y ai pas encore pensé.
GD	Si ça n'a pas marché, tu vas te représenter en septembre ou redoubler?
OH	Alors là, pas question! Le bahut, les études, j'en ai ras le bol. Je vais trouver un boulot, gagner du fric comme mes copains, profiter de la vie, quoi!
GD	Pff! Vous êtes tous les mêmes! Mais, nom d'une pipe, y a pas que l'argent dans la vie!

Insight

In familiar French, certain expressions are used to 'speed up' statements: **j'sais pas** for **je ne sais pas** (*I don't know*); **y a pas** for **il n'y a pas** (*there isn't/there aren't*); **non?** for **n'est-ce pas?** (*isn't that so?*); **pas question!** for **il n'en est pas question!** (*absolutely not/no way!*). They are not offensive.

QUICK VOCAB

le trimestre *three-month period/term. In France, the academic year is divided into three terms.*

faire une impasse *to skip one subject in your revision (in the hope it will not come up in the exam!). GD advised against* **impasses**. *The word also means a cul-de-sac or dead end.*

c'est la vie! *That's life! A philosophical or fatalistic view of things. The expression is also used in English.*

être recalé *to fail an exam*

le bahut *student slang for the (secondary) school they go to*

se représenter *to resit (usually in September) parts of a failed examination*

redoubler *to repeat the year, a possibility which is often not very appealing to students, since there is a stigma attached to being* **un redoublant** *(a repeater)*

Language learning tip 3

In the activity that follows, there are a number of 'clues' you can use to find the English meaning of the familiar French expressions listed. For instance in:

- **un boulot**, *the indefinite article* **un** *should lead you to look for a noun.*
- **des trucs**, *the word* **des**, *which normally precedes a plural noun in French, is often not translated in English.*

Try to use such detective skills before diving into the dictionary! This investigative approach should play a very important part in your language learning and therefore your progress!

Activity 2

Having studied the expressions listed below, which we met in the dialogue, match them according to meaning. Just write the number and, next to it, the letter of the matching translation.

1 ouais
2 j'ai paniqué
3 pas mal de
4 nom d'un chien
5 ça marcherait
6 des trucs
7 vachement
8 manque de pot
9 pas moyen
10 j'ai eu des trous
11 pas question!
12 le bahut
13 j'en ai ras-le-bol
14 un boulot
15 du fric

a *a job*
b *it would work*
c *(some) money*
d *unfortunately*
e *a fair bit of …*
f *the school*
g *for heaven's sake*
h *things*
i *impossible*
j *yeah!*
k *I'm fed up*
l *I lost my cool*
m *I couldn't remember*
n *extremely*
o *out of the question!*

Bof! is an interjection used to express a feeling of resignation or helplessness concerning a situation which cannot be changed easily or at all. It was one of the key words used by students in the 1968 period of unrest (**les événements de mai soixante-huit** – see Dialogue 2). It goes hand in hand with the expression **j'en ai ras-le-bol** (*I've had it up to here* or *I'm fed up to the back teeth*). Both were extensively uttered by young people to express their dissatisfaction about the way they were treated by the authorities and by their parents at that time. They are sometimes referred to as **les soixante-huitards** or **la génération bof**.

Insight

When using a foreign language, pay attention to the style and register needed in various circumstances. This will avoid creating feelings which may affect your relationship with native speakers. Do not be tempted to show off your knowledge of slang unless you are confident it is safe to do so.

Comprehension 1

Remember: in a comprehension exercise, you should read the questions first, and make sure that you understand precisely what you are required to do. This will help you to home in on the answers and may also give you helpful clues about content. Read/listen to the dialogue again, before answering the questions.

This activity is part of your self-assessment. Award yourself ten marks for each completely correct answer, and add this to your total in the self-assessment form.

1 What is the teacher's opening question to Olivier?
2 Why is the teacher surprised at Olivier's initial answer about his results?
3 Which two 'reasons' does Olivier give for his poor performance?
4 Why is the teacher indignant about the last of Olivier's 'reasons'?
5 What explanation does Olivier give for not having covered the whole of the syllabus?

6 What, according to the teacher, will be the reaction of Olivier's parents when the results come out?
7 What are the possibilities put forward by the teacher, if Olivier has failed?
8 How does Olivier respond to these?
9 What does Olivier want to do instead?
10 What is the teacher's final comment/criticism?

Activity 3

In Unit 4, we examined some of the 'tricks' used in familiar French to simplify or speed up conversation. Below are some of those tricks, used by Olivier (and his teacher) in the dialogue. Replace them by the standard forms, which should be in a less familiar style.

Example: **J'sais pas. = Je ne sais pas.**

1 Ces examens, ça s'est bien passé?
2 J'avais pensé que ça marcherait.
3 Oui mais ça, c'est pas une excuse.
4 J'avais pas eu le temps de réviser.
5 C'est tes parents qui vont être déçus, non?
6 Tu vas te représenter en septembre?
7 J'y ai pas encore pensé.
8 Y a pas que l'argent dans la vie!

Activity 4

Olivier's teacher uses some familiar turns of phrase which indicate that he is probably not much older than his students and adopts a fairly relaxed style with them. There are, however, two expressions which are usually thought to belong to standard or even elevated French. Can you spot them? Could you then put them into familiar French?

Activity 5

In the dialogue, the teacher uses the familiar form of address **tu** with Olivier (see Unit 2). There are, however, three instances when the **vous** form appears in his speech. Note them down. Can their presence be justified? Explain your point of view.

Language learning tip 4

In French, the verb **passer** should be treated with some caution as it can mean:

- *to pass* (when talking about the passing of time).

  le temps passe — *time passes*

- *to sit* (an examination), but not to pass it!

  Il va passer son bac. — *He's going to sit his A levels.*

- *to spend* (time) doing something.

  Ils passent des heures devant la télé. — *They spend hours in front of the TV.*

- *to cross a frontier/barrier.* In this case, it is used with **avoir** and not **être.**

  Nous avons passé la frontière. — *We have crossed the border/frontier.*

  J'ai passé l'âge! — *I'm too old (for this sort of thing).*

Activity 6

In the dialogue, the teacher uses two idiomatic expressions to voice his annoyance/irritation. Can you pick them out and give their literal translation? What register do you think they belong to?

In the following version of the dialogue between Gérard Dupuy and Olivier Heim, which we studied earlier, familiar and slang expressions have been replaced by the corresponding standard (S) or elevated (E) forms. Those are shown in ***bold italics*** for easy identification. Comparing the two versions will help you get a better feel for the different registers.

GD Alors, dis-moi, Olivier, ***tes examens se sont-ils bien passés*** (E)?

OH ***Eh bien*** (S), vous savez, non, pas vraiment. ***Je suis un peu déprimé*** (S)!

GD Ah bon? Pourquoi? Tu avais pourtant bien travaillé toute l'année, ***n'est-ce pas*** (S)? Tes résultats, sans être brillants, avaient été acceptables.

OH ***Oui*** (S), mais ***je ne sais pas*** (S). J'ai ***perdu mon sang-froid*** (S), j'ai eu des trous ***de mémoire*** (S). ***Je n'ai pas pu*** (S) me rappeler des ***choses très simples*** (S). Et ***d'autre part, je n'avais pas révisé bon nombre de sujets, donc*** (S/E) …

GD Mais, ***pourtant*** (S), je vous avais prévenus, toi et tes camarades! Je vous ***avais dit et répété bien des fois*** (S): 'surtout, ***révisez tous vos sujets***' (S)!

OH Je sais bien que vous l'aviez dit, mais j'avais pensé que ***cela serait possible*** (S). ***Et d'autre part*** (S), vous savez bien que j'avais été malade au deuxième trimestre.

GD Oui, mais ***ce n'est pas*** (S) une excuse!

OH Je sais, mais ***je n'ai pas eu*** (S) le temps de tout réviser. ***Malheureusement, j'ai eu des questions sur des sujets que je n'avais pas étudiés*** (S).

GD Mais tu a bien répondu à certaines questions tout de même?

OH ***Oui*** (S), mais pas assez en détail. J'ai l'impression que mes résultats ***ne*** (S) vont pas être brillants.

GD C'est la vie! Mais, si tu ***échoues*** (S), ***tes parents ne vont-ils pas être déçus*** (E)?

OH ***Si, extrêmement*** (S)! Mais je suis sûr que ***je n'ai*** (S) aucune chance.

GD Alors, que vas-tu faire maintenant?

OH ***Eh bien, je ne sais pas*** (S). ***Je n'y ai pas*** (S) encore pensé.

GD Si ***tu as échoué*** (S), ***vas-tu te représenter à la session de*** (E) septembre ou redoubler?

OH ***Certainement pas! J'en ai assez du lycée*** (S), et des études. Je vais trouver un ***travail*** (S), gagner ***de l'argent*** (S) comme mes ***amis*** (S), ***profiter de la vie*** (S)!

GD Pff! ***Vous avez tous la même attitude*** (S)! Mais ***enfin*** (S), l'argent ***n'est pas la seule chose importante*** (S) dans la vie!

3 Past participle agreement with *avoir* and *être*

As we have already seen, **avoir** and **être**, apart from having a meaning of their own, are used to form compound tenses, such as the perfect and pluperfect indicative, conditional perfect, perfect subjunctive, etc.:

1 Vous *avez fermé* le magasin à sept heures.	*You closed the shop at seven (perfect indicative).*
2 Nous *avions réservé* une table pour deux.	*We had reserved a table for two (pluperfect indicative).*
3 Elle *serait partie* sans vous.	*She would have gone without you (conditional perfect).*
4 Ils *seront revenus* à minuit.	*They will have come back at (by) midnight (future perfect).*

From the above examples, we can see that the past participles behave differently after **avoir** (Examples 1 and 2) and **être** (Examples 3 and 4). The past participle following **être** changes (i.e. agrees) according to the gender and the number of the performer(s) of the action or subject(s), whereas, in the case of **avoir**, there appears to be no agreement. So, with être, past participles agree with the subject (just as adjectives do with the noun they qualify):

Elle est *intelligente* et *travailleuse.* *(adjectives)*	*She is intelligent and hard working.*
Elle est *partie* hier matin et elle est *revenue* hier soir. *(past participles)*	*She left yesterday morning and she came back yesterday evening.*

When the auxiliary is **avoir** instead of **être**, the situation is a little less straightforward, but before we examine it in detail, we have to clarify the concept of direct and indirect object complements.

A complement is a phrase which gives additional information about the thing or being that is either:

1 Affected by the subject's action and identified by the answer to the questions *who/what/whom* (called a direct object complement (d.o.)) or

2 The recipient (beneficiary) of the subject's action identified by the answer to the question *to* (or *for*) *which/to what/to whom* (called an indirect object complement (i.o.)).

In the examples below, the abbreviations s. = *subject*, v. = *verb*, d.o. = *direct object* and i.o. = *indirect object* are used to identify the relevant parts of the sentence.

They give money. **Ils donnent de l'argent.**
| They | give | (*what?*) → money |
s. v. d.o.

They give money to the poor. **Ils donnent de l'argent aux pauvres.**
| They | give | (*what?*) → money | (*to whom?*) → | to the poor |
s. v. d.o. i.o.

But beware. In the sentence:
They give the poor money
| They | give | (*to whom?*) → (to) the poor | (*what?*) → money |
s. v. i.o. d.o.

it is still the money which is affected (= given), and the poor who are the recipients.

A number of English verbs appear in sentences which wrongly give the impression that we are dealing with a direct object whereas it is an indirect object construction which is needed:

On a *vendu* la voiture.	*We sold the car.*
On a *vendu* la voiture aux voisins.	*We sold the car to the neighbours.* or *We sold the neighbours the car.*

Note: **On a vendu les voisins la voiture** is not grammatically acceptable.

Let us now return to the problem of the agreement of the past participle with **avoir**. If the sentence constructed with **avoir** contains a direct object and if that direct object precedes **avoir**, there will be agreement. Conversely, if the sentence constructed with **avoir** does not contain a direct object, or if the direct object follows **avoir**, there will be no agreement!

As this may still be a little baffling, we will clarify with some examples.

The first thing is, of course, to determine what the direct object is, and where it is situated in the sentence. One simple – if not totally foolproof – way to do so is, as we suggested earlier, to ask the question **qui?** or **quoi?** (but not **à qui?** or **à quoi?**) after the past participle following **avoir**.

Il a *envoyé* la lettre.	*He sent the letter.*

He sent what? = *the letter*. The direct object (*the letter*) comes too late to influence the past participle: no agreement!

Voici la lettre qu'il a *envoyée*.	*Here is the letter he sent.*

He sent what? = *the letter*. The direct object (*the letter* – fem. sing.), is mentioned twice (**la lettre** and **qu'**) before the past participle: agreement! Here are two further examples:

Elle a *reçu* les documents ce matin.	*She received the documents this morning.*

She received what? = *the documents*. **Les documents** comes too late to influence the past participle: no agreement!

Elle a les documents? Oui, elle les a *reçus* ce matin.	*Does she have the documents? Yes, she received them this morning.*

She received what? = *them*. The pronoun **les**, which replaces **les documents**, occurs before the past participle: agreement!

Do not worry unduly about the agreement of the past participle with **avoir** in conversation: a good many French people make mistakes in applying the rules. In formal documents, however, it is important to try and be as accurate as possible.

Note:

a The compound tenses of **être** (*has been*, *had been*, *would have been*, etc.) are formed with **avoir** as the auxiliary: **Elle a été, elle avait été, elle aurait été**, etc.

b The past participle **été** never agrees, regardless of the position of the direct object.

La superbe danseuse qu'elle a été (*not* étée).	*The superb dancer that she was/ has been.*

c The compound tenses of **avoir** (*has had*, *had had*, *would have had*, etc.) are also formed with **avoir** as the auxiliary: **elle a eu, elle avait eu, elle aurait eu**, etc. Note that, in this case, the rules of agreement apply.

Les difficultés qu'elle a eues.	*The difficulties she (has) had.*

Insight

Making the correct past participle agreements in formal written French indicates a high level of grammatical sophistication which will be appreciated by native speakers. In oral exchanges, however, do not worry unduly about such agreements since, in most cases, they are not pronounced.

Activity 7

In the English sentences that follow, identify the direct objet (d.o.) and the indirect object (i.o.) by placing the abbreviation immediately after the appropriate phrase.

1 We sent an e-mail.
2 I gave the beggar two euros.
3 She brought her friends some flowers.
4 He returned the book to the bookshop.

5 They gave the owner the keys.
6 The director wrote the employees a letter.
7 The police permitted him to leave.
8 You have contacted the shop.
9 I have lent my neighbour a ladder.
10 His master sold him to a slave trader.

Activity 8

Using the perfect tense, translate the sentences of Activity 7 into French.

Activity 9

In the following sentences, check that the past participle agreement is correct. If not, make any amendments required. In one or two cases, you may have to use logic as well as grammar to find the right answer.

1 Ma femme m'a appelée au téléphone.
2 Ils avaient vendue leur maison.
3 Les garçons se sont sali en jouant dans la vase.
4 Le patron avait ouverte la porte.
5 Elle est arrivé à temps!
6 Mon frère était descendue dans la rue.
7 Elles se sont endormis très vite.
8 Elle aurait été furieux de me voir.
9 Mon dieu! Tu as changée.
10 Nous sommes revenu à sept heures.

4 Pronominal/reflexive verbs

Language learning tip 5

On several previous occasions, we have encountered the expression 'reflexive or pronominal verbs' which we used in a rather imprecise way. To be accurate, we should now distinguish between three categories of verbs which are constructed with the 'reflexive' pronouns **me, te, se, nous, vous, se.**

1 *Verbs which indicate that the action performed by the subject 'falls back' onto the performer:* **se laver** *(to wash oneself),* **se lever** *(to get up),* **se coucher** *(to lie down),* **se couper** *(to cut oneself),* **se raser** *(to shave oneself), etc.*

2 *Reciprocal verbs, which indicate that the action performed by the subject falls on the object, which in turn performs the same action on the subject:* **se battre** *(to fight with each other),* **se disputer** *(to argue with each other),* **s'embrasser** *(to kiss each other), etc.*

3 *Pronominal verbs such as* **se révolter** *(to revolt/rebel),* **s'enfuir** *(to run away),* **s'évanouir** *(to faint/vanish), etc. which, unlike the other two categories, cannot be used without the reflexive pronoun:* **Ils se sont enfuis**. *They ran away.*

As we have seen previously, pronominal verbs use être preceded by one of the following pronouns: **me, te, se, nous, vous, se,** to form their compound tenses. Normally, the past participles will agree in the appropriate way.

Elle *s'est couchée* très tard, mais elle *s'est levée* de bonne heure.	*She went to bed late but she got up early.*
Ils se *sont battus* comme des lions.	*They fought like lions (= bravely).*
Elles *s'étaient trouvées* sans argent.	*They had found themselves without money.*

There are some (rare) exceptions to this general rule. You will, if required, find them in your grammar.

Note: In many of the examples above, the perfect tense has been used for the sake of simplicity, but what has been said holds good for all compound tenses.

Although it is always rewarding to get things right, don't worry: not making the proper agreement will not prevent you from being understood!

Insight

In English there is often no need for a reflexive pronoun before a pronominal verb: *I wash*, *he shaves*, *you get up*, *they dress* ... In French, such verbs require one of the following: **me/m', te/t', se/s', nous, vous, se/s': je <u>me</u> lave, il <u>se</u> rase, vous <u>vous</u> levez, ils <u>s'</u> habillent ...**

Activity 10

In the following, replace the infinitive with the correct form of the past participle and make the agreement as appropriate.

1 La petite fille est (tomber) dans la rue.
2 Ils se sont (laver) dans la rivière.
3 Les enfants ont (pleurer) toute la nuit.
4 Elle a (voir) l'accident de sa fenêtre.
5 Ils sont (arriver) à huit heures.
6 Nous avions (oublier) notre parapluie.
7 J'ai (perdre) ma montre et je l'ai (chercher) partout.
8 C'est la veste que tu as (acheter).
9 Ils se seront (perdre) dans la forêt.

Activity 11

In the conversation below, two women are talking about a job interview which one of them has just attended. Translate the English responses into French, using some of the familiar structures we encountered in the exchange between Olivier and his teacher in Unit 5, Dialogue 1. Beware of agreements, and note that *they* should be translated by **ils**.

CD1, TR 5, 03:32

F1 Dis-moi, cette entrevue, ça s'est bien passé?
F2 *No, not really. There were a fair number of brilliant candidates. I'm sure I don't stand a chance!*
F1 Mais tu avais pourtant bien préparé ton entrevue et ta présentation!
F2 *Yes, but I panicked. I know it's not an excuse, but they asked me things I hadn't prepared.*
F1 C'est ton mari qui va être déçu.
F2 *Yes, I know, but that's life!*
F1 Qu'est-ce que tu vas faire maintenant?

F2	*I don't know. I haven't thought about it yet.*
F1	Tu vas chercher un autre emploi?
F2	*No way! I'm going to enjoy life.*
F1	Tu as raison. Y a pas que l'argent dans la vie!

5 The pluperfect

This tense is used to indicate an action which had been completed in the past (1), when another action (2) took place.

Past   Present

(1)   (2)

——————x——————x——————

J'avais fini **mon travail quand ils sont arrivés.**	*I had finished (pluperfect) my work when they arrived (perfect).*

If two perfects were used, the meaning would be quite different:

J'ai fini mon travail quand ils sont arrivés.	*I finished my work when they arrived (and not before).*

The two examples above clearly show the importance of using the right tense to express accurately the time relationship between events.

5.1 How to form the pluperfect

It is in fact very simple. All you need is the imperfect of the appropriate auxiliary **avoir** or **être** and the past participle of the main verb (the French equivalent of English verb forms such as *broken*, *seen*, *spoken* ...). These are shown below.

Avoir	*Être*
j'avais	j'étais
tu avais	tu étais
il/elle/on avait	il/elle/on était
nous avions	nous étions
vous aviez	vous étiez
ils/elles avaient	ils/elles étaient

Activity 12

In the following list, there are verbs which take **avoir** to form their compound tenses, and others which take **être**. Classify them appropriately, using A (for **avoir**) and E (for **être**).

monter, acheter, rester, tomber, manger, vendre, descendre, regarder, aller, prendre, sortir, pouvoir

Language learning tip 6

The pluperfect is often used to remind someone about what had been said or done before disaster struck:

Je t'*avais demandé* de payer la facture!	*I had asked you to pay the bill* (before now – but you didn't).
On vous *avait dit* de faire attention!	*We (rather than 'one') had told you to be careful* (before now – but you weren't).

Activity 13

In the following passage, replace the infinitives by the appropriate form of the pluperfect. Remember that French has two auxiliaries for the formation of this tense and that using them is not a matter of personal preference.

Nous (partir) de la maison à six heures du matin. Nous (penser) qu'il n'y aurait pas beaucoup de circulation sur l'autoroute. Avant le départ, nous (téléphoner) à nos amis pour leur annoncer l'heure de notre arrivée. Nous (faire) à peine une dizaine de kilomètres quand nous sommes tombés en panne: Jacques (oublier) de faire le plein d'essence! Heureusement, nous (emmener) notre téléphone portable. J'ai appelé notre garagiste. Il est venu nous dépanner tout de suite!

la circulation *Here, the English word is traffic. Note that* **le trafic** *can also be used, when referring to transport by train or lorry.*

l'autoroute *In France, there are approximately 2,500 kilometres of motorways. They are mostly two-lane and paying* (**à péage**), *except in the immediate vicinity of towns, where toll booths would create enormous traffic jams* – **des embouteillages monstres**.

à peine *hardly, or barely. In formal French, it usually appears as:* **à peine avions-nous fait une dizaine de kilomètres que ...**

tomber en panne *to have a mechanical breakdown. A nervous breakdown is:* **une dépression (nerveuse)!**

faire le plein (d'essence *or* **de gazole)** *to fill up (the tank) with petrol or diesel*

le (téléphone) portable *As in England, mobile phones are now a must with many people.*

le garagiste *the garage owner. Also called* **le mécanicien**, *or (in familiar French)* **le mécano**.

il est venu nous dépanner *he came and fixed the car for us. It is, however, possible to say:* **Est-ce que tu peux me dépanner?** *when you need somebody to do you a good turn or to lend you some money to be paid back later!*

tout de suite *at once. In familiar French, this expression is often confused with* **de suite** *(afterwards). However,* **je reviens de suite** *is taken to mean (I'll be) back soon!*

QUICK VOCAB

Insight

In English, the verb *to be* is used to state someone's age. In French, it is **avoir** (*to have*) which is required for the purpose: **'Marc <u>a</u> trente ans'** (*'Marc is thirty (years old)'*). Don't forget that the word **ans** must be used!

Dialogue 2

There follows a short extract from a discussion between a radio presenter (**RP**) and a sociology expert (**SE**) about the rise of children as consumers, highlighting some of the social changes which have taken place since the end of the sixties.

CD1, TR 5, 05:14

RP **(1)** Professeur, je crois avoir lu dans votre dernier livre que le rôle des jeunes en France avait profondément changé depuis 1968.

SE Absolument! Depuis la fin des années soixante, les jeunes ont pris une importance économique considérable dans notre société.

RP D'après vous, comment est-ce que cela s'explique?

SE Oh, c'est très simple! À partir de 68, les parents qui appartenaient à la génération du baby-boom, c'est à dire celle des gens nés entre 1945 et 1960, ont décidé de donner à leurs enfants plus de liberté et d'indépendance, de les traiter comme des adultes.

RP Comment cela s'est-il passé?

SE D'abord, on leur a donné la parole: autour de la table familiale, puis en public et enfin dans les médias. Ensuite, il y a eu l'argent de poche: les baby-boomers, qui avaient connu la période de vaches maigres de l'après-guerre, pour compenser ce que leurs parents n'avaient pas pu acheter, mais aussi pour avoir la paix, ont commencé à donner de plus en plus d'argent de poche à leurs 'chers petits'. Cela a d'abord permis non seulement aux 'ados' mais aussi à leurs cadets, de dépenser des sommes non-négligeables sur des magazines, des disques et, pour les filles, sur des produits de beauté et des cosmétiques. Puis, graduellement, ces enfants qui jusque là n'avaient pas eu droit à la parole, sont devenus non seulement des consommateurs, mais aussi des décideurs capables d'influencer leurs aînés.

RP **(2)** C'est vrai, et les gens de marketing n'ont pas mis très longtemps à se rendre compte du potentiel commercial de ce nouveau marché.

SE Absolument! Il ne faut pas oublier que dans les années soixante-dix, les moins de 20 ans représentaient grosso modo un tiers de la population de l'Hexagone. Alors, les grandes marques ont lancé des produits spécialement étudiés pour ce segment de clientèle! Les années quatre-vingt et quatre-vingt-dix ont vu l'explosion des produits griffés spécifiquement pour les jeunes. À mesure qu'ils ont eu plus d'argent et de pouvoir d'achat, les jeunes consommateurs sont devenus plus exigeants et ont demandé des produits marqués que Nike, Adidas, Diesel et j'en passe, se sont fait un plaisir de leur présenter. La pression des pairs a aidé, et nous en sommes arrivés aujourd'hui au point où, si un produit n'est pas griffé, les jeunes n'en veulent pas!

RP Merci de ces clarifications, Professeur.

Insight

In French, when referring to a group of people under or over a certain age, the expressions **les moins de …** or **les plus de …** are used as appropriate: **les moins de vingt ans** (*the under-twenties*); **les plus de soixante ans** (*the over-sixties*).

d'après vous (or **selon vous**) *according to you*
on leur a donné la parole autour de la table familiale *we/one allowed them to speak up at the dinner table. Children began to participate in conversation at the dinner table (instead of being seen and not heard).*
l'argent de poche *pocket money*
la période de vaches maigres *the lean years (lit. the period of lean cows). The opposite is* **la période de vaches grasses** *(a period of wealth or plenty).*
l'après-guerre *the post-war period*
les 'ados' *(short for* **adolescents***) More or less equivalent to the English word teenagers.*
de plus en plus d'argent *more and more money*
leurs cadets *their younger counterparts. The opposite is* **leurs aînés**, *their elders.*
des produits de beauté *beauty products*
des décideurs *decision-makers, from* **décider** *(to decide)*
grosso modo *roughly speaking. This expression is used with numbers/ quantities.*
les produits griffés *branded goods/designer goods.* **La griffe** *is the label/ logo of a famous designer. It can also mean the claw of an animal.*
le pouvoir d'achat *purchasing power*
se faire un plaisir de *(+ infinitive) to be only too glad to …*
et j'en passé *to name but a few*
la pression des pairs *peer pressure*

QUICK VOCAB

Insight

To rank the children of a family by age, you can use the expressions: **le (la) plus âgé(e)** or **l'aîné(e)** for *the elder/ oldest*. For a *younger child* use **le cadet (la cadette)**, and for the youngest **le (la) plus jeune.** Remember that gender and number agreement must be made.

Language learning tip 7

In the passage, there are a couple of nouns borrowed from English/American: **le baby-boom** and **le marketing.** Both are masculine as are the immense majority of borrowed nouns of the same origin, as mentioned in Appendix 5. In spite of the strenuous efforts of the French government, the number of English words and expressions is ever increasing, and it is said that **les teenagers** are partly to blame!

Le baby-boom refers to the period of sharp demographic expansion which occurred in France between the end of the Second World War and the late sixties. This **explosion démographique** (*population explosion*) was due not only to an increase in the number of births during that period, but also to a high level of immigration mainly from the French Colonies.

Mai soixante-huit (*May 68*). At that time, under the presidency of General de Gaulle, there was a huge social uprising caused, among other things, by students' frustrations in the face of antiquated educational methods, equipment, facilities and discipline. Schools and universities were occupied and managers locked in their offices. The unrest lasted for the whole of May. By mid-May the students were joined by workers. It is estimated that by 20 May, at least ten million people were demonstrating in the streets. During that month, 800 million working hours were lost. The consequences for the economy were catastrophic.

La révolution de mai dealt a deadly blow to de Gaulle's regime, and he retired from politics a year later.

Comprehension 2

Answer the following questions on the first section of the dialogue, from the beginning to ... **des décideurs capables d'influencer leurs** aînés. First read the questions, then the text, before answering each one as fully as you can. Before reaching for your dictionary, try to 'guess' some of the vocabulary. You will be pleasantly surprised to find that you can understand a good deal!

1 What were the key ideas put forward by the sociologist in his latest book?
2 How does he explain the start of the phenomenon?
3 What reasons does he give to explain the attitude of the baby-boomers towards their children?
4 How did teenagers spend the cash they were given?
5 Did the process only involve teenagers? Explain.
6 What were the consequences of those changes on the attitude and behaviour of the youngsters concerned?

Activity 14
Translate the remainder of the text (2) into English. Here again, use your language skills to make some initial sense of the passage before beginning your translation.

L'éducation, c'est ce qui reste quand on a tout oublié! *Education is what's left when all else has been forgotten!*

Il faut que jeunesse se passe! *Youth must have its fling!*

Insight

In French, months and days are masculine. As a consequence, related adjectives will be in the masculine form: **'Cette année, janvier a été froid'** (*'January was cold this year'*); **'Nous avons eu un mardi intéressant'** (*'We've had an interesting Tuesday'*). Note that neither of the two categories is written with a capital letter.

TEST YOURSELF

1. How do modern dictionaries indicate the register/level of language of a given word?
2. Why is it important to be careful about using slang?
3. When does été, the past participle of être, agree in gender and number with the subject of the sentence?
4. What is the difference between reflexive and reciprocal verbs?
5. Where would you see the word **péage** when travelling in France by car? What is its meaning?
6. Which of the following two forms is correct: **je suis été malade** or **j'ai été malade** (*I have been ill*)? Why?
7. What is the gender of most English nouns used in French?
8. What was **le baby-boom**?
9. What is the pluperfect tense used for?
10. How can the economic and political impact of May 1968 be measured?

6

Les grands départs

In this unit you will learn

- ***How to form and use the future and future perfect***
- ***How to say 'everyone', 'someone', 'no one', 'nothing', etc.***
- ***How to ask questions with interrogative pronouns (who/what/where/how/why)***
- ***How to translate 'without -ing'; 'neither ... nor ...'; 'from ... to ...'; 'between ... and ...'***
- ***How to distinguish between the two meanings of* quelque(s)**
- ***How to distinguish between direct and indirect (or reported) speech***
- ***How to express comparison***
- ***How to distinguish between the various meanings of* plus que *and* plus de**

1 Ways of expressing the future

As we have seen earlier, events which are going to take place in the near future can be expressed by using the present of **aller**, followed by the infinitive of the main verb, as shown in the example below:

Nous allons fermer le magasin. *We are going to close the shop.*

Sometimes, however, we need to use a tense that will situate actions further into the future. This tense is the future indicative.

The timeline below may help to clarify the relationship between the present, the immediate future, the future perfect and the future:

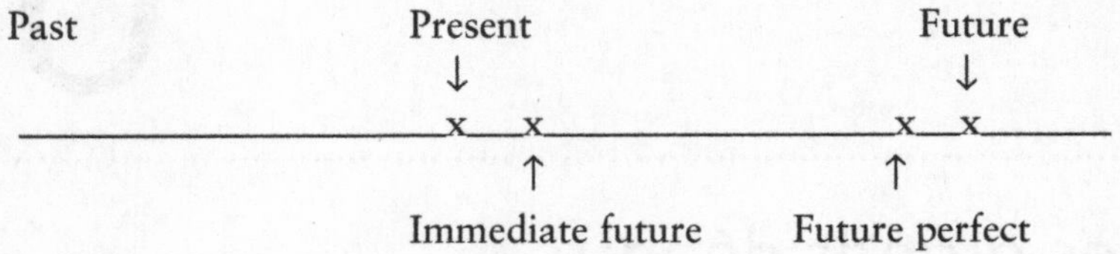

2 The future

In French the future tense is a simple (one-word) tense made up of a stem + an ending. In formal circumstances, it is still frequently used, but in familiar conversation it is often replaced by the immediate future.

2.1 How do you form the future?

Its formation is again quite simple: the appropriate endings (see the table on the following page) are added to the stem of the verb which, in the majority of cases, is very predictable:

a For most 1st group verbs (**regarder, marcher,** etc.), the stem will be the whole of the infinitive. However, first group verbs with infinitives ending in **-ayer, -oyer, -uyer** will change the **y** to **i**:

> **payer** (*to pay*) = **je paierai**, etc.;
> **essayer** (*to try*) = **j'essaierai**, etc.
> For **envoyer** (*to send*), the stem is **enverr-** (see the table on the following page).

b All 2nd group verbs (**finir, choisir,** etc.) will form their future by adding the appropriate endings to the infinitive.

> **finir** (*to finish*) = **je finirai**, etc.

c For 3rd group verbs, there are three possibilities:
1 With most infinitives ending in **-re** (**attendre, prendre,** etc.), the final **e** will be eliminated before the endings are added;

2 In the case of infinitives ending in **-ir** (**partir, sortir, etc.**), but not **-oir**, the stem will also be the whole of the infinitive;
3 For the rest, there will be a stem change, which unfortunately is not always predictable. To help you, some of the most common irregular stems are shown in the following table:

Infinitive	*Meaning*	*Stem for future*	*Future endings*	
aller	*to go*	ir-	je/j'	-ai
avoir	*to have*	aur-	tu	-as
envoyer	*to send*	enverr-	il/elle/on	-a
courir	*to run*	courr-	nous	-ons
devoir	*to have to/must*	devr-	vous	-ez
faire	*to do/make*	fer-	ils/elles	-ont
mourir	*to die*	mourr-		
pouvoir	*to be able to/can*	pourr-		
recevoir	*to receive*	recevr-		
savoir	*to know*	saur-		
voir	*to see*	verr-		
vouloir	*to want*	voudr-		

Language learning tip 1

Did you notice anything interesting about the endings in the right-hand column of the table?

They are, indeed, the same as the endings of **avoir** in the present tense, as a quick look at Unit 3 will confirm!

The stems we have identified for the future will also be useful to form another tense. From your earlier studies, can you remember which one? The answer will be revealed in the next unit!

Don't forget: playing detective pays off handsomely when you are learning a foreign language!

Insight

In spoken French, the future, sometimes perceived as a little highbrow, is often replaced by the immediate future (present of **aller** + infinitive of main verb). So, instead of **'Demain, elle ira à l'hypermarché'** (*'Tomorrow, she will go to the hypermarket'*), people will tend to say: **'Demain, elle <u>va aller</u> à l'hypermarché'**.

Reading

The 19th-century author Victor Hugo, whom we came across in Unit 3, was a prolific writer who had many strings to his bow. The following poem, which he wrote in September 1847, is still remembered by French people, who used to learn to recite it at primary school. If you have the recording, listen to it twice without looking at the text, then read it as you listen to it a third time. If you do not have the recording read it three times in preparation for the exercises associated with it.

Demain, dès l'aube ...

CD2, TR 1, 01:00

Demain, dès l'aube, à l'heure où blanchit la campagne,
Je partirai. Vois-tu, je sais que tu m'attends.
J'irai par la forêt, j'irai par la montagne.
Je ne puis demeurer loin de toi plus longtemps.

Je marcherai les yeux fixés sur mes pensées,
Sans rien voir au dehors, sans entendre aucun bruit,
Seul, inconnu, le dos courbé, les mains croisées,
Triste, et le jour pour moi sera comme la nuit.

Je ne regarderai ni l'or du soir qui tombe,
Ni les voiles au loin descendant vers Harfleur,
Et quand j'arriverai, je mettrai sur ta tombe
Un bouquet de houx vert et de bruyère en fleur.

dès l'aube *at the crack of dawn (lit. as soon as dawn breaks).* **Dès** *(which must not be confused with* **des***) is used to stress the immediacy of an action.*
je ne puis demeurer ... longtemps *The beginning of the poem seems to suggest that Victor Hugo is going to meet the woman he loves. In fact, he is going to visit the place where his daughter Léopoldine and her husband drowned in the river Seine.*
le dos courbé, les mains croisées *with back bent and hands crossed*
l'or du soir qui tombe *the gold of the setting sun (lit. ... of the falling evening)*
les voiles *(fem.) sails. Beware: the masculine* **le voile** *means veil.*
Harfleur *a small town on the river Seine*
la tombe *grave/tomb*
un bouquet de houx vert et de bruyère en fleur *a bunch of green holly and flowering heather*

QUICK VOCAB

Insight

Occasionally, accents are used in written French to differentiate between two words that have the same spelling. Such is the case for **a** (*has*) and **à** (*at/to/in*); **sur** (*on*) and **sûr** (*sure* – masc.); **la** (*the* – fem.) and **là** (there); **dès** (*as soon as*) and **des** (*some/of the*).

Comprehension 1

Having studied the poem, try to answer the following questions:

1 When will the poet set off on his journey? Give full details.
2 Why does he feel he must go (two reasons)?
3 Which details indicate that his journey may be tiring?
4 One of the lines of the poem suggests the idea of a pilgrimage. Which is it? Can you translate it into English?
5 Several lines suggest that the poet will be oblivious to the world around him. Can you say which ones, and for each give a 'fluid' translation?
6 Which two lines enable you to find out how long the journey will take?
7 Which words give the clue about the real purpose of the poet's journey?

Language learning tip 2

a In the expression **je ne puis** (*I cannot*), **puis** is an elevated form of **peux** and is normally used without the second part of the negation **pas.** So, **je ne puis = je ne peux pas.** It has nothing to do with the adverb **puis,** which as you know means *then* (*afterwards*).
b The preposition **sans** (*without*), is used with the infinitive and not as in English with the present participle (*-ing* form): **sans voir** (*without seeing*), **sans entendre** (*without hearing*).
c The expression **ni ... ni** used by Hugo in lines 9 and 10, meaning *neither ... nor*, can be used in the same way as its English equivalent. In French, however, it must be preceded by the negative particle **ne,** as can be seen in the text.

Activity 1

1 List all the future tense verbs used in the poem and, for each, give the infinitive and the present participle (*-ing* form).
2 There is one present participle in the text. Find it and give its infinitive form.

Activity 2

In addition to **puis**, given in the **Language learning tip** above, there are, in the poem, five verbs which are not in the future tense. Can you:

1 Note them down, giving their meaning and their infinitive;
2 Explain why, in your opinion, they are not in the future tense.

Activity 3

The activity which follows will be part of your self-assessment. Award yourself ten marks for each correctly spelt future, then enter your score in the self-assessment form.

In French, as in English, the future tense is frequently used for the weather forecast. In the following transcript, ten of the verbs have been numbered and put in the infinitive. Can you give the correct future form for each of them? Before you begin this exercise, you may wish to look back at the climate section of Unit 1.

Le bulletin météo

CD2, TR 1, 04:00

Dans la partie est de la France, de la frontière allemande aux Alpes, nous allons avoir un week-end printanier avec beaucoup de soleil. Seul inconvénient: les matinées (1 être) fraîches. Il (2 faire) beau également en Provence, sur la Côte d'Azur et la Corse: du soleil avec quelques petits nuages. De la frontière belge à la Normandie, la région parisienne et une partie du Massif Central, il y (3 avoir) beaucoup de soleil et un ciel souvent très bleu. Demain, dans le courant de la journée, il va y avoir quelques petits passages pluvieux sur l'Auvergne, mais les averses ne (4 durer) pas. Dans le sud-ouest, le soleil se (5 voiler) dans le courant de la matinée et les températures (6 baisser) légèrement en début d'après-midi. Des vents assez forts vont souffler sur la côte atlantique, où il (7 pleuvoir) dans la soirée et dans la nuit. Demain, nous (8 voir) un temps en général variable sur tout le pays, mais avec des températures très agréables pour la saison. Dans la région Midi-Pyrénées, le vent va se renforcer. Dans le Languedoc-Roussillon, un temps gris (9 persister) et les pluies (10 reprendre) dans la journée, sauf dans la vallée du Rhône, où le beau temps va persister au moins jusqu'à lundi.

Insight

To refer to a particular day, in the past or the future, do not use the article: **'Lundi, je vais aller à Paris'** (*'On Monday I'll go to Paris'*). The verb will indicate the time zone. If used, the article signals that the action is a regular event: **'Le mardi on va au cinéma'** (*'On Tuesdays we (fam.) go to the pictures'*).

Activity 4

There are, in the weather forecast, five examples of the immediate future. Note them down. Why do you think they have been used?

Insight

In French, the definite article is required before names of countries and regions: **l'Écosse** (*Scotland*), **le Kent** (*Kent*), **la Corse** (*Corsica*), **la Bretagne** (*Brittany*). If the article is used in English for geographical features, it will be used in French as well: *The* (*English*) *Channel* = **la Manche**, *The Alps* = **les Alpes**.

Activity 5

Translate into English the weather information given in the forecast for each of the areas listed below. Please note that the areas are not listed in sequence.

1 The South West.
2 The Atlantic Coast.
3 The Midi-Pyrénees region.
4 The Languedoc-Roussillon area.
5 The Provence-Côte d'Azur region.
6 The Rhône Valley.
7 Eastern France (from the German frontier to the Alps).
8 The North, Normandy and the Paris region.
9 Corsica.
10 The Auvergne.

Activity 6

With the help of the vocabulary and structures now at your disposal, translate the following weather forecast into French, using the future tense, except in the case of the underlined expression, which should be put in the immediate future.

The forecast for the weekend is excellent: <u>we are going to see</u> spring-like weather all over France, with a great deal of sunshine and blue skies. Early morning temperatures will be low, from 8 to 10 degrees, but they will rise during the course of the morning and in the afternoon they will reach 26 degrees in the South. Tomorrow night, temperatures will again drop to 6 to 8 degrees, but they will rise quickly on Sunday morning and we will have another sunny day. On Monday, there will be a good deal of sunshine in most areas, except in the Eastern regions where we will see some scattered morning showers, but they will not last. In the North, there will be a few small clouds, but they will not stay long. The good weather will continue until Tuesday. On Tuesday temperatures will drop and it will rain all over the country except in the Rhône Valley and in Provence, where the sunshine will continue at least until Thursday. Have a good weekend!

Language learning tip 3

▶ How to translate *between … and …* and *from … to …*

There are two expressions at your disposal to situate something between two values:

▶ **1 De … à …**

Nous aurons du soleil *de* vendredi *à* lundi.	*We will have sunshine from Friday to Monday.*

or:

▶ **2 Entre … et …**

Nous aurons du soleil *entre* vendredi *et* lundi.	*We will have sunshine between Friday and Monday.*

Beware: you cannot 'pick and mix' the two expressions!

▶ The two meanings of **quelque(s)**:

Generally, **quelques** is used as an indefinite adjective meaning *a few/some*:

Ils passent *quelques* jours avec nous.	*They are spending a few days with us.*

(Contd)

Sometimes, however, **quelque** is used as an adverb meaning *some/approximately*:

Ils passent *quelque* dix jours avec nous.	*They are spending some ten days with us.*

In this latter case it never takes an -s!

Insight

The future perfect serves to indicate that a future action will have taken place by the time another action occurs: **'Quand tu auras téléphoné, nous partirons'** (*'When you have telephoned, we will leave/go'*).

3 The future perfect

As we mentioned earlier, the future perfect is a compound tense: it is formed by adding the past participle of the main verb (with the appropriate agreement), to the future of **avoir** (*to have*) or **être** (*to be*). If required, the rules can be found in Unit 5.

The future of those two verbs is shown in the table below.

Avoir	*Être*
j'aurai	je serai
tu auras	tu seras
il/elle/on aura	il/elle/on sera
nous aurons	nous serons
vous aurez	vous serez
ils/elles auront	ils/elles seront

3.1 What is the use of this tense?

A look at the timeline below will give you the clue:

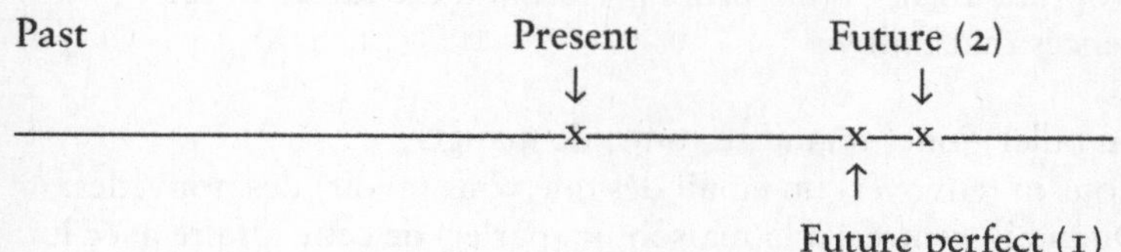

The future perfect will be very valuable when you want to state that the action indicated as (1) will have taken place before another, expressed by the main verb, and shown as (2) in the above diagram. To put it another way, the start of action (2) will be dependent upon completion of action (1):

Dès que nous *aurons fini* notre travail (1), nous irons nous promener (2).	*As soon as we have finished our work, we will go for a walk.*
Lorsque tu *seras partie* (1), je reviendrai (2).	*When you (*fem. sing.*) have gone, I will return.*

Action (2) will only take place when action (1) has occurred (or begun).

Note that this tense enables us to indicate a time-gap between the end of action (1) and the beginning of action (2), which we could not express if we used two futures:

Lorsque tu partiras, je reviendrai. *As soon as you go, I will return.*

In this case, the end of the first action and the start of the second will coincide exactly.

Activity 7

Using the principle set out above, put the infinitives in the appropriate form of the future perfect and the future in the sentences that follow:

1 Tu (aller) jouer quand tu (finir) de manger.
2 Vous m'(envoyer) un email dès que vous (avoir) des nouvelles.
3 Quand il (rentrer) à la maison, je (parler) de cette affaire avec lui.
4 Lorsque vous (payer) la facture, vous (pouvoir) prendre la voiture.
5 Après que vous (fermer) le bureau, vous (laisser) les clés à la réception.

Although French people appreciate the importance of work as a human activity, they like their holidays. In fact, France is probably the European country which has the greatest number of holidays in any given year. The expressions **faire le pont** (lit. *to do or make the bridge*), **un petit pont** and **un grand pont** often crop up in conversation. To the untrained ear, these could be quite confusing and sound like public works on a grand scale. But do not be fooled. Although the French are quite keen on DIY (**le bricolage**), they are not referring to building work, but to holidays; if, for instance, there is a bank/public holiday (**un jour férié**) on a given Friday, this will enable people to have three days free (**un petit pont**) to do some **bricolage** or to go to their **maison de campagne** or **résidence secondaire** (*second home*), if it is not too far. If, however, as happens at Easter, the Monday is also a holiday, there are four days of freedom (**un grand pont**) to take advantage of.

4 Indefinite pronouns

In language, there are situations when the speaker (or writer) wishes to refer to things or beings whose identity is not clear or not known. We have already seen some examples of this technique with **on** meaning *somebody*, and with **ça** meaning *that* (referring to things the gender and number of which is unspecified).

On the following page, there are a few more examples. For a complete list, you should refer to your grammar book.

Since the gender (and sometimes the number) of the noun phrase which these pronouns replace is not known or not clear, the verb will appear in the masculine (singular or plural as appropriate), as shown in the examples below:

1 Chacun a fait ce qu'il a pu.	Everyone has done/did what they could.
2 Beaucoup sont morts.	Many have died.
3 Tout est fini entre nous!	Everything is over between us!
4 Nul n'est obligé d'accepter.	No one is forced to accept.
5 Pas un d'entre vous n'a objecté.	Not one among you (has) objected!
6 Personne n'est infaillible!	Nobody/No one is infallible!
7 Rien n'est perdu!	The situation is not yet desperate! (lit. nothing is lost!)
8 Quelqu'un est entré ici.	Somebody came in here.

Note that, in French, indefinite pronouns with a negative meaning (Examples 4–7 above) take the negative particle **ne**, but that the **pas** element is not needed.

Activity 8

a Translate the sentences below. You may find it helpful to 'borrow' a few expressions from the examples above.

1 Nobody has seen the accident.
2 All is clear.
3 No one is a prophet in his own land (proverb).
4 Every man for himself!
5 There is somebody at the door.
6 All is lost.
7 Each one of you is going to sign this letter.

b In the following sentences, a few more indefinite expressions have been used, but some errors have 'slipped in'. Can you spot them, correct them, and explain what the problem is?

1 Aucun a fini son travail.
2 Plus d'une a refusé.

3 Pas un n'ont réussi.
4 Tout est en ordre.
5 Quelqu'un ont frappé.

Insight

The pronouns **qui, quoi, quand, où, pourquoi** and **comment** are used in French to ask the questions *who*, *what*, *when*, *where*, *why* and *how*? In elevated language, they are followed by an inversion: **'Quand es-tu arrivé?'** (*'When did you arrive?'*). In familiar language, they are simply added to the statement without inversion: **'Tu es arrivé quand?'**

5 Interrogative forms

In everyday communication, we often need to ask *who did what*, *when*, *where*, *why*, etc. Some of the pronouns needed for this are as follows: qui (*who/whom*) (often preceded by a preposition), que (*what*), où (*where*), lequel (*which*) and its variations, quand (*when*), pourquoi (*why*), comment (*how*):

***Qui* est-il?**	*Who is he?*
***Que* faites-vous là?**	*What are you doing there?*
***Où* allons-nous?**	*Where are we going?*
***Comment* allez-vous?**	*How are you?*
***Pourquoi* sont-elles restées?**	*Why did they (fem. plur.) stay?*

Note: quoi (*what*) is often used in relaxed conversation as a replacement to the standard form qu'est-ce que, perceived as too elevated for familiar language:

Tu lis *quoi?* (*for*: qu'est-ce que tu lis?)	*What are you reading?*
Vous aimez *quoi?* (*for*: qu'est-ce que vous aimez?)	*What do you like?*

In the next unit we shall meet some of the above again, but as relative pronouns.

Activity 9

In Unit 4 Section 3, we saw that in French there are three different ways of asking a question: elevated (*E*), standard (*S*) and familiar (*F*). As you may have noticed, the five sentences on the previous page are in the elevated style.

In this activity, each question is asked using one of the three registers specified in brackets above. Can you supply the other two forms? If, after looking at the eight questions, you are still not sure about how to complete the activity, you should revisit Units 4 and 5.

1 Tu fais quoi ce soir? (*F*) Que fais-tu ce soir? (*E*)
Qu'est-ce que tu fais ce soir? (*S*)
2 Quand est-ce que vous rentrerez? (*S*)
3 Où allons-nous? (*E*)
4 Pourquoi tu cries? (*F*)
5 Il va venir quand? (*F*)
6 Qui est-ce? (*E*)
7 De quoi vous parlez? (*F*)
8 Est-ce que nous allons attendre encore longtemps? (*S*).

6 Direct and indirect speech

When we want to report what someone says/said, we can either:

1 Quote what is/was said directly, using speech marks (direct speech):

Jean dit: 'je suis fatigué'. *John says 'I am tired'.*

or:

2 Use the form shown below (indirect speech):

Jean dit qu'il est fatigué. *John says he is tired.*

But beware: when using indirect speech, you must ensure that time zones are properly determined! Let us take an example to clarify this statement. If, using Sentence 2 above, we wish to report that Jean made, or had made, his statement earlier (using the indirect form), we would have to say:

Jean *a dit* qu'il était fatigué.	*John said that he was tired.*

The direct speech section (inside the speech marks) would remain unchanged:

Jean *a dit:* 'je suis fatigué'.	*John said: 'I am tired'.*

Note that, if the direct speech section contains the idea of a future action, it will have to be changed into a conditional in the indirect version:

Elle a crié: 'je n'*irai* plus jamais en vacances avec eux!'	*She shouted: 'never again will I go on holiday with them!'*
Elle a crié qu'elle n'*irait* plus jamais en vacances avec eux.	*She shouted that she would never again go on holiday with them.*

Activity 10

In the sentences that follow, replace the direct speech forms by the corresponding indirect ones. Make sure that the correct tenses are used.

1 Nous avions déclaré: 'nous sommes ruinés'.
2 Pierre a répondu: 'je suis occupé'.
3 Le patron m'a dit: 'vous avez bien travaillé!'
4 La secrétaire a ajouté: 'j'enverrai les documents ce soir'.
5 Le professeur s'est exclamé: 'demain il sera trop tard!'

Dialogue

The following dialogue is between Élise and Daniel Dufrêne who, as you may remember from Unit 2, live in Poitiers, in the département de la Vienne, and are friends of the Swift family.

They have a daughter, Audrey, who is a student at the local university. They are discussing their forthcoming holidays.

As usual, prepare yourself for the work that will follow by listening to the exchange at least twice and reading it carefully. Try to get the gist of the conversation first, and only use the dictionary as a last resort!

CD2, TR 1, 08:10

Élise	Daniel, les vacances approchent. Il faudra décider ce que nous ferons à Pâques ...
Daniel	Pour le week-end pascal, j'ai pensé qu'on pourrait descendre dans un petit hôtel du Midi, au milieu des pins et de la lavande!
Élise	C'est bien beau, mais tu te rends compte que c'est trop tard! Toutes les chambres seront prises!
Daniel	Pas de problème, j'ai déjà réservé.
Élise	Sans m'en parler?
Daniel	Ma foi, oui. Je savais que tu serais d'accord. Une semaine sans cuisine, sans ménage. Le paradis pour toi, non?
Élise	Tu es un amour de mari! Et en juillet, qu'est-ce que nous ferons?
Daniel	Ce que tu voudras, chérie.
Élise	Ça serait trop beau pour être vrai!
Daniel	Tu sais bien qu'il faudra aller en Dordogne passer quelques jours chez mes parents.
Élise	On restera combien de temps avec eux?
Daniel	Une semaine, je suppose. Après ça ils seront fatigués de nous.
Élise	Et nous d'eux!
Daniel	Tu n'es pas très charitable, mais tu n'as pas tort. Tu crois qu'Audrey viendra avec nous cette année?
Élise	Non! Elle veut aller en Grèce avec son copain. Déjà l'année dernière, elle a dit qu'elle ne viendrait plus jamais en vacances avec nous, parce qu'on était trop ringards et pas marrants du tout!
Daniel	Elle a dit ça?
Élise	Mais oui, tu sais bien. Elle n'a pas décroché les dents de toute une semaine!

(Contd)

Daniel	C'est vrai, je me souviens. Eh bien, tant mieux! On sera plus tranquilles, mais il faudra lui donner de l'argent. Elle a dit qu'elle était fauchée.
Élise	On verra. Et nous, alors?
Daniel	Nous? Ben, on ira passer quelques jours à la Charmandie!
Élise	Écoute, si on va là-bas tu travailleras tout le temps: la toiture, le carrelage de la cuisine. Et moi, qu'est-ce que je ferai pendant ce temps?
Daniel	Tu prendras la voiture et tu iras voir ta copine Évelyne. Vous pourrez discuter entre femmes.
Élise	Oui, mais je suis pas mariée avec Évelyne! Je voudrais bien passer quelques jours seule avec toi, au calme, à lire, à faire des promenades, pour décompresser. L'année a été longue et en septembre j'ai toute une série de réunions à Paris.
Daniel	Encore?
Élise	Évidemment, avec les élections présidentielles qui approchent!
Daniel	Dis-donc! Tu vas bien souvent à Paris depuis quelque temps. Est-ce que par hasard tu aurais un petit ami là-bas?
Élise	Pff! N'importe quoi!

QUICK VOCAB

Pâques *Easter. This, along with Christmas and the summer period, is the time of year which the French really look forward to.* **Le week-end pascal** *is a* **grand pont**, *which allows people to have four days of unbroken bliss.*

toutes les chambres seront prises *As in other countries, holiday accommodation (***les structures d'accueil***) is generally booked months in advance, and it is often virtually impossible to find something at short notice. Fortunately, Daniel has* **déjà réservé**.

à toi de … *(+ infinitive) it's your turn to …*

un amour de mari *a real darling (lit. a love of a husband)*

le (petit) copain *the boyfriend (also* **le petit ami** *or* **le boy friend***). The feminine is* **la copine**.

ringard *(masc.) behind the times/old fashioned (familiar)*

marrant *usually amusing (familiar). Here: fun to be with.*

ne pas décrocher les dents *to remain silent (lit. not to unhook your teeth)*

être fauché *to be flat broke/penniless.* **Faucher** *normally means to mow wheat or grass. The expression is also used for a pedestrian mown down by a vehicle.*

la Charmandie *The name of the family's second home. The name suggests that it is situated in the Charente or the Dordogne area (see map in Unit 1).*

décompresser *to get rid of stress (lit. to decompress/to let off steam). Also* **déstresser.**

les élections qui approchent *the forthcoming (presidential) elections. They used to take place every seven years, but are now held every five years. Élise, who is heavily involved in politics, attends frequent meetings in Paris. Daniel is teasing her by suggesting she may have* **un petit ami** *in the capital.*

dis-donc! *I say! This is the familiar form; the polite singular or plural equivalent is:* **dites-donc!**

n'importe quoi! *You are talking nonsense/rubbish! (familiar), lit. anything whatsoever.*

Comprehension 2

Answer the questions below using the information contained in the conversation between Élise and Daniel.

1 What has Daniel done about the Easter holiday without Élise's knowledge and consent?

2 Why will the couple go to the Dordogne?

3 Is Élise pleased at the prospect? Justify your answer.

4 What appear to be their daughter's plans for the summer holiday?

5 What led Élise to assume that Audrey would not want to go on holiday with them this year?

6 Why is Élise unhappy at the prospect of spending the summer holiday at La Charmandie?

7 What is Daniel's suggestion about his wife's activities while he repairs the roof and re-tiles the kitchen of their holiday home?

8 What would be Élise's preferred holiday activities and what are her reasons?

9 What reason does she give for her timetable of meetings in Paris?
10 What is her reaction to her husband's suggestion about a liaison in Paris?

Insight

English has an elegant way of indicating ownership by using **'s** (or sometimes just *'): Elise's husband, Daniel's parents' house*, etc. French, on the other hand, uses **de, du, de la** or **des** as appropriate, to convey that meaning: **le mari d'Elise, la maison des parents de Daniel**, etc.

Activity 11
In the conversation, there are indications that the style is familiar rather than standard or elevated (which is normal in the circumstances).

a Give examples to support this as regards:
- the vocabulary;
- the formation of questions;
- the use of other non-standard structures.

b List the expressions which in your opinion belong more specifically to the standard or elevated register.

Insight

Remember: in elevated French **on** means *one/somebody/people*, but in familiar French, it can also mean *we*. In the following radio broadcast, there are examples of both these meanings.

Radio broadcast

Every weekday between 8.50 a.m. and 9 o'clock, France Inter, one of the stations of Radio France (long wave 162 kHz), invites an expert or a political figure to answer listeners' telephone queries from all over France.

This morning, it is Monsieur Émile Bourdet, the government official in charge of road safety (**la sécurité routière**), who is in the studio to answer the listeners' questions.

1 Read the following passage several times;
2 Listen to the recording, at least once (if it is available);
3 Check the vocabulary you do not know in preparation for the language activities relating to it.

CD2, TR 1, 10:40

Presenter	Bienvenue à vous tous et à vos questions sur l'actualité. D'avance merci de poser des questions courtes, car vous êtes très nombreux à nous appeler ce matin. Monsieur Émile Bourdet, le responsable gouvernemental pour la Sécurité Routière, qui était notre invité pour 'questions directes' ce matin entre huit heures vingt et huit heures trente, est resté dans le studio pour répondre à vos questions. Un premier appel … Renée est en ligne. Bonjour et bienvenue à vous. Vous nous appelez d'où?
Renée	Bonjour, messieurs/dames. Je vous appelle de Lyon. Merci d'avoir pris ma question et merci pour votre émission.
Presenter	On vous écoute!
Renée	Bon, voilà. Comme chaque année au moment des grands départs, euh, il y a des embouteillages monstres dans notre région, et les Lyonnais ne peuvent pas circuler librement pour aller à leur travail. En périodes de vacances, il faut de trois à cinq fois plus de temps pour faire le même trajet. Est-ce que le gouvernement ne pourrait pas trouver une solution à ce problème?
M. Bourdet	Au cours des dernières décennies, le gouvernement a fait tout son possible pour remédier à cette situation: on a étalé les vacances scolaires et universitaires, pour empêcher les gens de partir tous en même temps; on a mis sur pied les opérations Bison Futé pour aider les automobilistes, les conseiller sur les itinéraires bis, leur signaler les meilleures périodes avec les

journées oranges, rouges ou noires, les heures les plus convenables pour les départs et les retours. Une solution serait de construire plus d'autoroutes, mais cela ne peut pas se faire du jour au lendemain, et de toute façon, le gouvernement ne veut pas bétoniser l'Hexagone! Patience, Renée, nous cherchons des solutions!

Presenter Merci, Renée, et bonne journée. Un autre appel! Bonjour, Anne, bienvenue à vous. Anne, vous êtes à Castres dans le Tarn.

Anne Oui, bonjour. Je voudrais simplement dire que … On dit en France que la peur du gendarme est le commencement de la sagesse. Alors, Monsieur Bourdet, pensez-vous que la réponse au problème des accidents de la route passe par la répression?

M. Bourdet Franchement, je ne le crois pas. Pendant sa campagne électorale le Président de la République avait clairement dit que l'une de ses grandes priorités serait la lutte contre la violence routière, l'autre étant la lutte contre le cancer. Il tient parole! Les actions policières sont devenues plus musclées; on applique maintenant la 'tolérance zéro' pour la majorité des infractions. On a également augmenté le nombre des points retirés pour les fautes graves comme les excès de vitesse et la conduite en état d'ivresse. Malheureusement, vous le savez aussi bien que moi, les Français sont beaucoup plus indisciplinés que les citoyens des autres pays européens! Le Premier Ministre vient d'annoncer que les effectifs des forces de l'ordre allaient être augmentés de 22.000 en prévision des grands départs. 22.000 policiers et gendarmes de plus sur les routes, ce n'est pas rien! Personnellement, je pense que ces mesures, en elles-mêmes, ne suffiront pas. La réponse n'est pas dans la répression mais dans l'éducation. Il faut convaincre les conducteurs, surtout les jeunes, que la voiture va moins vite que l'avion, comme disait le

	Major Thompson. Il faut prendre conscience du fait que les droits de chacun s'arrêtent où commencent les droits du voisin!
Presenter	Merci, Anne, et bonne journée. Un dernier appel. Christian?
Christian	Oui, bonjour.
Presenter	Vous nous appelez d'où?
Christian	De Chartres.
Presenter	Belle ville! Et votre question?
Christian	Euh! … Ce n'est pas exactement une question, c'est plutôt une constatation. … Il y a quelques années, mon fils a été victime d'un accident de la route: sur le chemin de l'école il a été fauché par la voiture d'un chauffard, un type en état d'ivresse qui conduisait comme un fou en ville. Bon, le type a été arrêté, on l'a condamné à deux ans de prison. Deux ans pour avoir tué mon gosse! Personnellement je trouve ça scandaleux!
M. Bourdet	Christian, je suis désolé et je sympathise avec vous. Comme je le disais tout à l'heure, le gouvernement a mis sur pied des mesures draconiennes, et en particulier les limitations de vitesse dans les agglomérations, qui ont permis, cette année, de faire passer le chiffre des victimes de la route au dessous de la barre des 8.000. Et nous ne nous arrêterons pas là!
Presenter	Merci, Christian, et merci Monsieur Bourdet, d'être resté avec nous. Le temps maintenant! …

Insight

Normally, the expression **plus de** indicates a greater amount (*more*), but sometimes it can mean *no more*, so, **plus de travail** could mean *more work* or *no more work*. Use the context to work out the meaning!

QUICK VOCAB

l'actualité *current events. In the plural, it refers to the television news bulletins.*
l'émission *Here: broadcast, but it can also mean emission (of gases, etc.).*
un embouteillage *a traffic jam, from the word* **une bouteille** *(a bottle). Also called* **un bouchon** *(a cork).*
une décennie *a ten-year period. Also called* **une décade.**
étaler *to spread/stagger (holidays). A few years ago, the government organized France into a number of administrative zones (A, B, C), in which school and university holidays would take place at a time different from those of the other zones. The measure has had some success.*
Bison Futé *Cunning Buffalo. Name of a fictitious Indian Chief used as a symbol to represent a service to motorists (see section below).*
du jour au lendemain *overnight. Used to indicate the quick occurrence of an event.*
bétoniser *to turn into a concrete jungle. From* **le béton** *(***armé***) (reinforced) concrete.*
franchement *frankly*
des actions … musclées *strong repressive measures to combat a problem (*lit. *muscly actions)*
une infraction *a law-breaking action*
les effectifs *the work force (the total number of people employed in a certain area of activity)*
le conducteur *the driver (of a motor vehicle)*
le Major Thompson *The fictitious English hero of a novel,* **Les carnets du Major Thompson**, *published (in French!) in the early fifties by Pierre Daninos. The (retired) Major married a Frenchwoman and went to live in France. Despite the novel's age, its analysis of the French and their idiosyncrasies is pithy, very amusing and amazingly accurate even today!*
un chauffard *Here: a dangerous driver. Normally, a road hog.*
en état d'ivresse *over the limit (*lit. *in a state of inebriation)*

Bison Futé (*Cunning Buffalo*) is the humorous name given to a very useful service sponsored by the government. **Bison Futé** supplies motorists with traffic information and travel advice: it publishes, in advance of the start of each holiday, a calendar of departures and returns grading the density of road traffic by colour: green = normal; orange = dense; red = difficult; black = very difficult (and best avoided). It also produces road maps showing alternative routes – **les itinéraires bis** (to rhyme with miss!) – and road signs in the shape of green arrows bearing the name of the ultimate destination (e.g. **Espagne** *Spain*). If you land in the North of France at the start of the holiday period, look out for a **Bison Futé** log cabin, where you will be able to pick up some freebies (maps and brochures), as well as non-alcoholic drinks, games for the children, etc. If you want to know more about this resourceful Indian Chief, why not visit its website: www.bison-fute.equipement.gouv.fr/.

Comprehension 3

1 What was the initial request made by the presenter to listeners wishing to ask M. Bourdet a question?

2 Did M. Bourdet arrive in the studio immediately before the start of the phone-in programme? Give appropriate details.

3 Renée made a statement and asked a question. Can you clarify both?

4 M. Bourdet quoted two measures already in place to alleviate the problem mentioned by Renée. What were they?

5 M. Bourdet mentioned another solution. What were his reasons for discarding it?

6 What was the question put by Anne?

7 In his reply, M. Bourdet mentioned the President of the Republic. Why did he do so?

8 What, according to M. Bourdet, is the answer to the problem?

9 M. Bourdet also mentioned a toughening up of government measures to combat road deaths. What were they?

10 Summarize the points made by Christian in his call.

11 What has been the result of the various measures taken by the government as regards road safety?

12 What, in your opinion, is the meaning of the presenter's last remark: **le temps maintenant!**

Insight

In principle, the French equivalents of *here is/here are* and *there is/there* are **voici** and **voilà** respectively. So, *'Here is the key'* should be **'Voici la clé'**, and *'There are the suitcases'* should be **'Voilà les valises'**. However, in spoken French, voilà is used in both cases: **'Voilà la clé'**; **'Voilà les valises'**. **'Voilà!'** on its own means: *'That's it!'*

Activity 12

In the passage there are a number of nouns, the gender of which can be easily determined by their endings (so long as the 'rules' are known):

-tion
-ence/-ance
-ssion
-té
-ment
-age

Make a list of the nouns from the conversation which share the same ending (there is no need to repeat the same noun if it occurs more than once), and state whether they are masculine or feminine; list any exceptions if applicable. For more information about the relation between endings and gender, go to Appendix 5.

Activity 13

How would you translate the following warning to motorists into French? In the first instance, try to complete the task without help. Should you encounter any vocabulary problems, however, a word list has been provided on the next page to help you.

Motorists, beware!

The government has recently introduced new legislation to reduce drink-driving. As you know, it causes more than 40 per cent of all road deaths every year!

If you drive, say 'no' to alcohol! If you want to drink, ask a friend or your partner to drive.

Do not let yourself be tempted by a generous but misguided host. Say 'no' to alcohol!

The Anti-Alcohol League

a motorist **un automobiliste**
watch out/beware! **attention!**
drink-driving **l'alcool au volant/la conduite en état d'ivresse**
a partner **un/une partenaire**
to drive (a vehicle) **conduire**
misguided **malavisé**
a host **un hôte** *(beware, this word can also mean guest)*
do not let yourself be tempted **ne vous laissez pas tenter**
the Anti-Alcohol League **La Ligue Antialcoolique**

QUICK VOCAB

7 Comparatives and superlatives

When we communicate with others, we frequently need to compare things or beings by stating that:

1 A is extremely big, beautiful, fast, etc. or,
2 A is bigger/smaller, more/less beautiful, faster/slower than B or,
3 A is as big, beautiful, fast … as B.

To do so we use superlatives or comparatives.

When we want to say that someone or something possesses an attribute to a very high degree, that cannot usually be surpassed, we use a superlative. In English, we use words like *extremely*, *extraordinarily*, *unbelievably*, etc., followed by an adjective (adj.) or an adverb (adv.). The same principle is used in French:

Cet ordinateur est *extrêmement* rapide.	*This computer is extremely fast.*
Ce problème est *terriblement* compliqué.	*This problem is terribly complicated.*

If we want to compare things or beings in French, we use one of the following expressions:

1 plus … que …	*More … than …*
L'avion va *plus vite que* la voiture.	*The plane goes faster than the car.*
Les pêches sont *plus chères que* les poires.	*Peaches are more expensive than pears.*
2 aussi … que …	*As … as …*
Je suis *aussi calme que* vous.	*I am as calm as you (are).*
Ce bifteck est *aussi dur que* du fer.	*This steak is as tough as old boots (*lit. *as hard as iron).*
3 moins … que …	*less … than …*
Il est *moins patient que* son frère.	*He is less patient than his brother.*
Il fait *moins chaud qu'*hier.	*It (the weather) is less hot than yesterday.*

If you want to express the idea of *as … as …* not in physical but in more abstract terms, you can replace **aussi … que …** by **comme**, as shown below:

Il est sage *comme* une image.	*He is as good as gold (*lit. *as well behaved, or as quiet, as a picture!).*
Elle est belle *comme* le jour.	*She is ravishing (*lit. *as beautiful as daylight).*

Sometimes, moins que can also be expressed as **ne … pas aussi …** que (*not as … as*)

L'idée n'est pas *aussi stupide que* vous croyez!	*The idea is not as stupid as you think!*

7.1 Double comparatives

Double comparatives (e.g. *more and more, less and less*) are expressed in French as:

1 de plus en plus

La vie devient *de plus en plus* stressante.	*Life becomes/is becoming more and more stressful.*

2 de moins en moins

Nous le voyons *de moins en moins* souvent.	*We see him less and less frequently.*

The more ... the more ..., and *the less ... the less ...*, or a combination of the two, becomes **plus ... plus ...** or **moins ... moins ...**:

***Plus* ça change, *plus* c'est la même chose!**	*The more things change, the more they are the same!*
***Moins* je le vois, *plus* je suis content.**	*The less I see him the better! (lit. the more contented I am).*

Language learning tip 4

Plus que and **plus de**

1 Plus que

As we have seen, **plus ... que ...** can mean *more ... than ...* In certain circumstances, however, it can also mean *only ... left.*

Plus que trois jours avant les vacances.	*Only three days left before the holidays.*

(Contd)

2 Plus de can either mean:

- *No more*:

Plus d'essence!	*No more petrol!*

In this case, the final **s** of **plus** is not sounded.

- *More*:

Nous voulons plus d'argent!	*We want more money!*

In this case, the final **s** of **plus** is often – but not always – sounded.

- *More than/over* (with a quantity/value):

Nous avons fait plus de cent kilomètres.	*We have done over 100 kilometres.*

In this last sense it is the opposite of **moins de** (*under/below* with an expression of quantity or value):

Il a moins de dix-huit ans.	*He is less than 18 (years of age).*

Beware: As we saw in Units 4 and 5, the negative particle **ne** is omitted in familiar/slang French. So, the sentence: **On veut plus de problèmes!** would mean *We want no more problems!* in that register.

Activity 14

Translate the following sentences into French. Give the required number of alternative forms for those marked (×2, ×3, etc.), but make sure that the original meaning is preserved.

Example: The kitchen is bigger than the bedroom (×3):

- ▶ La cuisine est plus grande que la chambre.
- ▶ La chambre est plus petite que la cuisine.
- ▶ La chambre n'est pas aussi grande que la cuisine.

1 The questions are extremely numerous.
2 Drivers are more and more impatient (×2).
3 It is more difficult to travel in July than in September (×5).
4 Alternative routes are quieter than motorways (×3).
5 Road accident figures are lower than last year (×3).
6 The police are becoming stricter and stricter with dangerous drivers.
7 French people are less disciplined than other Europeans (×3).

La peur du gendarme est le commencement de la sagesse. *Fear of the gendarmes marks the beginning of wisdom.*

Learners of French often seem baffled by the fact that members of **les forces de l'ordre** (*the forces of law and order*) appear to have two different names: **les policiers** and **les gendarmes.** Although their roles are broadly the same (the fight against crime and the protection of the security of citizens), there are two main differences, apart from the fact that their uniforms are not the same:

1 The **Police Nationale** tends to have a more urban role, whereas the **Gendarmerie** can cover the whole of the national territory and assist the police in all its crime-fighting and prevention duties.

2 As a body, the police force comes under the umbrella of the **Ministre de l'Intérieur** (equivalent to the Home Secretary in Britain), whereas the **gendarmes** are officers who come under the responsibility of the **Ministre des Armées** (Secretary of State for Defence in the UK).

Another body often mentioned at times of civil unrest, but also at the time of **les grands départs** (*the great holiday exodus*), is the **Compagnies Républicaines de Sécurité**, whose members are referred to as **les CRS**. They, too, come under the **Ministre de l'Intérieur**.

For more information type **la police nationale** into a French search engine such as http://www.yahoo.fr.

TEST YOURSELF

1 What is the relationship between the present of **avoir** and the endings used for the future tense?

2 In the first part of the sentence: **'Quand tu auras terminé ton travail, nous partirons'** (*'When you have finished your work, we will go'*) what is the tense used, how is it formed and what does it indicate on the time axis?

3 What does **faire le pont** mean when not referring to building work?

4 Is **embouteillage** anything to do with wine-making?

5 When are indefinite pronouns such as **on** (*somebody*), **quelqu'un** (*someone*), **personne** (*nobody*) ... used?

6 Is the word **chauffard** a compliment or an insult when applied to a motorist?

7 Who or what is **bison futé**?

8 Why is the novel **'Les carnets du Major Thompson'** a good book to read for learners of French?

9 Why do you have to be careful with the expression **plus de**?

10 How would you translate *more and more/less and less* into French?

7

Préparatifs

In this unit you will learn

- ***How to form and use relative pronouns***
- ***How to form and use the conditional***
- ***How to make an official telephone call***
- ***How to deal with official requests***
- ***How to structure formal and informal letters***
- ***How to fill in an official form***
- ***How to distinguish between the three 'si's***
- ***About modal auxiliaries***

1 Relative pronouns

We have already seen that in French, as in other languages, there are grammatical words that can be used to make our speech (or writing) more fluid and elegant. For example, when we want to build long sentences, we can link together two or more sections called clauses, which could function independently from each other, but which, when joined, form a more elegant construct.

1 Regarde l'homme. L'homme est assis sur la chaise.	*Look at the man. The man is seated on the chair.*
2 Regarde l'homme qui est assis sur la chaise.	*Look at the man who is seated on the chair.*

As we can see, the relative pronoun **qui** used in Example 2 helps us to avoid a clumsy repetition.

There are two sorts of relative pronouns: simple ones and compound ones. The latter are less frequently used and are made up of the article **le** or its usual variations (**la, les**) and the appropriate form of **quel** (based on the gender and number of the person/thing referred to – see Section 1.3 below).

1.1 One-word relative pronouns

Relative pronoun	*Usual meaning*	*Usage*
1 qui	*that, who, which* (subject); *whom* (with a preposition)	It refers to the performer or subject of the action. It can be used on its own, or with a preposition (**à, pour, avec**…).
2 que	*that, which, whom* (direct object)	It refers to the thing(s) or being(s) at the 'receiving end' of an action. It is followed by a noun phrase distinct from the one which appears before it. It cannot be used with a preposition. In English, it can be omitted without loss of clarity.
3 quoi	*what*	It refers to things only and must be preceded by a preposition (**à, avec, de, contre**…).
4 dont	*about/for/from/of which*	It can be used to replace a noun phrase introduced by the preposition **de**. It can be replaced by **de qui**, if it refers to a person or persons.
5 où	*where* (or, sometimes, *when* (as in *the day when*…))	It is used to indicate location or destination in space or time. It can be preceded by the prepositions **de**, **vers** and **par**.

1 C'est une décision qui m'a coûté cher.	*It's a decision which (has) cost me dear(ly).*
2 C'est une décision que je regrette.	*It's a decision (that) I regret.*
3 C'est quelque chose contre quoi je ne peux rien.	*It's something against which I can do nothing.*
4 C'est une décision dont je suis responsable.	*It's a decision for which I am responsible.*
5 C'est le moment où je dois décider.	*It's the moment when I must decide.*

Insight

As you know, French hates vowel clashes between two words, and uses simple tricks to avoid them: **le/la** becomes **l'**; **je** becomes **j'**; **ceci/cela** (before **être**) becomes **c'**. Another trick is to put a **t** at the end of **ce** (*this/that* – masc.). Compare: **ce monsieur** (*this gentleman*) and **cet ami** (*this friend*).

1.2 Another neutral form

As mentioned in the table on the previous page, **quoi** (*what*) is used when details about the noun phrase are unclear or unknown and cannot be used to refer to people:

Je ne sais pas de *quoi* il parle.	*I don't know what he talks/he is talking about.*
De *quoi* parlez-vous?	*What do you talk/are you talking about?*

Activity 1

Fill in the blanks with the appropriate relative pronoun. Pay particular attention to the 'usage' section of the table on the previous page.

1 Voilà l'occasion _______ j'attendais.
2 Vous avez lu les lettres _______ sont arrivées ce matin?
3 Avec _______ vas-tu ouvrir cette bouteille?
4 Le jour ______ nous partirons d'ici approche.
5 C'est le document _______ je vous ai parlé.
6 Je fais ce _______ je peux.
7 Je déteste les gens ______ sont intolérants!

1.3 Compound relative pronouns and simpler alternatives!

The set of pronouns which follows is a combination of the appropriate form of the pronoun **quel** (*what* or *which*) with the definite article (**le, la, les**), or the prepositions **à** and **de**.

Word combinations	*Masculine singular*	*Feminine singular*	*Masculine plural*	*Feminine plural*
with the definite article preceded by a preposition (except **de**)	**lequel** or, if it refers to a person: prep. +**qui**	**laquelle** or, if it refers to a person: prep. +**qui**	**lesquels** or, if it refers to people: prep. +**qui**	**lesquelles** or, if it refers to people: prep. +**qui**
with the preposition **à** (*to which/to whom*)	**auquel** or, if it refers to a person: **à qui**	**à laquelle** or, if it refers to a person: **à qui**	**auxquels** or, if it refers to people: **à qui**	**auxquelles** or, if it refers to people: **à qui**
with the preposition **de** (*of/from whom*)	[1]**duquel** or, if it refers to a person: [2]**de qui**	[1]**de laquelle** or, if it refers to a person: [2]**de qui**	[1]**desquels** or, if it refers to people: [2]**de qui**	[1]**desquelles** or, if it refers to people: [2]**de qui**

De ces deux costumes, lequel préférez-vous? *Of these two suits, which one do you prefer?*

Voici les collègues avec lesquelles/avec qui je travaille. *Here are the (female) colleagues with whom I work.*

C'est la raison pour laquelle je suis venu te voir. *That's the reason why I've come (I came) to see you.*

J'ai vu les clients auxquels/à qui tu as vendu la maison. *I saw/have seen the clients to whom you sold the house.*

Ce sont des gens desquels/de qui je ne parle jamais. *These are people of whom I never speak.*

Note: the pronouns marked 1 and 2 in the table above are frequently replaced by **dont**:

Ce sont des gens *dont* je ne parle jamais. *These/those are people of whom I never speak.*

Activity 2
In the sentences below, replace the relative pronouns *in italics* by less formal ones from the table on the previous page.

Example: C'est la femme *avec laquelle* j'ai déjeuné. = C'est la femme *avec qui* j'ai déjeuné.

1 Appelez les clients *auxquels* nous avons vendu la maison.
2 Vous connaissez la personne *pour laquelle* nous avons réservé la place?
3 Il n'a pas vu les visiteurs *desquels* vous parlez. (Two possible answers.)
4 C'est le monsieur *pour lequel* je travaille.
5 Je remercie mes professeurs, *sans lesquels* je ne serais rien.

2 The conditional

We have seen that the indicative mood allows us to express the reality of an action in the past, the present or the future. By contrast, as briefly mentioned in Unit 1, the conditional mood, which has two main tenses (one simple – the present – and one compound – the perfect), has a different function, similar to the one it fulfils in English.

It is mainly used:

1 To express what would happen, now or in the future, if certain conditions were met:

Si j'étais riche, j'*achèterais* une grande maison.	*If I was (or were) rich, I would buy a big house.*

2 To express a longing, a wish, or a desire which may or may not come to pass:

J'*aimerais* voyager.	*I would like to travel.*
Je *voudrais* bien la connaître.	*I would (dearly) like to know her.*

3 To express a polite request rather than a demand:

Compare:

Je *voudrais* parler au directeur.	*I should like to speak to the manager.*

and:

Je *veux* parler au directeur.	*I want to speak to the manager.*

2.1 How to form the present conditional

Unlike English, in which the auxiliary *would/should* is used before the infinitive (without *to*), the French present conditional is formed by adding a set of endings to the infinitive of the verb. There are, however, some exceptions, as is often the case in grammar, particularly in the case of third-group verbs.

je manger*ais*	*I would eat*
tu finir*ais*	*you would finish*
But **elle prendr*ait*** (and not **elle prendre*ait***)	*she would take*

Look at the endings shown in the chart below. Do they ring a bell?

Subject pronouns	*Endings*
je	-ais
tu	-ais
il/elle/on	-ait
nous	-ions
vous	-iez
ils/elles	-aient

They should! They are the same as those used to form the imperfect, which we studied in Unit 3.

There is another reason for us to be pleased: the roots/stems used for the conditional are the same as those used to form the future. Beware, though! Those roots are not the same as those used for the imperfect indicative!

Insight

The present conditional expresses an action which would happen if certain conditions were met: **'Si j'avais de l'argent, j'achèterais cette maison'** (*'If I had money I would buy this house'*). It can also be used to formulate a polite request or a wish: **'J'aimerais voyager'** (*'I would like to travel'*).

Activity 3

In the following sentences, replace the infinitives with the appropriate present conditional verb form. Please ensure that the verb form corresponds to the subject pronoun.

1 Si j'étais vous, je (téléphoner).
2 Si on avait le temps, on (passer) le voir.
3 S'ils étaient pressés, ils (prendre) le TGV.
4 Si vous arriviez à l'heure, on (boire) l'apéritif.
5 Si tu ne rentrais pas trop tard, nous (aller) au concert.
6 Si j'étais vous, j'(appeller) la police.
7 Papa, tu (pouvoir) me prêter trente euros?

2.2 The conditional perfect

Its formation follows the normal pattern for a compound tense:

The present conditional of **être** or **avoir** + the past participle.

To refresh our memory, the conditional form of those two verbs is as follows:

Avoir	*Être*
j'aurais	je serais
tu aurais	tu serais
il/elle/on aurait	il/elle/on serait
nous aurions	nous serions
vous auriez	vous seriez
ils/elles auraient	ils/elles seraient

So, now all we need is the past participle of the verb we want to use.

If the formation of the conditional perfect is relatively easy, the time zone it represents may be less obvious.

If I had been rich, I would have bought …

(1) (2)

If something had happened in the past, provided certain conditions had been met, then the actions expressed by the conditional perfect could have taken place at any time. As things turned out, (1) did not happen, so (2) didn't either!

Compare:

Si j'étais riche, j'*achèterais* une grande maison avec une piscine.	*If I was/were rich, I would buy a big house with a swimming pool.*
Si j'avais été riche, j'*aurais acheté* une grande maison avec une piscine.	*If I had been rich, I would have bought a big house with a swimming pool. (but I never was, so I didn't!)*

Activity 4

In the sentences that follow, change the present conditional into the conditional perfect.

1 Je voudrais te parler.
2 Elle viendrait nous voir.
3 Vous pourriez vous excuser.
4 On devrait prévenir la police.
5 Ils seraient les bienvenus.
6 Nous mangerions au restaurant.

Insight

As well as expressing an action which could have happened under certain circumstances (**'Si j'avais eu de l'argent, j'aurais acheté cette maison'**), the conditional perfect can be used to express regret about something which could have happened but did not: **'J'aurais aimé voyager'** ('*I would have liked to have travelled*').

Telephone conversation

As you will remember from the information given in Unit 1, Claudine Swift, Marc's mother, has kept her French nationality. She wants to go back to her birthplace for the summer holiday, but she has just realized that her passport needs renewing. She telephones the French consulate to ask what documents she needs to produce for the purpose.

If you have the recording, listen as usual to the dialogue before completing the activities that follow.

CD2, TR 2, 01:00

Claudine Allô, le consulat de France?
Operator Oui, bonjour. Vous désirez?
Claudine Est-ce ce que vous pourriez me passer le service du renouvellement des passeports, s'il vous plaît?
Operator Une seconde, ne quittez pas.
...
Secretary Allô, oui?
Claudine Le service des passeports?
Secretary Oui, vous désirez?
Claudine Je suis française, domiciliée en Angleterre et mariée à un Britannique. Je voudrais renouveler mon passeport qui vient d'expirer. Quelles seraient les pièces à fournir, s'il vous plaît?
Secretary Est-ce que vous êtes déjà immatriculée à ce consulat?
Claudine Oui.
Secretary Nom et prénom?
Claudine Pardon?
Secretary Quels sont vos nom et prénom?
Claudine Ah! Claudine Swift! Excusez-moi, j'avais mal entendu.
Secretary Ce n'est pas grave. Vous voudriez bien épeler votre nom de famille s'il vous plaît?
Claudine Bien sûr: S. W. I. F. T.

Secretary	Et votre nom de jeune fille?
Claudine	Lescaze: L.E.S.C.A.Z.E.
Secretary	Bien. Quelle est votre adresse actuelle?
Claudine	185, Wilson Street, Londres.
Secretary	Et votre code postal?
Claudine	EC2A 2BX.
Secretary	Un moment, je vous prie, je vérifie sur mon ordinateur … Dites-moi, vous avez changé d'adresse récemment?
Claudine	Oui, nous avons déménagé il y a deux ans. Avant, j'habitais au 387, Allen Street …
Secretary	Ah, d'accord. Vous savez que normalement il faudrait nous prévenir! Vous auriez dû nous contacter!
Claudine	J'ai complètement oublié, je suis désolée.
Secretary	Et vous désirez effectuer les démarches en personne ou par courrier? En principe, nous préférons la première solution.
Claudine	Par courrier, à cause de mes horaires de travail. Désolée.
Secretary	Bon! Dans ce cas, je vous envoie la liste des documents à fournir aujourd'hui même. Un conseil: renvoyez-les en recommandé, c'est plus sûr.
Claudine	Merci … le renouvellement prendra combien de temps à peu près?
Secretary	Il faudra compter un bon mois.
Claudine	Bon, je vous remercie. Bonne journée!
Secretary	Merci, à vous aussi!

Insight

The expression **bonne journée** is used at the end of a conversation to convey the meaning *have a nice day*. As such, it is different from **bonjour** (*hello/good morning/good day*), which is used as a greeting when meeting somebody. **Journée** is also used to stress the span of a day as in: '**Quelle journée!**' ('*What a day!*').

Activity 5

There are in the text examples of verbs in the present conditional used to soften a demand into a polite request. Could you:

a list them in the order they appear;
b for each give the corresponding conditional perfect.

Activity 6

This activity will form part of your self-assessment schedule. You should award yourself five marks for each correct answer (true or false), total 50. In addition, each correct explanation will attract ten points, total 50. This total is to be added to your score in the self-assessment form.

True or false? If you think the statement is false, give the correct version. Please note that the statements are not in sequence!

1 Claudine's passport is about to expire.
2 Claudine was previously registered at this consulate.
3 The secretary gives Claudine the list of documents needed over the telephone.
4 Claudine has been living at her present address for the last five years.
5 Claudine says she will send her application by mail.
6 The list of documents required will be sent in the next couple of days.
7 The consulate prefers applications to be made in person.
8 The renewal procedure will take four weeks at the most.
9 The secretary advises Claudine to send her documents by recorded delivery.
10 When she last moved house, Claudine failed to notify the consulate.

Activity 7

In the telephone conversation, find the French expressions which enabled you to discover whether the statements listed in Activity 6 were true or false. Make a list of those expressions, following the same sequence (1–10 above).

Activity 8

In the telephone conversation, there are expressions used to:

1 Enquire what a person wants;
2 Say 'please';
3 Apologize;
4 Express agreement;
5 State that something is not important;
6 Ask somebody to wait a while;
7 Ask somebody to repeat or confirm what has been said;
8 State that something is fine;
9 Express thanks or appreciation;
10 Soften a demand into a polite request with the help of a tense.

Make a list of them, bearing in mind that in some cases there will be more than one phrase to express the same idea. If the same expression occurs several times, there is no need for you to enter it more than once in your list.

Activity 9

In the telephone conversation, there are several verbs in the conditional. Make a list of them and, for each, give the infinitive.

3 Letter writing

When writing to close friends or relatives, the French are fairly casual about the language and organization of their letters. Writing formal letters, however, is a different matter. The 'Cartesian spirit', which is supposed to characterize the French, makes it essential that the content of such letters is clearly structured to help the reader understand what is required, or what needs to be done. In a formal letter, one of the following salutations will be used:

1 **Monsieur, Madame** *Dear Sir or Madam or* **Messieurs** *Dear Sirs* (*very formal*);
2 **Cher Monsieur** *or* **Chère Madame** (*a little less formal*);
3 **Cher Monsieur Castel** *or* **Chère Madame Swift** (*less formal still*).

For each of the above, there is a corresponding closing formula. Several possibilities are available, but they should not be used indiscriminately:

1 With Example 1, one of the following closing formulae may be used:

Veuillez accepter (*or* recevoir *or* agréer), Monsieur, Madame, l'assurance de mon profond respect, *or* l'assurance de mes sentiments distingués, *or* l'assurance de ma parfaite considération

2 With Example 2, you should select either:

Je vous prie d'accepter, Cher Monsieur (*or* Chère Madame), mes cordiales salutations, *or* l'assurance de mes sentiments respectueux

3 With Example 3, you may use one of the closing formulae listed below:

a Recevez, Cher Monsieur X (*or* **Chère Madame Y**), **mon amical souvenir** *or* **mes sentiments les plus cordiaux,** *or*
b Amicalement *or* **Cordialement** (*followed by your signature*).

Whenever you come across other salutations or closing formulae, you should make a note of them and try to gauge the level of formality associated with them.

Activity 10
On the next page are four sets of salutations (a) and closing formulae (b). Study them carefully, bearing in mind the person you are writing to, and state, for each set, the formula which is appropriate for the purpose. If you feel there is something wrong, explain what it is, and give an acceptable alternative.

1 Writing to your close friend Pierre Castel:
a Mon Cher Pierre,
b Reçois, Mon Cher Pierre, l'assurance de mon profond respect.

2 Writing to the French Minister for Education:
a Monsieur le Ministre,
b Je vous prie d'accepter, Monsieur le Ministre, mes sentiments respectueux.

3 Writing to the French Tourist Office to obtain some brochures:
a Monsieur, Madame,
b Veuillez agréer, Monsieur, Madame, l'assurance de ma parfaite considération.

4 Writing to a hotel to ask for a reservation:
a Messieurs,
b Bien amicalement.

Insight

The French expression **il y a**, is used to translate *there is* or *there are*. To indicate an isolated action in the past, use **il y a eu** (*there has been/was*): **'Il y a eu un accident'** ('*There has been/was an accident*'). For repeated past actions, use **il y avait** (*there used to be*).

Reading

Official letters and forms

Claudine has just received the following document, as promised by the consulate secretary. Read it carefully in preparation for the activities that follow.

CONSULAT GÉNÉRAL DE FRANCE À LONDRES
21 CROMWELL ROAD
LONDON SW7 2EN

Horaires d'ouverture au public:

Du lundi au mercredi: 8h45–15h.
Le jeudi et le vendredi: 8h45–12h.

DEMANDE DE RENOUVELLEMENT DE PASSEPORT

Madame, Monsieur
Vous avez sollicité la délivrance ou le renouvellement d'un passeport.
Veuillez trouver ci-dessous la liste des pièces nécessaires.

DOCUMENTS À FOURNIR

1 Deux photographies de format 35 × 45 mm, identiques, récentes, sur fond blanc, de face et tête nue.

2 Votre passeport périmé ou, si vous n'avez jamais eu de passeport, votre carte nationale d'identité.

3 La copie intégrale récente de votre acte de naissance.

4 Votre livret de famille (pour les personnes mariées ou les parents célibataires).

5 Un justificatif de six mois minimum de résidence en Grande-Bretagne, avec preuve d'adresse: un contrat de travail avec six mois de bulletins de salaire, et justificatif d'adresse (quittance de loyer, facture ...). Indiquez également la couleur de vos yeux et votre taille.

Le prix du passeport est de 69 euros payables en numéraires, en livres sterling ou par carte bancaire (le taux de change sera celui en vigueur le jour de la délivrance du document).

La validité du passeport est de dix ans.

Les enfants de moins de 15 ans peuvent figurer sur le passeport de leurs parents.

Si vous êtes dans l'impossibilité de vous présenter en personne au consulat, pour des raisons d'éloignement ou d'empêchement majeur, vous pouvez nous adresser votre demande par courrier. Dans ce cas, envoyez uniquement votre dossier complet à l'exclusion de tout paiement. Le mode et le montant de ce dernier, qui dépend du taux de change en vigueur, vous seront précisés ultérieurement (indiquez si possible un numéro de téléphone ou l'on peut vous joindre pendant les heures de bureau). Joignez également une enveloppe timbrée à £3,65 pour un retour en recommandé. Notez, cependant, que la procédure normale est la présentation au Consulat pour la remise des documents.

Le Consulat Général de France à Londres décline toute responsabilité concernant d'éventuels problèmes liés à l'acheminement du courrier.

le justificatif *documentary evidence.* **Justifier** *to justify*; **une justification** *a justification.*
le livret de famille *The family record book. The French, who are very Cartesian, issue a booklet in which all administrative details concerning a family have to be entered (date and place of birth/marriage/death of each member, etc.). It is kept by the head of the family* **(le chef de famille).**
la quittance *official receipt for monies paid. Related to the expression* **être quitte** *(to be quits, free of an obligation), rather than* **quitter** *(to leave)!*
le loyer *rent. A tenant is* **un(e) locataire.**
le bulletin de salaire *salary slip. In modern French the distinction which exists between wage and salary is no longer made. All employees are* **salariés.**
en numéraire *(masc.) in cash (as opposed to any other form of payment). Sometimes called* **(argent) liquide.**
le taux (de change) *rate (of exchange)*
en vigueur *in force (of a law, an official decree, etc.)*
éventuel *possible or likely. This is a false friend. Eventual is* **final.**

QUICK VOCAB

Activity 11

After reading the instructions for the renewal of a French person's passport, answer the questions below in full sentences, if you can.

1 What are the precise requirements regarding identity photographs?
2 What is the alternative given to applicants under instruction 2?
3 Is anything other than a full birth certificate acceptable?
4 What documents does the applicant have to supply to show that he/she has been in the UK for at least six months?
5 What physical details is the applicant required to supply?
6 What methods can the applicant use to pay for the passport?
7 How long will it be before Claudine has to apply for renewal of the passport?
8 There is one reference to minors in the document. Can you clarify it?

Activity 12

Using your 'deductive skills' and the information contained in the latter part of the document, answer the following questions. Please note that the questions are not in sequence.

1 What may be the reason why Claudine chose to apply for her passport through the post?
2 Why is the cost of the passport not specified in the case of applications made through the post?
3 What is the applicant advised to supply 'if possible'?
4 Why is a pre-paid recorded delivery envelope required by the consulate?
5 Can you clarify the nature and purpose of the final sentence?

Insight

In the French expressions translating the last three months, the next two years, etc., the numeral is placed before the adjective: **les *trois* derniers mois, les *deux* prochaines années.** Note that *next year* is **l'année prochaine** or **l'an prochain** and *last year* is **l'année dernière** or **l'an dernier.**

Form filling

Below is a form similar to those that French people have to produce for administrative purposes, in particular when requesting official documents such as a passport or a visa.

Study it carefully before you begin the activities relating to it.

Fiche de renseignements

À remplir par l'intéressé(e):

1 Nom de famille ([1]M., Mme, Mlle):[2] ____________________

2 Prénom(s) usuel(s): ____________________

3 Sexe: [1]Masculin/féminin

4 Nationalité: ____________________

5 Date de naissance: ____________________

6 Lieu de naissance: ____________________

7 Situation de famille: célibataire, marié(e), veuf/veuve, autre: ____________________

8 Profession: ____________________

9 Domicile:[3] ____________________

____

____

10 Nom de famille et prénom(s) du [1]père/tuteur: ___________

11 Nom de famille et prénom(s) de la mère: ___________
____

12 Nom de jeune fille de la mère: ___________________

13 Domicile des parents:[3] ___________________
____
____

14 Profession des parents:
père: ___________________
mère: ___________________

[1]Rayer la (les) mention(s) inutile(s).
[2]À remplir en majuscules svp.
[3]Donner l'adresse complète.

Activity 13

Using the information given to you about Marc Swift and his family, fill in the form above as fully as you can, as if you were him. Marc is single and is currently living at 75, Belmont Terrace, London, EC1 4UP. He is a marketing manager.

Activity 14

Following receipt of the list of documents she has to submit for the renewal of her passport, Claudine has now produced a letter of application. Study the letter carefully before answering Questions 1–8 overleaf.

Londres, le 2 février 2010

Mme Claudine Swift
185 Wilson Street
Londres
EC2A 2BX

Consulat Général de France
Service des passeports
21 Cromwell Road
London
SW7 2EN

Madame, Monsieur

Demande de renouvellement de passeport

Suite à ma demande d'informations sur les pièces nécessaires au renouvellement de mon passeport, veuillez trouver ci-inclus les documents requis, à savoir:

- Mon passeport (périmé);
- Ma carte d'identité consulaire (également périmée);
- La copie de mon acte de naissance;
- Quatre photos d'identité (deux pour le passeport et deux pour la carte d'identité consulaire);
- Mes bulletins de salaire des trois derniers mois.

Pour mémoire, je rappelle que les documents dont je sollicite le renouvellement ont été précédemment délivrés par le Consulat Général de Londres.

Dans l'attente de votre notification d'établissement des frais à régler et du retour des documents, je vous prie d'accepter, Madame, Monsieur, l'assurance de mes sentiments respectueux.

Claudine Swift

Pièces jointes (voir ci-dessus).

Using the language you have learnt in this unit, how would you say in formal French (using the **vous** form when appropriate):

1 I am sorry but your passport is out of date!
2 I do not have your current address.
3 Following my visit to your office, I should like to thank you for your advice.
4 My mother wishes to renew her identity card.
5 Could you please spell your Christian name?
6 We are going to move house in two months.
7 Just a moment, I am checking your application.
8 He is sorry, but you are not on his list.

The French, as we know, are very keen on their freedom and individuality, and do not take kindly to too much interference from the state. It is therefore interesting to note that national identity cards (**les cartes nationales d'identité**) have been compulsory for a number of years and that French citizens are expected to carry them 'at all times'.

4 The three '*si*'

There are three meanings of the word **si** in French:

1 One is used when someone asks you a negative question for which the answer is positive:

Tu es malade? Oui!	*Are you ill? Yes!*
Tu n'es pas malade? *Si*!	*Aren't you ill? Yes!*

2 The si used to express doubt (*if* or *whether*):

Je ne sais pas *si* tu aimeras ce film.	*I don't know if you will like this film.*

3 The si expressing a condition. We have already seen this one when studying the imperfect (Unit 3) and the conditional tenses (earlier in this unit).

A few more details may be helpful for you to bear in mind. Whereas there is no tense restriction for the si expressing doubt, si expressing a condition can only be used in three prescribed ways.

Tenses to be found in clauses containing si (or s'+ vowel)		*Tenses to be found in the corresponding main clauses*
1 present (indicative) ***S'*il te donne un cadeau,**	→	present or future (indicative) **tu le remercies.** or **tu le remercieras.**
2 imperfect (indicative) ***S'*il te donnait un cadeau,**	→	conditional (present) **tu le remercierais.**
3 pluperfect (indicative) ***S'*il t'avait donné un cadeau,**	→	conditional (perfect) **tu l'aurais remercié.** Note that this indicates a possibility which did not happen.

Activity 15

This activity is part of your self-assessment. You should award yourself ten marks for each correct answer, total 50. This total should then be added to your score in the self-assessment form.

In the sentences below, one of the verbs is given in the appropriate tense, the other appears in the infinitive. Using the advice given in the above table, put the infinitive in the correct tense.

1 Si l'hôtel (être) complet, nous dormirons dans la voiture.
2 S'il (faire) beau demain, nous irons à la plage.
3 Si je (savoir), je ne serais pas venu.
4 Si nous avions eu le temps, nous (visiter) la cathédrale.
5 Si nous voulions, nous (pouvoir) partir en vacances.

Activity 16

Examine the following sentences and state whether each is correct or wrong. If it is wrong, make the necessary correction(s).

1 Si nous aurions de l'argent, nous achèterions une maison à la campagne.
2 Si les invités arrivent, tu leur offriras l'apéritif.
3 Si tu voulais, nous restions une semaine à Paris.
4 Si les circonstances le permettent, nous passons chez vous ce soir.
5 Si les voisins étaient là, nous irions les voir.
6 Si vous êtes d'accord, nous pouvons signer le contrat.
7 Si elle avait réussi à son examen, je lui aurais acheté une voiture.
8 Si j'aurais su, j'aurais pas venu! *(famous line from a children's film)*

Insight

As well as expressing a condition in the future (present conditional) or in the past (conditional perfect), **si** is used as an emphatic replacement for **oui** (yes) in response to a negative question. Compare: **Tu es malade? – Oui!** (*Are you ill? – Yes!*) and **Tu n'es pas malade? – Si!** ('*Aren't you ill? – Yes!*).

5 Modal auxiliaries

In addition to aller and venir used to form the immediate future and immediate past (see Unit 4), some other verbs can be used with an infinitive to express shades of meaning similar to those we saw when studying moods (Unit 1). These verbs, called modal auxiliaries, can express ability, obligation, necessity, probability, demand, etc. They are:

1 **devoir** (past participle **dû**): obligation or probability.
2 **pouvoir** (p.p. **pu**): ability or permission.
3 **savoir** (p.p. **su**): capability/knowledge.
4 **faire** (p.p. **fait**): transfer of responsibility to another.
5 **laisser** (p.p. **laissé**): permission granted.
6 **vouloir** (p.p. **voulu**): strong desire.

Nous devons payer.	*We must pay* (obligation).
Il doit être arrivé.	*He must have arrived* (conjecture/probability).
Vous pouvez nager.	*You can swim* (ability).
Vous savez nager.	*You can swim* (knowledge).

Je fais faire une maison. *I am having a house built* (transfer of responsibility).
Il nous laisse passer. *He is letting us (go) through* (permission).
Ils veulent l'arrêter. *They want to arrest him* (strong desire).

Activity 17

In the sentences below, fill in the gaps with what you feel is the right verb from the list opposite. Be sure to use the right person.

1 Il n'est pas venu. Il ________ être malade.
2 Vous ________ conduire? Oui, mais en ce moment, je ne ________ pas.
3 Nous allons ________ construire une piscine dans le jardin.
4 Ne répondez pas immédiatement, je vous ________ réfléchir un peu.
5 Elle ________ payer ses taxes!
6 Attendez un moment! Non, je suis fatiguée. Je ________ partir maintenant!

Avec des si, on mettrait Paris en bouteille! *With 'ifs' anything is possible* (lit. *with 'ifs' one/we would put Paris in a bottle)!*

English equivalents of the above proverb are:

If wishes were horses, beggars would ride.
If 'ifs' and 'ands' were pots and pans, there'd be no need for tinkers.

Le règlement, c'est le règlement! *Official rules are not there to be broken!*

Insight

When writing official letters in French, it is important to use the correct style and opening/closing formulae as shown in this unit. Failure to do so may be construed by the recipient as uncaring or impolite and work against you in your attempts to get something done.

TEST YOURSELF

1 In English it is possible to say or write: *the man I saw*. Can the same be done in French?

2 What three meanings can the conditional convey?

3 What is the difference between: '**Je voudrais parler au directeur**' and '**Je veux parler au directeur**'?

4 What characterizes French official letter writing?

5 Are there any rules concerning the photographs required for passports and other official documents?

6 When writing a letter, what opening formula would be appropriate to match the following closing one: '**Veuillez accepter l'assurance de mon profond respect**'?

7 **Si** can have three meanings. What are they?

8 What is the difference in meaning between **pouvoir** and **savoir**?

9 What shade of meaning is the conditional perfect used to express?

10 What two meanings can the modal auxiliary **devoir** convey?

8

Au travail!

In this unit you will learn

- ***About the economy and population of France***
- ***Business vocabulary***
- ***How to distinguish between* en fait *and* en effet**
- ***How to create new words from 'old ones' with prefixes and suffixes***
- ***How to be aware of the different ways to express figures in the two languages***
- ***How to recognize and handle political vocabulary and expressions***
- ***How to form and use the perfect infinitive ('to have done', 'to have been ...')***
- ***About the present continuous***

Reading 1

La population française

This section aims to 'complete the picture' by giving you a few more basic facts and figures about the French economy. Read it with care, taking your time to focus on the vocabulary. By doing so, you will realize how much you understand without referring to the notes or the dictionary. Some of the more difficult phrases will, as usual, be given after the text.

La France compte actuellement 62,5 millions d'habitants et une densité moyenne de 110 habitants au kilomètre carré. Les importantes variations de densité au sein de l'Hexagone s'expliquent par les différences géographiques, le climat et les activités économiques de chaque région. Aujourd'hui, les trois quarts de la population habitent dans les villes et l'agglomération parisienne compte environ dix millions de personnes. Depuis plusieurs années, la population augmente très peu, malgré le fait que la majorité des Français sont catholiques. Le taux de natalité est en régression grâce à la contraception, et le taux de mortalité reste stable du fait des progrès de la médecine et de la qualité des soins offerts par la Sécurité Sociale. On compte aujourd'hui en moyenne 1,9 enfants par famille. Ce faible taux de natalité, qui ne peut plus assurer le renouvellement des générations, est dû en partie aux incertitudes de la conjoncture économique internationale, mais aussi au fait que bon nombre de femmes travaillent maintenant à l'extérieur, comme leurs homologues masculins, pour améliorer les revenus de la famille et lui assurer un meilleur niveau de vie. Jusqu'en 1968, les femmes mariées restaient très souvent au foyer. Depuis la révolution de mai 68 et le Mouvement de Libération des Femmes (MLF), les Françaises sont devenues des citoyennes à part entière dans la vie sociale et économique et elles sont maintenant dans tous les domaines, y compris celui de la sexualité, égales aux hommes. Cependant, s'il est vrai qu'elles ont accès à toutes les carrières de la vie professionnelle, elles sont souvent, malgré la législation égalitaire qui déclare qu'à travail égal doit correspondre un salaire égal, moins bien payées que les hommes et restent à la traîne au hit-parade des promotions. En moyenne, et selon les branches d'activité concernées, leurs salaires sont inférieurs de 13 à 25% à celui des hommes.

La population active et les trois secteurs de l'économie française

La population active de l'Hexagone est actuellement d'environ 28 millions de personnes. Dans ce total on compte ceux qui ont un emploi et ceux qui en recherchent activement un. Selon les prédictions officielles, ce chiffre va augmenter jusqu'en 2015 pour ensuite diminuer d'une façon significative et alarmante. Le nombre des chômeurs s'élève aujourd'hui à 2,2 millions de personnes à peu près. Traditionnellement l'activité économique du pays se divise en trois secteurs:

1 Le secteur primaire, qui regroupe les travailleurs employés dans l'agriculture, les mines et la pêche. Il représente aujourd'hui grosso modo 4,5% de la population active.
2 Le secteur secondaire, qui concerne l'activité industrielle. Il compte actuellement près de 26% des actifs.
3 Le secteur tertiaire ou secteur des services. Comme dans tous les pays industrialisés, c'est celui qui augmente continuellement, au détriment des deux autres. Il représente aujourd'hui approximativement 72% du total des actifs et regroupe tous les emplois qui ne sont pas compris dans les deux autres secteurs. La gamme est très vaste et couvre les cols blancs, chefs d'entreprise et employés de banque, aussi bien que les serveurs de restaurant et le personnel domestique.

la densité moyenne *the average density (average number of people living within a specified area is expressed in inhabitants per square kilometre (abbreviated as hab./km²))*
au sein de *within (a place). Literally, it means in the bosom of …* **Les seins** *is used to refer to breasts.*
compter *Here: to number. Normally to count.*
le taux de natalité *the birth rate. Its opposite is* **le taux de mortalité.**
en régression *falling (for a trend or a figure). The opposite is* **en progression.**
en moyenne *on average*
le renouvellement *Lit. the renewal (of generations). This refers to the fact that in order to keep the population level stable, you need over two children per family to replace the parents.*
la conjoncture économique *the general economic climate*
un homologue *a (male) counterpart*
bon nombre de *(+ noun phrase)* **au foyer** *a fair number/a good many at home.* **Le foyer** *means the hearth and is also used to refer to a household.*

QUICK VOCAB

le MLF *the Women's Liberation Movement. It was late in reaching France but has caught up now!*
à part entière *fully fledged/fully paid up (for members of a group or an association)*
y compris *(invariable) including*
un chômeur *an unemployed person*
le secteur primaire *primary sector. The expression is also used in education, as is* **le secteur secondaire.**
un actif *an employed person. The opposite is* **un inactif***, usually referring to a retired person.*
la gamme *the range (of products, activities ...)*
les cols blancs *white-collar workers. The secondary sector equivalent is* **les cols bleus** *(blue-collar workers).*
le personnel domestique *people employed in private homes as cleaners, etc.*

Insight

In the reading section, there is a large number of nouns whose gender can be guessed thanks to their endings: **-té/-tion/-sion/-tude/-ture** = feminine; **-ment/-eur** = masculine. Use your detective skills to extend this list as you listen to native speakers.

Language learning tip 1

How to use dots and commas when expressing figures

You have no doubt already noticed that, when stating numbers in French, dots and commas are used differently. The rule is simple: it's precisely the reverse of English. So, if you see **2.000€,** it means two thousand euros, and not two euros with a very high level of accuracy! Conversely, if you see **boulangerie: 2,300 kilomètres,** it means that it is just under 2½ km away. So, don't lose heart. You will get your baguette in time for breakfast!

Activity 1

True or false? Now that you have become fully familiar with the text, state whether the following statements are true or false. If partially or totally false, give the accurate answer.

1 The population of France is evenly spread across the whole of the country.
2 For the last few years, and despite the fact that France is a Catholic country, the population has been declining.
3 The mortality rate remains stable thanks to the improvement in the quality of care given by the French Health Service.
4 The low number of children per family is solely due to the general economic climate.
5 The 'Revolution of 1968' and the Women's Liberation Movement have done nothing to improve the fate of French women.
6 Women do not have access to all careers.
7 The figure of 28 million represents the number of people in full employment.
8 The tertiary sector is concerned with industrial production.

Activity 2

In the text there are a number of phrases meaning *about*, *nearly*, *on average*, *roughly speaking*, *partly*, *approximately*. Make a list of them. They will prove useful in everyday conversation.

Activity 3

Using the appropriate expressions from the text and the knowledge you now possess, how would you translate the following?

1 On average, the salaries of blue-collar workers lag behind those of people working in the tertiary sector.
2 Since May 68, a good many women work outside the home, to improve the family income.
3 Despite legislation introduced by the government after May 68, the salaries of women are, on average, lower than those of their male counterparts for the same type of work.

4 In all industrialized countries, the tertiary sector increases in a significant way to the detriment of the other two sectors.
5 Currently, France's active population numbers approximately 28 million people.
6 At the moment, there are approximately 2 million workers who are unemployed in France.

Insight

The French have the irritating habit of referring to England, Wales and Scotland collectively as **l'Angleterre** and the inhabitants of all parts of the UK as **les Anglais**. They should be forgiven for they mean no offence!

Dialogue 1

Marc Swift, in his capacity as the marketing manager of the leisure and sportswear company Eurofitness Ltd, has made an appointment to meet Madame Sylviane Moréno, the sourcing and purchasing manager of Carrefour, the French hypermarket chain which has now become a multinational concern. The meeting is taking place in Agen, the head town of the Lot-et-Garonne area, where Marc arrived two days ago. He hopes that this contact may lead to a contract for the supply of equipment to a large number of Carrefour outlets throughout France. This dialogue contains a wide range of vocabulary which will be useful in a business context. Read the text carefully at least twice and, if you have the recording, listen to it before attempting the questions.

CD2, TR 3, 01:55

Madame Moréno Monsieur Marc Swift, je suppose! Bonjour. Je suis désolée de vous avoir fait attendre. Un problème urgent à résoudre.
Marc Je vous en prie, ce n'est rien.
Madame Moréno Je peux vous offrir une tasse de café? Un thé peut-être?
Marc Non, merci. J'espère que je ne vous dérange pas.

Madame Moréno	Non, pas du tout! J'ai sous les yeux votre lettre du 28 avril, dans laquelle vous nous proposez de nous fournir une large gamme d'équipements de sport et de loisir, à des prix qui me paraissent euh … disons … assez intéressants.
Marc	C'est exact. Je vous ai envoyé, par le même courrier, un catalogue de nos produits. Comme vous avez pu le constater, nous fabriquons une très large gamme d'équipements de milieu et haut de gamme. Nos prix sont en fait très compétitifs par rapport aux autres producteurs spécialisés dans cette branche, et la qualité et la finition de nos produits ne craint aucune concurrence! Je vous ai d'ailleurs apporté quelques échantillons qui vous donneront une idée du niveau de la qualité de notre gamme.
Madame Moréno	Vous savez certainement que Carrefour est aujourd'hui une société multinationale qui est implantée aux quatre coins du monde. Nous avons d'ailleurs plusieurs de nos hypermarchés en Angleterre.
Marc	En effet! Je connais la réputation de votre société et j'approuve votre politique sur la croissance soutenue, la protection de l'environnement, le recyclage des déchets. Je suis moi-même partisan du marketing sociétal, du marketing vert.
Madame Moréno	Bravo! Vous semblez être très au courant de notre philosophie. Mais dites-moi, pourquoi êtes-vous venu chez nous pour faire le marketing de vos produits?
Marc	Eh bien, pour tout vous dire, nous n'avons pas encore de représentants en France. C'est pourquoi j'ai décide de venir moi-même me rendre compte. Votre pays constitue en fait un marché très porteur pour le type de produits

	que nous fabriquons, puisque, selon les statistiques les plus récentes, les Français sont les plus gros consommateurs de produits de sport et de loisir de la Communauté après les Allemands. En outre, le climat de l'Hexagone est très favorable aux activités sportives et de loisir.
Madame Moréno	Sur ce point, vous avez parfaitement raison! La France est, en effet, le pays européen où il y a le plus grand nombre de jours de congés par an. Autrefois les Français travaillaient beaucoup plus dur que maintenant. Aujourd'hui, c'est le carpe diem!
Marc	Pardon?
Madame Moréno	Le carpe diem. C'est une expression latine qui veut dire 'saisir le jour', vivre pour le présent.
Marc	C'est une excellente philosophie pour les fournisseurs de produits comme les nôtres!
Madame Moréno	Sans aucun doute. Mais dites-moi, au niveau de la productivité et des livraisons, l'Angleterre a une terrible réputation à cause des grèves! Chez nous, on appelle ça 'la maladie anglaise'.
Marc	Madame Moréno, je peux vous assurer la main sur le cœur que c'est du passé. Selon les statistiques de l'Union Européenne, les ouvriers anglais – je devrais dire britanniques – sont ceux qui travaillent le plus grand nombre d'heures hebdomadaires pour des salaires inférieurs à la moyenne européenne.
Madame Moréno	Est-ce que ça veut dire que vos produits sont moins chers que ceux de vos concurrents?
Marc	Ils seront certainement très compétitifs.
Madame Moréno	Mmm! Nous allons voir!

désolé *sorry. In learned French, it could also mean desolate (of a landscape).*
résoudre *to solve or resolve*
avoir sous les yeux *to have in front of oneself (lit. to have under the eyes)*
une gamme *a range (of products). Also refers to the scale of musical notes.*
loisir *(masc.) leisure.* **Les loisirs** *are leisure pursuits.*
intéressant *Here: affordable or attractive (prices). It can also mean interesting.*
milieu et haut de gamme *middle and top of the range (of products)*
par rapport à *in relation to*
une branche *a branch (area of activity or part of a tree)*
la finition *the finish (of a product)*
craindre *to fear*
la concurrence *competition (commercial)*
implanté(e) *set up (also implanted)*
la société *Here: company. Can also mean society.*
sociétal *socially responsible (marketing). The expression* **le marketing vert** *refers to environmentally aware marketing.*
se rendre compte *to realize.* **Réaliser** *is also used in this sense in informal French.*
les congés (payés) *(paid) holidays*
le fournisseur *supplier*
la livraison *delivery*
la maladie *illness/sickness*
hebdomadaire *weekly. Monthly is* **mensuel** *and yearly* **annuel.**
la main sur le cœur *hand on heart (in all honesty)*
le concurrent *competitor*

QUICK VOCAB

Insight

Adjectives and nouns ending in **-if** in the masculine singular change **-if** into **-ive** in the feminine: **actif – active; compétitif – compétitive; objectif – objective,** etc.

Language learning tip 2

En fait *and* en effet

Although they sound similar, these two words have different meanings in French.

1 En effet is used to confirm something which has just been stated. It is the equivalent of the English *indeed* or *that is true*.

Vous êtes représentant? En effet!	*Are you a representative? Yes, indeed!*

2 En fait is used to introduce further information. It is the equivalent of *in fact, as a matter of fact* or even *in effect*.

Je vous avais dit que je viendrais à la réunion. En fait, je ne serai pas disponible.	*I had told you I would come to the meeting. In fact, I will not be available.*

Activity 4

How would you translate the following into French:

1 They wanted to go to the cinema, but in fact they stayed at home and watched television.
2 You are a blue-collar worker. In effect, you should not be here!
3 Did you like the film? Indeed (I did)!
4 May I see your passport please? As a matter of fact, I have left it at home.
5 People think that our products are expensive, but in fact they are very competitive.

1 Prefixes and suffixes

As you know, these two words refer to meaningful elements (called morphemes), which can be 'glued' to the beginning (prefixes), or the end (suffixes), of words, to change their meaning. Although using this method is very rewarding, some care must be exercised, as we shall soon see.

New French words can be created by this method, but a clear distinction must be made between:

1 Elements which change the meaning while preserving the grammatical category of the original word.

real (adj.) ~ *unreal* (adj.); *possibility* (noun) ~ *impossibility* (noun).

2 Elements which change the grammatical category of the original.

to motivate (verb) ~ *motivation* (noun); *cruel* (adj.) ~ *cruelty* (noun).

Using the right technique and looking for rules will enable you to enrich your vocabulary considerably with relatively little effort.

1.1 Prefixes

Here are some of the most frequently encountered French prefixes:

1 in- (meaning *not*), and the other forms with the same meaning (ill- or irr- or im-):

In the following examples, - indicates that the word is the same in English.

> incapable (-); inaudible (-); incroyable (*incredible*); insupportable (*unbearable*); impossible (-); immobile (-); imbuvable (*undrinkable*); illégal (-); illogique (*illogical*), irrégulier (*irregular*); irresponsable (*irresponsible*)

Despite their different appearance, all the above prefixes have the same meaning. The different shape is merely conditioned by the first letter (or sound) of the word to which the prefix is glued.

Beware, however, because **in-** and **im-** can also mean *inside* as in **incorporer** (*to incorporate*), **importer** (*to import/to bring in*).

2 **dé-** or **des-** (indicating *the opposite of*):
déformer (*to damage the shape of*); **déranger** (*to disturb*); **défaire** (*to undo*); **déshabiller** (*to undress*); **déstabiliser** (*to destabilize*)

3 **re-** (*to do something again/to get back*):
refaire (*to redo*); **redescendre** (*to go down again*); **revendre** (*to sell again*); **ressortir** (*to go out again*)

4 **sur-** (*to exceed/go over*):
surpasser (*to surpass*); **surestimer** (*to overestimate*); **surévaluer** (*to overvalue*)

5 **mal-** (*not …*):
malheureux (*unhappy*); **malchanceux** (*unlucky*)

6 **sous-** (*under*):
sous-estimer (*to underestimate*); **sous-évaluer** (*to undervalue*)

1.2 Suffixes

Whereas adding a prefix does not require any change to the shape of the word which it attaches itself to, suffixes often involve modifications to the end of the word to which they are to be added.

arranger (*to arrange*)	→ arrangement
changer (*to change*)	→ changement
contempler (*to gaze at*)	→ contemplation
développer (*to develop*)	→ développement
essayer (*to try*)	→ essayage (*also* essai for 'a trial/try')
évaluer (*to evaluate*)	→ évaluation
finir (*to finish*)	→ finition (*also* finissage for industrial processes)

nourrir (*to feed/nourish*) → nourriture
passer (*to pass*) → passage
rafraîchir (*to refresh*) → rafraîchissement
beau (*beautiful*) → beauté
nouveau (*new*) → nouveauté
social (*social*) → socialisme

Beware: if two formations are possible, they usually have very distinct meanings:

laver: lavage (*washing*); lavement (*enema*)!

Activity 5
On the strength of what we have learnt about prefixes, try and form the opposite of each of the following:

1 actif
2 buvable
3 destructible
4 légitime
5 moral
6 personnel
7 rationnel
8 supportable

Activity 6
With the help of the appropriate prefix, express for each of the words below the idea of 'doing something again':

1 couper
2 décorer
3 faire
4 monter
5 placer
6 prendre
7 vivre

Activity 7

From the following list of suffixes (**-ment, -age, -tion, -té, -ture**), choose the one which will help you change each of the following words into nouns. Beware, some stem changes are needed in order to create the new word, but careful study of the language information provided above should help you solve most of the problems.

1 avertir
2 changer
3 construire
4 laver
5 modifier
6 nettoyer
7 opérer
8 ouvrir
9 préparer

Venture a guess for the gender of each noun and check against the list given in Appendix 3.

Activity 8

This activity is part of your self-assessment. You should award yourself five marks for each correct answer, total 50. Add the total to your score in the self-assessment form.

In the dialogue between Marc and Madame Moréno, find the nouns which have been created from the verbs listed below and, for each, give the gender. Once again, these verbs are not in sequence.

1 consommer
2 croître
3 équiper
4 exprimer
5 finir
6 fournir
7 produire
8 protéger
9 représenter
10 livrer

Insight

In French, such expressions as *once a month*, *twice a week*, *three times a day*, etc., are constructed with **par** (*per*): **une fois par mois, deux fois par semaine, trois fois par jour.**

Dialogue 2

Marc's meeting at Carrefour with Madame Moréno went well and he hopes that something concrete will emerge from that first encounter. He had planned to go back to Britain the next day (13 May), but this proves impossible: there are general strikes throughout France, and all trains and flights have been cancelled. Fortunately, Pierre Castel has invited him to spend a couple of days in Villeneuve. This will allow the situation to get back to normal and will also give Marc time to look at some property. He is now at Studio Belvert, a photographer's shop, to buy a film for his camera. As usual, he cannot resist striking up a conversation with the manager and his assistant.

CD2, TR 3, 06:49

Marc	… Comme je vous le disais il y a un moment, ma mère est française et mon père est anglais. Ils ont vaguement l'intention d'acheter une résidence secondaire en France pour leur retraite. Étant donné que je voyage beaucoup du fait de mon travail, j'ai pensé que ce serait une bonne idée de jeter un coup d'œil dans la région.
Jean-Claude	En toute honnêteté, vous pourriez tomber plus mal! Le Lot-et-Garonne est encore un bon endroit pour acheter. D'ailleurs, il y a pas mal d'Anglais et de Hollandais qui se sont installés ici, et nous en avons beaucoup comme clients au magasin.
Marc	Ah bon?
Jean-Claude	Oui, absolument. Mais il faut dire que la majorité d'entre eux ont acheté des propriétés il y a quelques années au moment où les prix étaient

(Contd)

encore très abordables. Aujourd'hui les choses ont bien changé; les prix ont tendance à flamber, comme partout d'ailleurs, mais il y a encore de bonnes affaires à faire.

Marc On m'a dit que Villeneuve était une ville calme, où le coût de la vie était raisonnable et où les affaires marchaient bien.

Jean-Claude C'est vrai. Il ne faut pas se plaindre! Villeneuve est une ville de bourgeois et de retraités. Les gens qui, dans leur jeunesse, avaient quitté la région pour aller chercher fortune dans les grandes villes, ont tendance à revenir au moment de la retraite pour retrouver leurs racines. Pour les étrangers, elle est aussi très pittoresque, et d'ailleurs, n'oublions pas qu'historiquement, l'Aquitaine est une région qui a appartenu aux Anglais au Moyen Âge.

Marc D'après ce que j'ai cru comprendre, il n'y a plus beaucoup d'industries par ici.

Jean-Claude C'est vrai que les industries qui étaient liées à l'agriculture ont plus ou moins disparu. Ceci dit, il existe encore pas mal de jardiniers et de fermiers dans la région. Deux fois par semaine, il y a au centre-ville un marché où les paysans des environs viennent vendre leurs fruits et leurs légumes frais, mais la grande majorité des Villeneuvois vont s'approvisionner à Carrefour ou à Auchan, les hypermarchés du coin.

Marc Hier, je suis allé voir la responsable des achats de Carrefour à Agen. C'est impressionnant, c'est vrai, mais … est-ce que les grandes surfaces ont eu un effet négatif sur les petits commerces?

Jean-Claude Alors là, aucun doute! Il y a pas mal de petits commerces qui ont dû fermer leurs portes.

Michèle Ce qui m'énerve le plus, c'est que vous avez des clients qui viennent poser des tas de questions sur un produit, sur son prix, ses performances, etc. Ils passent une demi-heure à vous casser les pieds. Ils ont aucune envie de faire leurs achats chez vous. Une fois qu'ils ont les renseignements nécessaires, il vont acheter l'appareil à l'hypermarché. Ça, ça me tue!

Marc	Pourquoi est-ce qu'ils n'y vont pas directement alors?
Michèle	Tout simplement parce que le personnel des hypers a pas les compétences techniques. Ce sont des vendeurs, pas des spécialistes. Ils donnent des détails de base sur le prix, les caractéristiques générales du produit mais ça ne va pas plus loin. Alors ils viennent d'abord chez nous. Vous savez, quelquefois, c'est dur de garder le sourire!
Marc	Mais, vous ne pouvez pas vous organiser, faire quelque chose?
Jean-Claude	On a essayé de former des groupements pour acheter en gros, mais sans grand succès. Le petit commerce ne peut pas lutter contre les prix cassés que les grandes surfaces sont capables d'offrir à la clientèle.
Michèle	Vous comprenez, la puissance des centrales d'achat des hypers est trop grande. Leurs volumes d'achat sont énormes.
Jean-Claude	Michèle est jeune, voilà pourquoi ces choses-là la mettent en colère. Moi, je prends ma retraite dans trois mois. Comme disait l'autre, après moi, le déluge!
Marc	Je vois. Mais pour revenir à ce que je disais tout à l'heure, quelle serait la meilleure solution pour trouver des maisons à vendre, d'après vous?
Jean-Claude	Ben, la meilleure solution serait de consulter un agent immobilier. Il y en a plusieurs ici ...
Michèle	Et puis, y a *Les Échos*.
Marc	*Les Échos?*
Michèle	Oui, c'est le journal local gratuit. Y a toujours des maisons et des propriétés à vendre; vous pouvez prendre rendez-vous et visiter, sans obligation d'achat.
Marc	Je vous remercie de tous ces renseignements. Ah! Voilà un client. Je ne veux pas vous déranger plus longtemps. Au revoir!

QUICK VOCAB

vaguement *vaguely. Here it means toying with the idea.*
étant donné que … *given the fact that …*
jeter un coup d'œil (à) *to have a quick look/to cast a glance (at)*
une propriété *property. It can also mean a farm (with grounds and outbuildings).*
abordable (prix) *low/affordable (price)*
mal tomber *to get a rough deal or to arrive at the wrong time. The expression* **vous tombez bien!** *usually means 'you arrive just when we need you' (unless a sarcastic tone is used).*
flamber (prix) *to soar (prices). Also to burn brightly.*
une bonne affaire *a real bargain. Sometimes used in the expression* **une affaire d'or** *(a golden bargain not to be missed!).*
les racines (fem.) *roots (for plants, teeth, etc.)*
un étranger *a stranger, but also a foreigner*
un jardinier *Here: a market gardener. Also a gardener.*
d'après … *according to …*
le paysan *farmer. Sometimes considered derogatory, but not here.*
casser les pieds *to make a nuisance of oneself (lit. to break someone's feet – but stands for something much ruder!).*
le coin *Here: the locality/area* (lit. *the corner)*
en gros *wholesale. The opposite is* **au détail.**
un prix cassé *a knock-down price*
la centrale d'achat *central purchasing agency (for large stores)*
après moi, le déluge *An oft-quoted expression which means 'I don't care what happens when I'm gone'. Variously attributed to Louis XIV, Napoleon, and General de Gaulle.*
un agent immobilier *an estate agent*

Insight

Unlike adjectives, French adverbs are invariable. Consequently, you should distinguish between **'Elle est dure'** (*'She is hard'* – adj.) and **'Elle travaille dur'** (*'She works hard'* – adv.), and between **'Elle est forte'** (*'She is strong'* – adj.) and **'Elle parle fort'** (*'She speaks loudly'* – adv.).

Language learning tip 3

Capital or no capital?

Generally, there is little difference between the use of capital letters in the two languages. One, however, does stand out, in the case of words referring to nationality. Look at the sentences below: can you work it out (if you do not know)? The answer is quite simple, as we will see:

Un visiteur français est arrivé dans le village anglais.	*A French visitor arrived in the English village.*
Les Allemands sont très disciplinés et les Français ne le sont pas.	*The Germans are very disciplined and the French are not.*

Have those of you who did not know the rule managed to work it out? If the word indicating nationality is an adjective, as in the first example, there is no capital. If the word is a noun, as in the second example, the capital is needed.

Comprehension 1

After listening to and reading the conversation between Marc and the staff of Studio Belvert, answer the following questions in English.

1 What are the arguments and the advice put forward by Jean-Claude in response to Marc's intention to look at property in the area?
2 How does Jean-Claude explain the original departure of people from the area and their eventual return?
3 What information does Jean-Claude give about the price of property in the area?
4 Has agricultural activity completely vanished in the region?
5 What are Michèle's feelings about time-wasters and why?

6 What is Michèle's explanation for the level of technical advice given in a hypermarket?
7 What is Jean-Claude's response to the suggestion that small retailers should fight back?
8 How can the difference in attitude between Michèle and Jean-Claude be explained?

Activity 9

Can you clarify the type of language (register) which Michèle uses in the conversation? Give clear examples to support your view. If you want to refresh your memory on this point, you can go back to Units 4 and 5.

Activity 10

Translate the following sentences using expressions from the dialogue.

1 We have tried to organize ourselves, but without much success.
2 Let's not forget that …
3 This being said, we have tried to fight against the competition.
4 The best solution would be to ask for an appointment.
5 I'm going to Paris to seek my fortune.
6 We go to the restaurant twice a week.
7 People have changed a lot. Now they tend to go to hypermarkets to do their shopping.
8 Why aren't the customers coming to your shop?
9 What irritates me most is that a fair number of small businesses have had to close down.

Insight

English makes a distinction between the two nouns *stranger* and *foreigner*. In French, there is only one word: **étranger** (fem. **étrangère**) to cover both meanings. Note also that **à l'étranger** = *abroad*.

Reading 2

Because of government proposals to introduce new legislation regarding pension contributions and working conditions, French workers, following the adage **En mai fais ce qui te plaît** (*In May, do as you please*), have taken to the streets. In an effort to appease the demonstrators, the Prime Minister has decided to speak to the country. The text of his speech is given below.

🔈 CD2, TR 3, 10:53

Mes chers concitoyens,

Depuis plusieurs semaines, un certain nombre de secteurs sont affectés par des mouvements de grève liés aux conditions de travail, aux salaires et au problème des retraites.

Je suis conscient du fait que tous les travailleurs veulent maintenir, et si possible améliorer, leur niveau de vie. C'est dans l'ordre normal des choses. Mais la majorité d'entre vous comprend fort bien que la conjoncture internationale n'est pas favorable à des demandes d'augmentation de salaires allant jusqu'à 15%, compte tenu d'un niveau d'inflation qui, cette année, se situe à 2%. Le monde a récemment traversé une période d'instabilité politique qui a eu des répercussions désastreuses sur notre situation économique. Dans un pays démocratique comme le nôtre, il est normal que la rue exprime son mécontentement. Mais à ceux qui veulent nous mettre des bâtons dans les roues, je dis, n'attendez de moi ni faiblesse ni sympathie! Je voudrais donc demander à tous ceux d'entre vous qui en ce moment ont cessé le travail pour appuyer leurs revendications, de faire preuve de patience et de modération. Le gouvernement étudiera les demandes comme il le fait régulièrement et, dans la mesure du possible, essaiera d'y donner satisfaction.

Les mouvements de protestation frappent également le secteur de l'éducation à un moment crucial, celui des examens. Des centaines de milliers d'écoliers et d'étudiants vont voir leurs épreuves retardées ou annulées pour cause de grève. Est-il raisonnable de jouer avec l'avenir de nos jeunes en cette période vitale pour eux? Je ne le crois pas!

Iciencore, je m'engage à rencontrer les représentants des divers syndicats de l'Éducation Nationale, afin qu'ensemble nous puissions mettre sur pied un programme susceptible de les satisfaire. Mais il faut bien se rappeler que toute réforme est coûteuse et que l'état doit organiser des priorités d'action.

Le problème des retraites est une autre des causes de mécontentement parmi vous. Comme vous le savez, le déficit de la Sécurité Sociale est énorme et si rien n'est fait, nous ne pourrons bientôt plus garantir à ceux qui arrivent à la fin de leur vie active, les allocations auxquelles ils pensent avoir droit. C'est pourquoi nous avons augmenté la durée des cotisations à 40 ans sans pour cela en relever le niveau. Cette mesure, qui nous permettra de garantir une retraite au moins égale à 75% du salaire final, est la seule façon pour le gouvernement de faire face à la crise qui frappe actuellement notre système de sécurité sociale.

Les engagements qu'avait pris le gouvernement ont étés tenus dans la mesure des possibilités financières.

Confrontés à une conjoncture difficile et à une situation internationale instable, nous devons faire de notre mieux pour nous assurer que les progrès économiques et sociaux de ces dernières années ne seront pas perdus. J'ai dans cette lutte, le soutien du Chef de l'État!

Merci de votre attention et de votre compréhension.

QUICK VOCAB

un concitoyen *a fellow-citizen. As you would expect, the feminine is* **une concitoyenne.**
lié a *(+ noun phrase) linked with/to*
la grève *strike (work). A military strike is* **une frappe.**
maintenir *to preserve. Also to maintain.*
la conjoncture *general economic climate*
une augmentation de salaire *a salary increase*
mettre des bâtons dans les roues *to put spokes in the wheels*

la rue *the street. Here: the striking workers.*
la sympathie *sympathy. Beware however of* **sympathique** *(false friend) which means friendly/amicable.*
les revendications (salariales) *wage/salary claims*
faire preuve de *(+ noun phrase) to demonstrate/show (feelings)*
au cas par cas *treating each case individually (and on merit)*
s'engager (à ...) *to undertake (to ...)*
mettre sur pied *to set up (lit. to put on foot)*
la cotisation *premium (money due to an official body)*
relever (un salaire ...) *to increase (of a salary, an allowance ...)*
le soutien *support. The verb is* **soutenir**. *Beware:* **un souteneur** *is a pimp!*

Insight

In French, the present tense is used to indicate that an action which has been going on for a while is likely to continue, or that it is happening now: '**Il travaille bien**' means '*He works well*' or '*He is working well*'. It can also express an action about to happen: '**Ils partent demain**' ('*They leave tomorrow*').

In France, as in other developed countries, there are a number of workers' trade unions called **les syndicats**. Their number is currently estimated at about 100. Their power and influence varies according to the number of their paid-up members. The most important syndicats are:

1 la CFDT (Confédération Française Démocratique du Travail);
2 la CGT (Confédération Générale du Travail);
3 la CGT–FO (Confédération Générale du Travail – Force Ouvrière);
4 la CGC (Confédération Générale des Cadres);
5 la CFTC (Confédération Française des Travailleurs Chrétiens);
6 la FEN (Fédération Française de l'Éducation Nationale)

The unionization rate of workers, which was around 25% 30 years ago, is said to be currently below 10%. But workers are generally quite militant and ready *to take to the streets* (**descendre dans la rue**) to support their *claims* (**revendications**), having first obtained the agreement of the government about their intentions through a **préavis de grève** (*advance notification of a strike*)!

Their demands usually range from salary increases and shorter working hours (currently set at 35 hours a week for many employees), to better working conditions and the improvement of pensions, to name but a few.

For further information about French trade unions, you may visit http://yahoo.fr and type in **syndicats français** or **le syndicalisme en France.**

Comprehension 2

Having read the Prime Minister's declaration at least twice, listen to the recording, if you have it. Make a note of any 'unfamiliar' words, and check their meaning before answering the questions which follow.

1 What appear to be the three main causes of the current demonstrations?
2 What reasons does the Prime Minister give to brush aside the 15 per cent pay claims which have been put forward by some trade unions?
3 What will be his attitude towards those who try to put 'spokes in the government's wheels'?
4 What are his comments about strikes in the education sector? Give as much detail as possible.
5 What does he promise to do, if people are patient and moderate in their demands?
6 What does he pledge to do in response to the demands of the education trade unions?
7 What measures have been taken to try to solve the enormous deficit of the French National Health Service?
8 What do you judge the tone of the declaration to be? Support your views with carefully selected quotations.

2 The perfect infinitive

Few people tend to use the expression 'perfect infinitive', but it clearly indicates that we are dealing with a compound tense, and clarifies the way it is constructed. Predictably, the perfect infinitive is composed of the infinitive of **avoir** or **être**, as appropriate, and the past participle of the main verb:

Infinitive	*Perfect infinitive*
acheter	avoir acheté
commander	avoir commandé
partir	être parti
pouvoir	avoir pu
venir	être venu

2.1 What is the purpose of this tense?

Whereas the infinitive is used to situate an action in the present or the future, the perfect infinitive places the action in the past:

Il doit *payer* sa facture ce soir.	*He must (or is due to) pay his bill tonight (present or future).*
Il doit *avoir payé* sa facture ce soir.	*He must have paid his bill by tonight (idea of a completed action by a certain deadline (past, present or future)).*

The perfect infinitive is sometimes used to avoid the perfect subjunctive (see Unit 9):

Ils ne croyaient pas qu'ils *aient gagné*. **Ils ne croyaient pas *avoir gagné*.**	*They did not think they had won.*

This tense is often found in constructions involving an impersonal verb (**il faut que, il est nécessaire que, il est vital que, il est essentiel que**), where **il** does not refer to a specific person:

Il faudra être partis demain.	*It will be necessary to have left by tomorrow.*
Il sera nécessaire d'avoir fini ce soir.	*It will be necessary to have finished by tonight.*

In this sense, it is the equivalent of the perfect subjunctive, but, because of its impersonal quality, it does not carry any information about the performer(s) of the action. So, if needed, a pronoun will have to be inserted before the infinitive:

Il faut être partis à trois heures.	*One (presumably we) must be gone by three o'clock.*
Il nous faut être partis à trois heures.	*We must be gone by three o'clock.*

Activity 11

This next activity will be part of your self-assessment. You should award yourself ten marks for each correct answer, total 50. This total is to be added to your score in the self-assessment form.

In the sentences below, replace the present infinitive (underlined) with the appropriate form of the perfect infinitive to situate the action clearly in the past. Remember to check which auxiliary is required.

1 Ta sœur déclare avoir une maladie grave.
2 Nous espérons vous être utiles.
3 Il faut se trouver dans la même situation pour comprendre sa réaction.
4 Il est incapable de vouloir nous frapper.
5 Je ne crois pas devenir trop dur avec eux.

3 How to say that an action is/was/will be in progress when ...

In English, we use the present continuous and other similarly formed tenses to indicate an action in progress at the time of speaking (or writing).

1 ***I am working*** *in the garden.*
2 ***They were watching*** *the match.*
3 *This time next week,* ***we will be travelling*** *in Germany.*

This is rendered in French by the expression **être en train de** + infinitive. The appropriate time zone will be indicated by the tense of the verb être. So, the examples above will be translated as:

1 **Je suis en train de** travailler dans le jardin (*present*).
2 **Ils étaient en train de** regarder le match (*imperfect*).
3 La semaine prochaine à cette heure-ci **nous serons en train de** voyager en Allemagne (*future*).

Activity 12
Using the above method, translate the following into French:

1 When I get back, he will be washing his car.
2 I have just phoned Marc. He is in the process of preparing the document.
3 If all goes well, tomorrow at this time I will be signing the contract.
4 When I arrived, they were in the process of finishing their lunch.
5 We knew that he would be in the process of redecorating his room.

Insight

The infinitive is used to express present or future actions in relation to the main time zone, whereas the perfect infinitive situates those actions in the past. Compare: **'Il veut partir à sept heures'** ('*He wants to go at seven o'clock*') and **'Il veut être parti à sept heures'** ('*He wants to be gone by seven o'clock*').

On ne peut pas être et avoir été! (lit. *One cannot both be and have been!*) A better rendering may be *One cannot hope to keep forever one's youth, dashing looks, stamina, etc.*

Vouloir, c'est pouvoir! *Where there's a will there's a way!*

TEST YOURSELF

1 What is **une gamme** when it is not a musical scale?

2 Which of the following two distances is the greater: 2.500 kilometres or 2,500 kilometres? Explain.

3 What is **un Carrefour** when it is not a crossroads?

4 What is the difference in meaning between **en fait** and **en effet**?

5 What is the difference in meaning between **fermer sa porte** and **fermer ses portes**?

6 Which expression meaning *I don't care about what will happen when I'm gone* has been variously attributed to three French heads of state?

7 Why should you beware of the adjective **sympathique**?

8 Give three examples of the changes that happen to the privative prefix **in-** (= *not*) in certain contexts.

9 How is the perfect infinitive formed in French?

10 What is the difference between the present infinitive (e.g. **partir**) and the perfect infinitive (e.g. **être parti**) when it comes to situating an action in time?

9

Un coin de paradis

In this unit you will learn

- ***How to form and use the subjunctive (present and perfect)***
- ***How to use alternative ways of expressing commands, guidance and suggestions using the infinitive and the imperative***
- ***How to form and use adverbs of manner***
- ***How to use alternative ways of expressing the passive***
- ***How to connect clauses using conjunctions***
- ***How to use* en *and* y**

1 The subjunctive – what is it for?

For some reason, the word 'subjunctive' seems to create fear in the minds of learners of French. In fact, it is a useful tool and is quite easy to cope with, so long as its purpose is clearly understood. The subjunctive mood is composed of a set of tenses only two of which are in current use. It serves to express very specific shades of meaning: possibility, command, hope, doubt, fear, longing, or the fact that something may or may not happen in the future, or may or may not have happened in the past. So, unlike the indicative, which expresses reality, the subjunctive deals with hypothesis and conjecture.

A few examples will, we hope, help clarify the matter further:

Elle *téléphonera.*	*She will telephone (this will happen: indicative mood; simple future).*
Il est possible qu'elle *téléphone*.	*She may telephone (this could/might happen, either now or in the future).*
Elle a *téléphoné.*	*She (has) telephoned (this has happened; indicative mood; perfect tense).*
Il est possible qu'elle ait *téléphoné.*	*She may have telephoned (possibility in the recent or distant past).*
Je crois qu'ils *sont partis.*	*I think they have gone (this has now happened; indicative mood; perfect tense).*
Je ne crois pas qu'ils *soient partis.*	*I don't think they have gone (expression of doubt about an action in the recent or distant past).*

1.1 How to form the present subjunctive

The present subjunctive, as other simple (one-word) tenses, is formed by putting together a stem and a set of endings. With a couple of exceptions, the endings are the same for the three groups. The stem is usually predictable and, in many cases, stays the same throughout the tense. Below are examples of verbs from each group which follow a 'regular' pattern:

Subject pronoun	*Endings for all verbs*	*1st group (parler)*	*2nd group (finir)*	*3rd group (sortir)*	*3rd group (vouloir)*
que je	-e	parle	finisse	sorte	veuille
que tu (fam. sing.)	-es	parles	finisses	sortes	veuilles
qu'il/elle/on	-e	parle	finisse	sorte	veuille
que nous	-ions	parlions	finissions	sortions	voulions
que vous (pol. sing./plur.)	-iez	parliez	finissiez	sortiez	vouliez
qu'ils/elles	-ent	parlent	finissent	sortent	veuillent

The present subjunctives of **avoir** and **être**, which are also irregular, are presented separately in Unit 9, Section 2.

Language learning tip 1

Although the pronoun **que** is generally associated with the subjunctive, its presence does not automatically mean that a subjunctive must follow. Here again, the difference will be between reality (indicative), and possibility, doubt, command, etc. (subjunctive).

Sometimes, the decision to choose between the indicative and subjunctive moods will require you to assess the level of certainty of the action concerned:

1 **Il est probable que** (*it is probable that …*) suggests that the action considered is very likely or nearly certain. It is therefore the indicative which is required.
2 **Il est possible que** (*it is possible that …*) suggests that the action considered is by no means certain. It is therefore the subjunctive which is needed.

Il est probable qu'ils *abandonneront*.	*It is probable that they will give up (indicative).*
Il est possible qu'ils *abandonnent*.	*It is possible that they may give up (subjunctive).*
Je suis presque certain qu'elle *acceptera*.	*I am almost certain she will accept (indicative).*
Je ne suis pas certain qu'elle *accepte*.	*I am not certain she will accept (subjunctive).*

It has to be said that the subjunctive is considered as rather ponderous and it is therefore not overly popular in ordinary conversation. So, in spite of what we have just said, do not be too surprised if you hear: ***Il est possible qu'ils abandonneront!** Although, strictly speaking it is incorrect, you may get away with using it yourself!

Insight

In French, the indicative expresses the reality of an action (past, present or future). By contrast, doubt, vague possibility, fear are rendered by the subjunctive. Compare: '**Je suis sûr qu'elle viendra**' ('*I am sure she will come*') and '**Je ne suis pas sûr qu'elle vienne**' ('*I'm not sure she will come*').

1.2 How to find the stem to form the present subjunctive

For the majority of verbs, the stem will consist of the infinitive minus its ending. This will hold good for most 1st group verbs, all 2nd group ones and a fair proportion of 3rd group ones, particularly those ending in -ir and -re.

Some of the most common (but troublesome) verbs are listed below.

Infinitive	*Meaning*	Stem
apercevoir	*to catch sight of*	aperçoiv-/apercev-
boire	*to drink*	boiv-/buv-
connaître	*to know*	connaiss-
croire	*to believe*	croi-/croy-
devoir	*to have to*	doiv-/dev-
faire	*to do*	fass-
mourir	*to die*	meur-/mour-
pouvoir	*to be able*	puiss-
recevoir	*to receive/welcome*	reçoiv-/recev-
savoir	*to know*	sach-
voir	*to see*	voi-/voy-

1 When there are two stems shown in the above table, the second one is used for the **nous** and **vous** forms only.
2 The subjunctive of **avoir** and **être**, which are presented in the next section, does not follow the regular pattern of formation.

Language learning tip 2

Quite often – but not always – the stem used to form the subjunctive of irregular 3rd group verbs is the same as that of the present participle (the equivalent of the *-ing* form in English). This may guide you in the construction of the subjunctive.

Remember: don't be afraid to experiment, and modify your 'theories' in the light of what you have heard/seen!

2 How to form the perfect subjunctive

As in the case of all compound tenses, we need an auxiliary (either **avoir** or **être**) to form the perfect subjunctive. All that's required is the present subjunctive of the auxiliary, followed by the past participle of the main verb.

Present subjunctive of avoir	*Present subjunctive of être*
que j'aie	que je sois
que tu aies (fam.)	que tu sois (fam.)
qu'il/elle/on ait	qu'il/elle/on soit
que nous ayons	que nous soyons
que vous ayez (pol. sing./plur.)	que vous soyez (pol. sing./plur.)
qu'ils/elles aient	qu'ils/elles soient

2.1 How and when to use the perfect subjunctive

This tense normally refers to an action already completed and situated in the past:

Nous sommes contents qu'ils *soient revenus.*	*We are glad they have returned.*

However, it can also be used to refer to an action which should be completed by a given deadline situated in the future.

Je ne suis pas sûr que vous *ayez fini* ce soir.	*I'm not sure you'll have finished by tonight.*
Je veux que tu *aies signé* le contrat quand je reviendrai.	*I want you to have signed the contract when (by the time) I get back.*
Il faut que vous *soyez parties* avant son retour.	*You must be gone before his return (he returns).*

Clearly, the expressions **ce soir**, **je reviendrai** and **son retour** refer to an action which has not yet taken place.

Activity 1

In each of the following sentences turn the present subjunctive into the perfect subjunctive. Before you start, you may wish to go back to Unit 3, to check which verbs take **avoir** and which take **être** for the formation of their compound tenses.

1 Il faut que je paie mes impôts dès demain.
2 Je ne crois pas que nous finissions ce soir.
3 Il est possible qu'il rentre à neuf heures.
4 Nous doutons qu'ils réussissent à nous persuader.
5 Il n'est pas certain que vous puissiez le convaincre.
6 Elle a peur que nous ayons un accident.
7 Nous aimerions qu'elle parte avant midi.

Activity 2

This next activity will be part of your self-assessment. You should award yourself five marks for each correct answer, total 50. This total should be added to your score in the self-assessment form.

Look at each of the following expressions, and indicate whether it should be followed by the subjunctive or by the indicative.

1 Je crois que …
2 Il est possible que …
3 Il est douteux que …
4 Je pense que …

5 J'ai peur que …
6 Il est vrai que …
7 Je suis certain que …
8 Il n'est pas sûr que …
9 Nous aimerions que …
10 J'exige que …

Language learning tip 3

Demander *and* exiger

Beware of the false friend **demander**: in French, it simply means to ask. If you want to say *to demand*, you will need the verb **exiger**.

Insight

In addition to **demander**, there are many other 'false friends' to beware of in French: **attendre** = *to wait;* **la drogue** = *drug (noxious substance)*; **énerver** = *to irritate*; **formidable** = *wonderful/great*; **inhabité** = *uninhabited*; **la manifestation** = *demonstration*; **le médecin** = *doctor*; **le préservatif** = *condom*; **le récipient** = *container*; **résumer** = *to sum up*; **la retraite** = *retirement (as well as retreat).*

3 How to avoid the subjunctive when expressing orders, suggestions, advice …

We now know that, in French, the subjunctive can be used, among other things, to express commands or orders, but that, nowadays, particularly in informal conversation, it is often avoided because it is perceived as heavy. Native speakers will often replace it by a variety of grammatically acceptable alternatives (e.g. the infinitive, the imperative, or noun phrases):

Elle attend que vous *partiez*. **Elle attend *votre départ* (noun).**	*She is waiting for you to go.*
Il faut que nous *rentrions* à la maison. **Il (nous) faut *rentrer* à la maison *(infinitive)*.**	*We must get back home.*
Nous doutons qu'ils *soient* courageux. **Nous doutons *de leur courage* (noun).**	*We doubt their courage.*
Il est urgent que voustéléphoniez! **Téléphonez, c'est urgent *(imperative)*!**	*It's urgent for you to telephone!*

Activity 3

In each of the sentences that follow, replace the subjunctive by a simpler expression. Note that, in some of the sentences, there may be more than one way of doing it! Try as much as possible to remain faithful to the general meaning.

1 Il faut que nous fermions le magasin.
2 J'aimerais que nous puissions voyager toi et moi.
3 Nous voulons attendre que tu arrives.
4 Il est essentiel que vous finissiez ce travail.
5 J'exige qu'il rembourse cet argent.
6 Ils ont peur que le consulat refuse.
7 Ils aimeraient que vous donniez votre accord.

Activity 4

In the sentences below, replace the simpler expressions by the subjunctive.

1 L'arrivée du message est encore possible.
2 Il nous faut changer de l'argent.
3 Refuser serait impossible pour nous.
4 Combien de temps me faudra-t-il attendre?
5 Il nous faut réserver une place au restaurant.
6 Je ne crois pas pouvoir réussir.

Reading 1

The South-West of France (**le sud-ouest**) is well known for the quality of its cuisine and its regional wines. Despite fears about the dangers of fatty diets and regular intake of alcohol, the longevity of the inhabitants of that region seems to be above the national average. Below is a recipe for goose with chestnuts. Both of the main ingredients are found in abundance in the area.

CD2, TR 4, 00:28

Recette régionale du sud-ouest – l'oie rôtie aux marrons

Ingrédients: 1 oie; le foie de l'oie; 100 g de viande de veau; 100 g de viande de porc; 100 g de lardons; 1 kilo de marrons; 75 centilitres de bouillon; 2 échalotes. On peut également, si l'on veut, utiliser une truffe pour améliorer la recette. Dans ce cas, couper la truffe en très fines lamelles. Entailler (faire des entailles dans) la peau de l'oie et glisser dans chacune les morceaux de truffe avant la cuisson.

Temps de cuisson: variable selon le poids de la volaille (mais compter 30 minutes de cuisson par 500 grammes de viande).

Préparation (45 minutes): Enlever les abats de l'oie. Saler et poivrer intérieurement. Faire un hachis avec le foie, le veau, le porc et les lardons. Éplucher les marrons et les faire cuire dans le bouillon. Les réduire en purée. Hacher finement les échalotes et les faire cuire au beurre. Mélanger le tout et ajouter, si désiré, des épluchures de truffes. Saler. Poivrer. Remplir l'intérieur de l'oie avec ce hachis. Ficeler et faire rôtir dans un four préchauffé à 175 degrés C (Celsius).

Attention: Bien surveiller la cuisson qui doit se faire à chaleur modérée. Une cuisson trop forte risque de dessécher la viande. Au besoin, couvrir l'oie avec un papier d'aluminium beurré, pour ralentir la coloration du rôti. Déglacer le plat de cuisson et servir le jus en saucière.

QUICK VOCAB

la recette *recipe*
l'oie *goose*
le marron *chestnut (cookery); otherwise, horse-chestnut (inedible!)*
(le temps de) cuisson *cooking (time)*
la volaille *fowl (here: the goose)*
le foie *liver*
la viande *meat*
le veau *veal*
le bouillon *stock (also broth)*
l'échalote *shallot*
les abats *giblets*
le hachis *minced meat to which the chestnuts and shallots are added*
la truffe *truffle (very flavoursome, but horrendously expensive)*
l'épluchure *peel (when removed from potatoes, carrots, etc.)*
préchauffé *pre-heated*
Note: the verbs used in this recipe are listed in Activity 5.

Truffles are a type of fungus found, among other places, in the South-West of France. They grow in the ground, usually at the foot of old oak trees, and farmers go with specially trained pigs or dogs to look for them. Truffles are normally black or brown in colour and look like small, oddly shaped potatoes. They can cost up to €1,700 (just under €1,150) a kilo. For this reason they are sometimes referred to as 'the black pearls of Périgord' (the area where, according to the locals, the best truffles are produced (see map in Unit 1)).

Insight

Like the infinitive, but in a less impersonal way, the imperative is used to give advice, instructions and orders. It has no subject pronouns, and uses only the second person singular and the first and second persons plural. The imperative of **regarder** (*to look*) is **regarde** (*look* – fam.), **regardons** (*let's look*), **regardez** (*look* – polite sing./plural).

Activity 5

In Column A of the table below, there is a list of the infinitives used to give instructions in the above recipe; Column B contains the second person plural of the imperative of the same verbs. This, as we know, is the other main tense used to give instructions or advice, but in a more friendly, less impersonal way. Column C contains the English translation of the verbs of Column A, but the meanings have been jumbled up. Can you match them up again?

Example: 20 déglacer = i *to deglaze (to make a sauce from the residue in the pan)*

A French infinitives	*B Equivalent imperatives*	*C Jumbled-up translations*
1 couper	**1** coupez	**a** *to peel (vegetables)*
2 entailler	**2** entaillez	**b** *to serve*
3 glisser	**3** glissez	**c** *to cook*
4 compter	**4** comptez	**d** *to make*
5 enlever	**5** enlevez	**e** *to chop*
6 saler	**6** salez	**f** *to add*
7 poivrer	**7** poivrez	**g** *to remove*
8 faire	**8** faites	**h** *to slit*
9 éplucher	**9** épluchez	**i** *to deglaze*
10 faire cuire	**10** faites cuire	**j** *to watch*
11 réduire	**11** réduisez	**k** *to truss*
12 hacher	**12** hachez	**l** *to add pepper*
13 mélanger	**13** mélangez	**m** *to fill*
14 ajouter	**14** ajoutez	**n** *to add salt*
15 remplir	**15** remplissez	**o** *to mix*
16 ficeler	**16** ficelez	**p** *to count*
17 faire rôtir	**17** faites rôtir	**q** *to roast (something)*
18 surveiller	**18** surveillez	**r** *to slide*
19 couvrir	**19** couvrez	**s** *to cut*
20 déglacer	**20** déglacez	**t** *to wrap/cover*
21 servir	**21** servez	**u** *to reduce*

Language learning tip 4

Did you notice anything about the list of verbs in Column A? How many 1st group verbs are there? How many 2nd group ones? How many 3rd group ones?

The answer is: 14 1st group; 2 2nd group (**remplir**, **rôtir**); 5 3rd group (**faire** (also in **faire cuire** and **faire rôtir**), **réduire**, **cuire**, **couvrir** and **servir**).

There are approximately 5,000 1st group verbs in French, and virtually all of them are regular i.e. they behave in a predictable way in terms of the formation of their stems and endings. There are about 350 2nd group verbs, and they are all regular; that means that for a given tense, their ending will be exactly the same. There are approximately 130 3rd group verbs. This last category is the one for which there will be the greatest variations in the stem and the formation of tenses. Many of them are very frequently used, but don't worry, you will soon develop 'a sixth sense' about their endings.

Insight

With a few exceptions, adverbs of manner are formed in French by adding **-ment** to the end of the feminine adjective concerned: **complet** (*complete* masc.) – **complète** (fem.) – **complètement; heureux** (*happy* masc.) – **heureuse** (fem.) – **heureusement.** A different rule applies to adjectives ending in **-ent** or **-ant.**

Activity 6

Translate the following recipe into French, using some of the vocabulary we met in the previous exercise. This time, however, you should use the correct form of the imperative instead of the infinitive. This will give a 'more friendly feel' to your instructions.

First, read the recipe carefully, several times, and try to translate it into French without looking at the vocabulary! If you need to, you may then use the key words given after the recipe to complete your task successfully.

Onion soup (soupe à l'oignon)
Ingredients:
1½ litres of stock
3 medium-sized onions
60 grams of butter
80 grams of flour
one teaspoonful of sugar

Preparation: 12 minutes. **Cooking time:** 20 minutes.

Peel and slice the onions. Place in a pan, add the butter and the sugar, and cook until golden. Sprinkle with the flour. Add the stock, bring to the boil and cook slowly for 15 to 20 minutes. Add salt and pepper. Line the bottom of a soup tureen with thin slices of bread. Pour the soup onto the bread. If desired, add grated Gruyère cheese. Serve hot.

an onion **un oignon**
a pan **une casserole** (false friend!)
to cook until golden **faire dorer**
to sprinkle **saupoudrer**
flour **la farine**
to bring to the boil **porter à ébullition/faire bouillir**
to line **couvrir** (3rd group)
a soup tureen **une soupière**
to pour **verser**
grated **râpé** (of cheese, etc.)
Gruyère cheese **le (fromage de) gruyère**

QUICK VOCAB

As we have seen earlier, the French are bons viveurs, but they sometimes fall victim to the abundance of good things they have at their disposal. There are currently approximately 5 million people whose drinking habits may lead to health problems. Most of them are men. Women drink less. As a result, their average lifespan is longer than that of their male counterparts (approximately 84 years as against 77). Thanks to systematic campaigns by the government to reduce alcohol-related road accidents, the yearly number of casualties has fallen from 16,000 in the seventies to under 5,000 today. If caught driving 'under the influence', drivers are dealt with very severely and subjected to on-the-spot fines, immediate impounding of their vehicle and/or a prison sentence as well as penalty points on their driving licence.

4 Adverbs of manner

Having already clarified the use and position of adverbs in Unit 4, we shall now examine how to create adverbs of manner from adjectives.

4.1 How to form adverbs of manner

In English, adverbs of manner are created by adding the ending *-ly* to the appropriate adjective (e.g. *slowly*, *quickly*, etc.). In French, the situation, although broadly similar, is a little more complex.

The general rule is that, normally, to form such adverbs, you take the feminine singular form of the adjective and add the ending **-ment**:

Masc. sing.	Fem. sing.	Adverb
régulier (*regular*)	→ **régulière**	→ **régulièrement**
curieux (*curious/strange*)	→ **curieuse**	→ **curieusement**
franc (*frank*)	→ **franche**	→ **franchement**
grave (*serious/grave*)	→ **grave**	→ **gravement**

Note: As you can see from the last of the above examples, if an adjective ends with -e (without an accent) in the masculine singular, its feminine singular form is identical. This is not the case if it ends in -é.

The following adjustments are needed to cover the rest of the possibilities:

1 If, in the masculine singular, the adjective ends in **-é**, **-ai** or **-u**, the adverbial ending will be built on the masculine, not the feminine:

modéré (*moderate*)	→ **modérée**	→ **modérément**
vrai (*true*)	→ **vraie**	→ **vraiment**
absolu (*absolute*)	→ **absolue**	→ **absolument**

2 If, in the masculine singular, the adjective ends in **-ent**, that ending will be deleted and **-emment** added to form the adverb:

violent (*violent*) → **violemment**
prudent (*prudent*) → **prudemment**

One exception, which follows the general rule:

lent (*slow*)	→ **lente**	→ **lentement**

3 If the adjective ends in **-ant** in the masculine singular, that ending will be deleted and **-amment** added to form the adverb:

méchant	**méchamment**
vaillant (*brave/valiant*)	**vaillamment**

There are no exceptions to this last rule.

Reading 2

Marc, eager to find out more information about Villeneuve, goes to the local **office du tourisme** where he picks up a brochure advertising the charms of the town and the surrounding area. Read and listen to the following extract from the brochure in preparation for the activities which follow.

🔊 CD2, TR 4, 03:51

Villeneuve est une charmante petite ville de 25.000 habitants, agréablement située au cœur de la campagne verdoyante du Lot-et-Garonne. Malgré son nom, c'est une très vieille ville qui était anciennement fortifiée. Aujourd'hui, la plupart des murs d'enceinte qui entouraient la ville ont disparu, mais on peut encore y voir quelques vestiges de remparts, ainsi que les deux tours qui contrôlaient l'entrée de la cité. Elle est traversée par le Lot, une charmante petite rivière qui la sépare en deux parties réunies par trois ponts dont l'un, le Pont Vieux, date du 13e siècle, à l'époque où les Anglais occupaient encore l'Aquitaine dont Villeneuve fait partie.

Villeneuve se trouve à 60 km au sud de Bergerac, ville de Dordogne maintenant internationalement renommée pour ses vins. Elle est à mi-chemin entre Bordeaux et Toulouse, deux métropoles régionales qui ont largement bénéficié de la décentralisation décidée il y a quelques années par le gouvernement.

Le climat de la région se caractérise par des étés chauds et secs et des hivers froids, mais sans excès. Les paysages vallonnés et verdoyants font que la région attire les vacanciers, les retraités et les étrangers qui rêvent de s'établir en France.

Autrefois, du fait de son climat et de la richesse des sols, la région avait une vocation essentiellement agricole. Elle était célèbre pour ses fruits et ses légumes, et en particulier pour les pruneaux d'Agen qui, comme vous le diront les gens du coin, se cultivent principalement autour de Villeneuve. Il y a quelques années, le célèbre slogan 'Villeneuve, la seule ville au monde où on travaille pour des prunes' a fait rire plus d'un visiteur car, comme chacun sait, 'travailler pour des prunes' veut dire travailler pour rien, sans être payé!

Malgré la concurrence des produits importés de Californie, les pruneaux d'Agen sont connus et très appréciés des connaisseurs. Une fois récoltés, en septembre, les fruits sont cuits dans des fours spéciaux où la température et l'humidité sont rigoureusement contrôlées.

Les activités liées à la production agricole ont sérieusement décliné en partie à cause de la concurrence étrangère, mais il existe encore actuellement des petits fermiers et des jardiniers qui deux fois par semaine, le mardi et le samedi, viennent au centre-ville, sur la place Lafayette, plus connue sous le nom de Place des Cornières, vendre aux Villeneuvois leurs produits fraîchement cueillis.

Venez nous rendre visite et juger par vous-mêmes que Villeneuve est vraiment une ville accueillante où il fait bon vivre. Un paradis en somme!

au cœur de *in the heart/the centre of (a place)*
verdoyante *(fem.) verdant/green and pleasant (landscape)*
malgré son nom *despite its name. Villeneuve literally means Newtown. There are dozens of places called Villeneuve, but only one on the river Lot!*
fortifié *walled. Also fortified in the general sense.*
le mur d'enceinte *surrounding wall built as fortification to protect a town. Note that* **être enceinte** *means to be pregnant.*
une métropole *a large town/city, but as we have seen,* **en métropole** *means in mainland France. The adjective* **métropolitain** *has been made into a noun which refers to the Paris underground (***le Métro** *for short).*
renommé *famous/renowned*
vallonné *hilly/undulating (for landscape)*
le vacancier *holidaymaker*
s'établir *Here: to settle (in a place). Also to establish oneself.*
les gens du coin *the people of the area (informal)*
le pruneau *dried plum (or prune). The French appear to be totally ignorant of the fruit's reputation as a laxative and turn them into a delicacy by preserving them in Armagnac, the local equivalent of Cognac.*
comme chacun sait *as everyone knows*
travailler pour des prunes *to work without any payment*
le jardinier *market gardener. Note that the verb* **jardiner** *normally refers to pottering around the garden.*

Comprehension 1

Having read and listened to the passage several times, answer the following questions:

1 What basic things do we learn about Villeneuve and its geographical situation? Give as much detail as possible, but do not give information out of sequence.
2 How can you situate Villeneuve in relation to the other three towns mentioned in the text?
3 What historical details do we learn about the town?
4 What types of people are attracted to the area and why?
5 State the economic changes which have taken place in the area.
6 The text omits to mention one feature about the climate of the region, which appeared in Unit 1. Which is it? Can you give a possible explanation for the 'omission'?
7 What do we learn in the passage about 'les pruneaux d'Agen'?

Activity 7

True or false? If a statement is false, give the correct answer with all the relevant details.

1 Villeneuve is situated in the Aquitaine region, formerly occupied by the English.
2 The river Lot separates the town in two.
3 One of the bridges linking the two sections was built in the 13th century.
4 Villeneuve is internationally renowned for its wines.
5 The town has greatly benefited from the government's decentralization policy.
6 Agricultural activity in the area is as buoyant as it ever was. Once a week, there is a market in the town centre.

Activity 8

Without looking at the text, in which agreements would give the game away, give the gender of the following nouns. In each case, justify your statement:

1 décentralisation
2 gouvernement

3 slogan
4 concurrence
5 septembre
6 température
7 humidité

Note that information about the gender of nouns appears in Appendices 3 and 5.

Activity 9

In the description of Villeneuve, there are a number of adverbs of manner.

1 List them in the order they appear in the text.
2 For each, give the masculine singular form of the adjective used to create them.

Activity 10

Using the information from the brochure extract and the 'cut and paste' technique, translate the following sentences into French:

1 Villeneuve is a charming little town.
2 The area is famous for its vegetables and fruit.
3 In earlier times, Villeneuve was a fortified town.
4 The people of the area will tell you that the town attracts a great many tourists.
5 Production is tightly controlled.
6 Fruits and vegetables from the region are greatly appreciated.
7 In the 13th century, the English still occupied Aquitaine.

5 Another way of expressing the passive

We have seen that, in order to form the passive, the normal structure of an active sentence has to be modified to indicate that someone is/has been/will be subjected to an action:

Le touriste a acheté la maison.	*The tourist (has) bought the house.*
La maison a été achetée par le touriste.	*The house was/has been bought by the tourist.*

If, however, the performer of the action is not stated or is represented by the indefinite pronoun **on** meaning *somebody* (not *we!*), it is often possible to use a reflexive form, as if the person or thing subjected to the action was doing it to him-/her-/itself.

On construit la maison. **La maison se construit.**	*The house is being built.*
La région est caractérisée par … **La région se caractérise par …**	*The area is characterized by …*
Les légumes sont cultivés dans la région. **Les légumes se cultivent dans la région.**	*Vegetables are grown in the area.*
Villeneuve est situé en Aquitaine. **Villeneuve se situe en Aquitaine.**	*Villeneuve is situated in the Aquitaine region.*

Activity 11

This next activity is part of your self-assessment. You should award yourself ten marks for each correct answer, total 50. This total should be added to your score in the self-assessment form.

Change the following passive sentences into active ones using the technique shown above:

1 Les œufs sont vendus à la douzaine.
2 Les pruneaux sont récoltés en septembre.
3 L'espagnol est appris facilement.
4 Ce signal sera vu de loin.
5 Ces produits peuvent être achetés au supermarché.

6 Linking words (conjunctions)

When we speak or write, we tend to link several utterances together to produce fuller, longer sentences, thereby avoiding the feeling of a clipped, 'chopped up' style. To this end, we use words or expressions called conjunctions, which fall into two categories:

1 *Co-ordinating conjunctions*. These are used to link clauses of equal status which could function as independent sentences separated by full stops (or pauses in speech).

Examples: et (*and*), ou (*or*), ni (*nor*), mais (*but*), or (*yet*), car (*for/ because*), donc (*therefore*) ...

Le photographe est arrivé. Il a pris une douzaine de photos. La mariée n'était pas contente. Elle en voulait beaucoup plus. *The photographer arrived. He took a dozen photographs. The bride was not pleased. She wanted many more.*

Le photographe est arrivé *et* il a pris une douzaine de photos, *mais* la mariée n'était pas contente *car* elle en voulait beaucoup plus. *The photographer arrived **and** took a dozen photographs **but** the bride was not pleased **because** she wanted many more.*

It is clear that the inclusion of et, mais and car in the second sentence gives a pleasanter, more fluid style to the utterance.

2 *Subordinating conjunctions*. These are used to add to the main idea when we wish to express supplementary information which is not vitally important, but which gives additional details and helps 'to complete the picture'. To distinguish between the two clauses, the phrases 'main clause' and 'subordinate clause' are often used in grammar:

a Vous dormiez | *quand* nous sommes rentrés.
main clause — subordinate clause
*You were asleep **when** we got back.*

b Nous n'avons pas dormi | *parce que* vous faisiez trop de bruit.
main clause — subordinate clause
*We did not sleep **because** you were making too much noise.*

c Nous n'avons pas fait de bruit | *pour que* vous puissiez dormir.
main clause — subordinate clause
*We did not make any noise **so that** you would be able to sleep.*

Note:
1 A subordinate clause cannot be used on its own.
2 As mentioned in the section about the subjunctive, it is important to find out whether the subordinating conjunction is expressing reality (in this case the verb will be in the indicative – examples **a** and **b**) or doubt, fear, etc. (in which case the subjunctive will be needed – example **c**).

Some common subordinating conjunctions are listed below. If they are followed by + S, it means that the subjunctive must be used in the subordinate clause:

afin que + S (*so that*); **alors que** (*as/whilst*); **après que** (*after*); **bien que** + S (*although*); **jusqu'à ce que** + S (*until*); **pour que** + S (*so that*); **selon que** (*depending on the fact that*); **vu que** (*in view of the fact that*)

We will do a reinforcement activity on conjunctions after the dialogue. For a fuller list, you should consult your grammar.

Activity 12
The sets of sentences numbered from 1 to 3 below are made up of short sentences separated by full stops. Using some of the co-ordinating conjunctions listed above, can you turn them into a single, logically organized and more 'fluid' sentence?

1 Nous avons pris nos parapluies. Il pleuvait. Nous sommes allés nous promener.
2 Elle voulait nous accompagner. Elle avait beaucoup de travail. Elle est restée à la maison.
3 Je pense. Je suis (*famous saying*).

Insight

Depuis can be used with a precise date to translate the English *since*: '**Il habite ici depuis 1990**' ('*He has been living here since 1990*'), or with a time span to translate *for*, for example: '**Il habite ici depuis dix ans**' ('*He has been living here for ten years*'). The present is used in both cases.

Dialogue

Marc has now decided to investigate the housing market in the Lot-et-Garonne area on behalf of his parents. The following conversation takes place between him and Pierre Castel, who has invited him to stay for a couple of days. If you have the recording, you should listen to it at least twice, in preparation for the activities.

CD2, TR 4, 08:37

Marc	Ce matin j'ai discuté avec Monsieur Belvert, le patron du studio …
Pierre	Je ne crois pas. Monsieur Belvert est mort depuis déjà plusieurs années. Je pense que vous voulez dire Jean-Claude Dumas! Il n'est pas le propriétaire du magasin, il n'est que le gérant. Belvert est le nom du studio! Mais, je croyais qu'il avait pris sa retraite!
Marc	Non, pas encore, dans trois mois, d'après ce qu'il m'a dit! Je lui ai expliqué que mes parents étaient à la recherche d'une maison secondaire.
Pierre	Ils veulent quitter l'Angleterre définitivement?
Marc	Non, pas pour l'instant. Mais ils approchent eux aussi de la retraite. Je crois que ma mère a un peu le mal du pays et dans quelques années …
Pierre	C'est normal. Les racines! Dans ce cas vous avez plusieurs solutions. La plus logique serait de consulter une agence immobilière afin que vous puissiez avoir une idée des prix.
Marc	C'est aussi ce que Monsieur … euh … Dumas m'a recommandé.
Pierre	Vous n'aurez que l'embarras du choix! Il y en a une bonne douzaine à Villeneuve, dont un rue de Paris, à 200 mètres d'ici. Vous pourrez donc regarder dans les vitrines, comparer les prix, et même, sans obligation d'achat, consulter les agents pour qu'ils vous donnent des informations. Après tout, ils sont là pour ça!
Marc	Monsieur Dumas m'a aussi parlé des *Échos* de Villeneuve.

Pierre Bonne idée! C'est un journal gratuit où on trouve pas mal de propriétés à vendre. Ça vous donnerait une idée des prix. Un conseil, tout de même: si vos parents décident d'acheter quelque chose, il faudra qu'ils se méfient, parce qu'il y a malheureusement des gens malhonnêtes, ici comme partout. Je connais un couple d'Anglais qui, l'an dernier, ont acheté sur un coup de cœur: ils ont craqué pour une jolie petite villa sur la colline, au sud de la ville. La vue était superbe, le prix semblait abordable. En définitive, la remise en état de la maison leur a coûté les yeux de la tête et cette année ils ont décidé de la revendre et de repartir chez eux. Mais, vu que votre mère est française, je suis sûr qu'elle sera au courant de tous ces pièges.

Marc Probablement, mais elle a un peu perdu pied. Il y a longtemps qu'elle a quitté la France.

Pierre Bon, attendez une minute. Je crois qu'il me reste encore quelques copies des *Échos*. Je vais vous en chercher une de sorte que vous puissiez y jeter un coup d'œil.

Marc Merci beaucoup, Pierre!

QUICK VOCAB

le/la propriétaire *the owner. The person who deals with the day-to-day running of a business without being the owner is* **le gérant/la gérante.**

l'Angleterre *Quite often, the French use this term to mean Britain or the UK. The same vagueness applies (no offence intended) to the use of* **les Anglais***!*

définitivement *for good (and all). Beware of this word: it does not mean definitely, which is normally translated by* **sans aucun doute.**

avoir le mal du pays *to be homesick*

une agence immobilière *an estate agent's (run by* **un agent immobilier***)*

n'avoir que l'embarras du choix *to be spoilt for choice (lit. to have only the embarrassment of choice)*

la vitrine *shop window.* **Le lèche-vitrine** *(lit. shop-window licking) means window shopping.*

ils sont là pour ça *that's what they are here for. Remember that in conversation,* **là** *(there) is often used in preference to* **ici** *(here).*

pas mal de … *quite a few/a lot of …*

sur un coup de cœur *on an impulse (about something which really takes your fancy)*
craquer *to be unable to resist or say 'no' (lit. to crack)*
en définitive *in the final analysis/at the end of the day*
remettre en état *to put something back in working order*
coûter les yeux de la tête *to cost an arm and a leg*
être au courant *to (be in the) know. Similar to* **être branché** (*or* **chébran**), *seen in Unit 5.*
un piège *a trap. In familiar language* **se faire piéger** *usually means to be caught in a swindle or scam.*

Insight

In the two words **donc** (*therefore*) and **dont** (*of which/of whom*), the final letter is normally silent. As a result, both sound the same, but the context will help you distinguish between them. Compare: **'Je pense, donc je suis'** ('*I think therefore I am*') and **la maison dont j'ai parlé** (*the house of which I talked*).

Language learning tip 5

An and **année:** Both words can be used to translate *year*, but there are a couple of things to be aware of:

1 Either **an** or **année** can be used to refer to last year or next year without any overtone:

L'*an* dernier/L'*année* dernière, il a passé son 'bac'.	*Last year he sat his baccalaureate.*

2 For *this (current) year, only* **cette année** must be used.

***Cette année* il va à l'université.**	*This year he is going to university.*

3 An is used to express an objective number of years without any overtone:

Ils ont passé trois *ans* en Afrique.	*They spent three years (3 x 365 days) in Africa.*

4 Année gives extra subjective information about the period concerned:

Ils ont passé trois *années* en Afrique.	*They spent three years (either delightful or dreadful) in Africa.*

5 Années is also used after **quelques, plusieurs, un certain nombre d'...** expressing an unspecified number:

Ils se sont installés ici il y a quelques *années*.	*They settled here a few years ago.*

Comprehension 2

Having read the passage a few times, answer the questions which follow:

1 Why does Marc's mother wish to buy a house in France?
2 What does Pierre first suggest to Marc about finding houses for sale?
3 In what way could *Les Échos* de Villeneuve help Marc in his search?
4 What piece of advice does Pierre volunteer as regards buying property?
5 What were the reasons why the 'English couple' mentioned by Pierre fell in love with the villa?
6 What was the result of their hasty decision and what are they doing this year?
7 How does Marc counter Pierre's confident statement about his mother?

Activity 13

In the text you will find examples of the use of subordinating conjunctions. Can you spot them and say whether they require the subjunctive or the indicative?

Insight

Tout (adjective) means *all*, *the whole of* or *every*: **tout le temps** (*all the time*), **toute la journée** (*all day*), **tous les jours** (*every day*). As an indefinite pronoun, it means *everything*: **'Tout est prêt'** (*'Everything is ready'*) and the final **t** is sounded. In the plural, it means *all* (*of them*): **'Ils sont tous là'** (*'They are all here'*), and the final **s** is sounded.

7 Using the pronouns *en* and *y*

The pronouns en and y replace a noun phrase which has already been mentioned, and are used as follows:

1 en means *from*, or (*out*) *of*, and is used to replace a noun phrase:

Tu viens de l'hypermarché?	*Are you coming from the hypermarket?*
Oui, j'en viens.	*Yes, I am (coming from it/there).*
Attention! Un train peut en cacher un autre!	*Be careful! One train can hide another one (of it/them, i.e. another train)! (Sign on level crossings in France)*

2 y means *there*, indicating either position or movement towards:

Ils sont allés en France? Oui, ils y sont allés.	*Have they gone/did they go to France? Yes they did (go there).*
Les enfants vont au cinéma?	*Are the children going to the cinema?*
Non, ils n'y vont pas!	*No they are not (going there)!*

Note: In the future, when the verb **aller** is used, y is omitted because of the unpleasant sound it would make. So, we should not say ***nous y irons**, but simply **nous irons.**

Activity 14

In the sentences below, the noun phrase is repeated. This does not make for good style! Try improving matters by using **en** and **y** as appropriate.

1 Tu viens de Paris? Oui, je viens de Paris.
2 Vous êtes revenues de Marseille? Nous ne sommes pas allées à Marseille!
3 Vous avez parlé de cette affaire? Oui, nous avons parlé de cette affaire.
4 Vous habitez dans la région? Oui, nous habitons dans la région.
5 Tu viens d'Espagne? Oui, je viens d'Espagne et je retourne en Espagne!

Activity 15

Look at the dialogue again and try to find examples of **en** and **y**. Make a note of the full sentences in which they appear.

Activity 16

Looking at *Les Échos*, the local paper, Marc has found four properties which he feels may be of interest to his parents. He cannot decide which one – if any – he should like to go and have a close look at. Imagine that, like his father, you are a healthy DIY enthusiast about to retire. Bearing in mind the prices quoted, and the description of each property, rank them in descending order of preference, giving sound reasons for your choice.

1

À vendre: Villeneuve, villa de construction récente en excellent état comprenant 4 pièces principales, séjour, salon, salle de bains et salle d'eau, cuisine équipée, 3 chambres. Garage, chauffage central gaz de ville, jardin clos et arboré de 500 m^2.

Prix: 142.500,00 €.

2 À vendre: Villeneuve, proche du centre, villa pierre sur sous-sol, excellent état, 6 pièces principales, 4 chambres, séjour, cuisine aménagée, salle de jeux, buanderie, garage, chauffage central gaz de ville. Jardin clos 750 m^2.

Prix: 70.000 €.

3 À 5 km de Villeneuve, maison de campagne à rénover sur 5.000 m^2 de terrain. Surface habitable 105 m^2; séjour, salon, 4 chambres. Possibilités d'aménagement. Garage. Site calme et agréable avec superbe point de vue sur la vallée du Lot.

Prix: 63.000,00 €.

4 Dans un petit village à 5 minutes de Villeneuve, grande maison avec superbe point de vue sur le Lot. Surface habitable 150m^2. Jardin clos et arboré de 130 m^2 environ.

Prix: 82.000,00 €.

Il faut manger pour vivre et non pas vivre pour manger (a saying which does not go down too well in the South-West!). *One must eat (in order) to live and not live (in order) to eat!*

Il faut cultiver son jardin! *One must cultivate one's garden!* (This is a line which appeared at the end of **Candide,** a satirical novel written in 1759 by the French author Voltaire. The adventures of the hero are recounted in the 'biographical mode', using the simple past. It is witty, amusing and very easy to read.) One of the interpretations of the above quotation is: 'One should not seek faraway adventures, but try to find happiness and fulfilment close to home.'

Insight

To indicate where someone comes from or where they are going, use the pronouns **en** and **y: Ils sont devant l'hypermarché. – Ils en viennent? – Non, ils y vont!** – *They are in front of the hypermarket. – Are they coming from it? – No, they are going (to it)!.*

Note, however, that y can also mean *about it*: **j'y ai pensé** (*I've thought about it*).

TEST YOURSELF

1. What is the subjunctive used for?
2. Do the endings of the present subjunctive vary according to the group which the verb belongs to?
3. Is the pronoun **que** introducing a subordinate clause a reliable marker for the subjunctive? Explain.
4. The subjunctive is a fairly ponderous mood. How can it often be avoided?
5. What are the black pearls of Périgord and how are they gathered?
6. Which are the two categories of adjectives which do not form their adverbs of manner in the usual way (feminine singular form + **-ment**)?
7. What are the three geographical clues which will enable you to locate Villeneuve-sur-Lot on a map of France?
8. How can one tell that, in the Middle Ages, Villeneuve was a **bastide** (i.e. *a walled town*)?
9. Has Villeneuve ever been an important industrial centre?
10. What, in gastronomic terms, is Villeneuve famous for?

10

Liberté, égalité, solidarité

In this unit you will learn

- ***How to form the past definite to say that something happened in the past***
- ***What happens when two verbs follow each other***
- ***How to say 'nobody', 'no one', 'nothing', 'none' in French***
- ***How to use the present participle to lighten your style***
- ***How to refine your use of the subjunctive***
- ***How to say 'having done', 'having been', etc.***
- ***More on giving orders***

1 How to say that something happened (once) in the past

We have already seen that, in informal French, one of the roles of the perfect is to indicate that an action happened in the past, but without insisting on its duration or repetition.

1 L'an dernier ils *sont allés* en Italie.	*Last year they went to Italy* (statement of fact, without stress on duration or repetition).
2 Chaque année ils *allaient* en Italie.	*They used to go to Italy every year* (stress on repetition).

It is clear that, in Example 1, the action may have lasted quite a while, but the role of the perfect is only to state that it took place at a certain point in the past. Expressing duration or repetition is the job of the imperfect (Example 2).

There is a sophisticated equivalent of the perfect, called the past definite, which fulfils the same role as the one mentioned above, but which is not normally seen or heard, except in formal language. However, since you are likely to find it in quality literature and journalism, you should be able to recognize it, even if you are not called upon to use it.

If we replace the perfect by the past definite, Example 1 above

L'an dernier ils *sont allés* en Italie. becomes: **L'an dernier ils *allèrent* en Italie.**	*Last year they went to Italy.*

Here is another example:

Ce jour-là, ils *ont vu* la pièce et ils *ont été* enchantés (perfect). **Ce jour-là, ils *virent* la pièce et ils *furent* enchantés** (past definite).	*That day, they saw the play and they were delighted/ enchanted.*

Before we turn to the formation of this simple (one-word) tense, it may be helpful to visualize it along the time-axis.

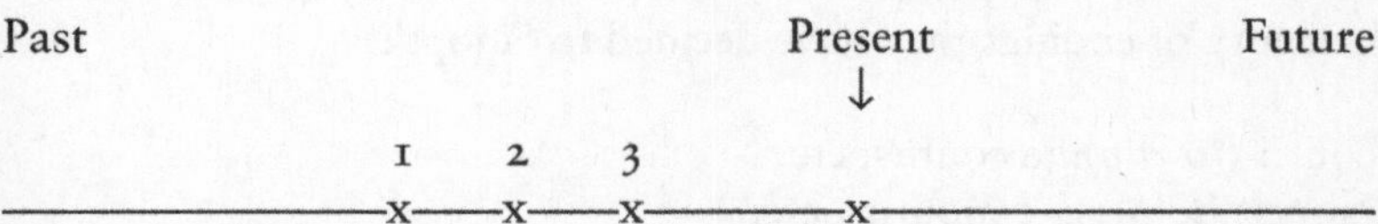

The past actions indicated by 1, 2 and 3 above are seen as distinct and separate. It is interesting to note that each action may have lasted some time, but that is unimportant: the emphasis is on the fact that they happened and not on their duration or repetition.

The past definite is therefore ideal for recounting discrete past events, and for writing formal biographies:

Un jour, les parents de Pierre *quittèrent* Charleville et *allèrent* habiter à Villeneuve où ils *restèrent* jusqu'à la retraite.	*One day, Pierre's parents left Charleville and went to live in Villeneuve where they remained until their retirement.*

2 How to form the past definite

As is the case with simple tenses, it is made up of a stem to which endings are added. These depend on the group (1st, 2nd or 3rd), which the verb belongs to.

	1st group (e.g. regarder)[1]	*2nd group (e.g. finir)*[1]	*3rd group (-ir endings)*[2]	*3rd group (-re endings)*[1]	*3rd group (-oir endings)*[3]
je	-ai	-is	-is	-is	-us
tu (fam.)	-as	-is	-is	-is	-us
il/elle/on	-a	-it	-it	-it	-ut
nous	-âmes	-îmes	-îmes	-îmes	-ûmes
vous	-âtes	-îtes	-îtes	-îtes	-ûtes
ils/elles	-èrent	-irent	-irent	-irent	-urent

[1]No exceptions; [2]few exceptions; [3]some exceptions.

It is helpful to note that 'irregular' verbs (i.e. those which do not follow the normal pattern for their group) will stay faithful to the category of endings they have decided to 'adopt':

courir (*to run*): je courus, etc.
mourir (*to die*): je mourus, etc.
s'asseoir (*to sit down*): je m'assis, etc.

Insight

In standard spoken French, the past definite is considered too elevated for everyday use and is replaced by the perfect: **je partis** (*I went/left*) becomes **je suis parti**; **elle écouta** (*she listened*) is replaced by: **elle a écouté**, etc.

2.1 How to find the stem for the formation of the past definite

There are a couple of methods used for this purpose. Sadly, none of them is foolproof.

The simplest way is to remove the infinitive marker and to add the appropriate ending. This works in all cases for 1st and 2nd group verbs, and in the vast majority of cases for 3rd group verbs:

donner (*to give,* 1st group) → donn-
investir (*to invest,* 2nd group) → invest-
vendre (*to sell,* 3rd group) → vend-
sortir (*to go out,* 3rd group) → sort-
vouloir (*to want,* 3rd group) → voul-

There are, however, several 3rd group verbs which do not follow this pattern. The most common ones are listed below:

Verb	*Meaning*	*Stem/root*
avoir	*to have*	e- (j'eus, tu eus …)
boire	*to drink*	b- (je bus, tu bus …)
connaître	*to know*	conn- (je connus, tu connus …)
craindre	*to fear*	craign- (je craignis, tu craignis …)
croire	*to believe*	cr- (je crus, tu crus …)
croître	*to grow* (sophisticated)	cr- (je crûs, tu crûs …)
devenir	*to become*	dev- (je devins, tu devins …)
devoir	*to have to*	d- (je dus, tu dus …)
être	*to be*	f- (je fus, tu fus …)
faire	*to do/make*	f- (je fis, tu fis …)
joindre	*to join*	joign- (je joignis, tu joignis …)
naître	*to be born*	naqu- (je naquis, tu naquis …)
peindre	*to paint*	peign- (je peignis, tu peignis …)
pouvoir	*to be able to*	p- (je pus, tu pus …)
prendre	*to take*	pr- (je pris, tu pris …)
réduire	*to reduce*	réduis- (je réduisis, tu réduisis …)
résoudre	*to resolve/solve*	résol- (je résolus, tu résolus …)
savoir	*to know*	s- (je sus, tu sus …)
voir	*to see*	v- (je vis, tu vis …)

Notes:

1 All verbs ending in **-aindre, -eindre** and **-oindre** will follow the same patterns for the formation of their stem.
2 **Tenir** and its compounds (**retenir, soutenir maintenir …**) follow the same pattern: **je tins, tu tins, il/elle/on tint, nous tînmes, vous tîntes, ils/elles tinrent.**
3 Verbs with infinitives ending in **-cer** and **-ger** require small additional adjustments:

-cer endings. Whenever the elimination of the ending leads to the presence of **a, o,** or **u** immediately after the **c,** this letter must be changed to **ç**. Failure to do so would cause it to be pronounced as the *c* in *cap* and not as the *c* in *city*:

lancer *(to throw/launch)* → **je lançai**
recevoir *(to receive)* → **je reçus**

Note that the value of **c** (as pronounced in *city*) is not affected if **e** (or **i**) follows e.g. **nous recevons.**

-ger endings. Whenever the elimination of the ending leads to the presence of **a, o,** or **u** immediately after the **g,** an **e** must be inserted after that letter to preserve the sound quality of the second *g* in *garage*. Failure to do so would cause **g** to be pronounced as the first *g* in *garage*:

charger *(to load/charge)* → **je chargeai**
plonger *(to plunge/dive)* → **je plongeai**

Note that the value of **g** (as heard for the second *g* of *garage*) is not affected if **e** (or **i**) follows: e.g. **nous chargions, vous plongiez.** This holds good throughout the conjugation of verbs in **-cer** and **-ger.**

For a more exhaustive study of the past definite, you should refer to your dedicated grammar.

Activity 1

Below is a list of infinitives from the three groups. For each, indicate the first person singular of the past definite. This will be sufficient to determine which series of endings is needed for the other persons.

1 réduire
2 rougir
3 déclarer
4 suivre
5 émigrer
6 se réfugier (*beware, this is a reflexive!)*
7 vendre
8 couvrir

Activity 2

This activity is part of your self-assessment. There are 20 verbs in the following biography. For each completely correct answer, award yourself five marks. Any error on a given verb will lead to no mark being awarded for it. Your score should be added to your current total on the record sheet at the end of the book.

Below is the biography of Pierre Castel, whom we have met several times in previous units. In it, the verbs appear in the infinitive. Using your knowledge and the information given above, replace them by the appropriate form of the past definite.

Pierre Castel (naître) à Villeneuve-sur-Lot en 1972. Ses parents, originaires du nord de la France, (devoir) quitter la région de Charleville peu avant sa naissance, quand le père (être) muté dans le sud-ouest. Les Castel (aller) s'installer d'abord dans un modeste appartement près du centre-ville. À la suite d'une promotion bien méritée, le père (acheter) une charmante villa au bord de la rivière. Pierre (faire) ses études primaires et secondaires à Villeneuve, puis il (décider) d'aller à l'Université de Bordeaux, où il (effectuer) des études littéraires et (préparer) une Licence de Lettres Modernes. À la fin de ses études supérieures, il (devoir) faire dix-huit mois de service national. Son service militaire terminé, il (acheter) une petite librairie. Il (être) obligé d'emprunter une assez forte somme, mais ses parents l'(aider) considérablement. Son affaire (prospérer), et lorsque les locaux (devenir) trop petits, il (résoudre) de faire l'acquisition, place Lafayette, d'un magasin beaucoup plus grand. Il (savoir) rendre sa librairie accueillante et, grâce à sa formation littéraire, il (pouvoir) donner des conseils à ses clients. Cela lui (valoir) une excellente réputation qu'il (entretenir).

As was the case for all able-bodied young Frenchmen between the ages of 18 and 21 (except for students successfully following a course in higher education, who were allowed a **sursis** or *postponement*), Pierre Castel had to do his national service. This long-established custom, in which conscripts spent between two years (in the fifties and sixties) and one year (from 2000) **sous les drapeaux** (lit. *under the flags*), could only be avoided if the future conscript had very severe (and medically attested) physical or mental problems. The **service militaire** or **service national** was abolished in 2002. Instituted soon after the French Revolution, it had lasted over two centuries.

The custom for soon-to-be released conscripts was to make (or purchase) *a skittle* **une quille** as a symbol of the end of their 'ordeal'.

So, if you have seen the film **Jean de Florette**, you will now know why the young 'Galinette' was wearing a skittle round his neck in the opening scene!

Activity 3

Armed with all the information given about the past definite, you should now try to write your own (or someone else's) biography. There will obviously be no model answer for this activity, but to help you, we suggest the following headings:

1 Date and place of birth;
2 Start and end dates of primary, secondary and, if appropriate, further or higher education;

3 Employment history with dates (if appropriate);
4 Current and former addresses with dates (if appropriate);
5 Changes in civil or job status (if appropriate).

You may find the following expressions helpful for the purpose of 'your' biography:

1 Fréquenter une école;
2 Commencer *ou* terminer ses études;
3 Entrer dans le monde du travail;
4 Le premier emploi;
5 Rencontrer un/une partenaire;
6 Déménager;
7 Se marier;
8 Avoir un (des) enfant(s).

3 What happens when two verbs follow each other?

Without looking at the information below, can you formulate a simple rule which will take care of the problem?

If you need some help, the rule is as follows:

When two verbs follow each other, the second one is in the *infinitive*, except if the first one is avoir or être, in which case the second verb is a past participle (since these are the auxiliaries needed to form compound tenses).

Elle désire *rester* ici.	*She wishes to stay here.*
Nous voudrions *réserver* une chambre.	*We would like to reserve a room.*
Il aime *être* tranquille.	*He likes to be/being quiet.*
Pierre Castel a *acheté* le magasin.	*Pierre Castel (has) bought the shop.*
Il était *descendu*.	*He had gone down(stairs).*

Activity 4

In Pierre Castel's biography, you will have noticed:

a A few constructions with two infinitives immediately following each other;
b A couple of expressions in which the second infinitive is introduced by a preposition;
c Two constructions in which the first of the two verbs is **être**.

Make a list of those constructions under each of the headings above.

Reading 1

The text below is an extract from the **Déclaration des Droits de l'Homme et du Citoyen** (*The Declaration of the Rights of Men and Citizens*), which was written in August 1789. It is made up of a 'preamble' and 17 'articles', of which only ten have been included. If you wish, you can view the whole document on the web. Simply go to http://fr.yahoo.com and then type **Déclaration des Droits de l'Homme et du Citoyen** in to the 'Recherche' box.

Read and listen to the passage several times before answering the questions that relate to it.

CD2, TR 5, 01:41

Préambule

Les représentants du peuple français, constitués en Assemblée nationale, considérant que l'ignorance, l'oubli ou le mépris des droits de l'homme sont les seules causes des malheurs publics et de la corruption des gouvernements, ont résolu d'exposer, dans une déclaration solennelle, les droits naturels, inaliénables et sacrés de l'homme, afin que cette déclaration, constamment présente à tous les membres du corps social, leur rappelle sans cesse leurs droits et leurs devoirs; afin que les actes du pouvoir législatif et ceux du pouvoir exécutif, pouvant être à chaque instant comparés avec le but de toute institution politique, en soient plus respectés; afin que les réclamations des citoyens, fondées désormais sur des principes simples et incontestables, tournent toujours au maintien de la Constitution et au bonheur de tous.

En conséquence, l'Assemblée nationale reconnaît et déclare, en présence et sous les auspices de l'Être Suprême, les droits suivants de l'homme et du citoyen.

Article premier
Les hommes naissent et demeurent libres et égaux en droits. Les distinctions sociales ne peuvent être fondées que sur l'utilité commune.

Article 2
Le but de toute association politique est la conservation des droits naturels et imprescriptibles de l'homme. Ces droits sont la liberté, la propriété, la sûreté et la résistance à l'oppression.

Article 4
La liberté consiste à pouvoir faire tout ce qui ne nuit pas à autrui: ainsi, l'exercice des droits naturels de chaque homme n'a de bornes que celles qui assurent aux autres membres de la société la jouissance de ces mêmes droits. Ces bornes ne peuvent être déterminées que par la loi.

Article 5
La loi n'a le droit de défendre que les actions nuisibles à la société. Tout ce qui n'est pas défendu par la loi ne peut être empêché, et nul ne peut être contraint à faire ce qu'elle n'ordonne pas.

Article 7
Nul homme ne peut être accusé, arrêté ou détenu que dans les cas déterminés par la loi et selon les formes qu'elle a prescrites. Ceux qui sollicitent, expédient, exécutent ou font exécuter des ordres arbitraires doivent être punis; mais tout citoyen appelé ou saisi en vertu de la loi doit obéir à l'instant; il se rend coupable par la résistance.

Article 8
La loi ne doit établir que des peines strictement et évidemment nécessaires, et nul ne peut être puni qu'en vertu d'une loi établie et promulguée antérieurement au délit, et légalement appliquée.

Article 9
Tout homme étant présumé innocent jusqu'à ce qu'il ait été déclaré coupable, s'il est jugé indispensable de l'arrêter, toute rigueur qui ne serait pas nécessaire pour s'assurer de sa personne doit être sévèrement réprimée par la loi.

Article 10
Nul ne doit être inquiété pour ses opinions, même religieuses, pourvu que leur manifestation ne trouble pas l'ordre public établi par la loi.

Article 11
La libre communication des pensées et des opinions est un des droits les plus précieux de l'homme; tout citoyen peut donc parler, écrire, imprimer librement, sauf à répondre de l'abus de cette liberté dans les cas déterminés par la loi.

Article 17
La propriété étant un droit inviolable et sacré, nul ne peut en être privé, si ce n'est lorsque la nécessité publique, légalement constatée, l'exige évidemment, et sous la condition d'une juste et préalable indemnité.

QUICK VOCAB

l'Assemblée nationale *One of the two Chambers in the French legislative system. The other is called* **le Sénat.**
sans cesse *continually/ceaselessly*
les droits et les devoirs *the rights and duties.* **Les devoirs** *can also mean homework.*
tout *any (whatsoever). It can also mean every(thing).*
les membres du corps social *the members of society (lit. ... of the social body)*
les auspices *the auspices*
l'Être Suprême *the Supreme Being (i.e. God)*
fondé *based.* **La fondation** *means foundation.*

nuire (à ...) *to be detrimental (to ...)*
autrui *other people. This word belongs to elevated style and occurs in such expressions as* **le bien d'autrui** *(the property of others). It is only used in the singular.*
une borne *a limit or boundary. It can also be used to mean a kilometre marker/milestone.* **Sans bornes** *means boundless.*
la jouissance *the enjoyment (the verb is* **jouir***)*
défendu *forbidden. It can also mean defended.*
nul (+ ne) *nobody/no one*
préalable *(adj.) prior/previous. Often found in the expression* **au préalable** *(beforehand).*
exiger *to demand*

As you will know, the motto of the French Republic is **Liberté, Égalité, Fraternité**, which, of course, means *Liberty*, *Equality*, *Fraternity*. This motto appeared during the French Revolution, as did the **Déclaration des Droits de l'Homme et du Citoyen** (note that the masculine singular is intended to represent all human beings).

The egalitarian ideas and statements enshrined in this document were adopted by many budding democracies in the 19th century and served as a model for the writing of their Constitutions. Unfortunately, in France as elsewhere, the sentiments expressed in those documents have sometimes been forgotten!

Insight

To illustrate the importance of looking at the ending of nouns to work out their gender, what better example than the motto of the French Republic: '**Liberté, Égalité, Fraternité**'? In French, all abstract nouns ending in -té are feminine!

Comprehension 1

Read the preamble again and answer the following questions in English:

1 Who formulated the **Déclaration**?
2 What is the main purpose of the document?

3 What, according to the text, are the sole causes of public misfortune and government corruption?
4 What will be the ultimate results of the application of the principles laid out in the **Déclaration**?

Activity 5

Each of the following statements A–G is taken from one of the articles of the **Déclaration.** Can you match the letter with the number of the article to which it corresponds? Please note that:

1 In a few cases, minor adjustments have been made to the English wording.
2 The presentation of the statements is not sequential.
3 Since the document was written long before the advent of political correctness, any reference to men should be read as applying to both sexes.

A No one should be harassed for his opinions so long as the expression of these opinions does not disrupt public order.
B The law does not have the right to forbid anything that is not legally prohibited.
C Within the framework of the law, the natural rights of any man are only limited by those of others.
D All men are born and remain free and equal.
E Any citizen who resists lawful arrest or fails to comply immediately with a lawful request made by the forces of law and order is by that very fact guilty.
F Any man must be presumed innocent until found guilty.
G No man can be accused, arrested or detained except in cases determined by the law and according to the prescribed legal procedures.

Activity 6

In the **Déclaration des Droits** (including the preamble), there are several adverbs of manner.

1 Find them and give their meaning;
2 Give the masculine singular form of the adjective from which they are derived.

4 How to say 'nobody', 'no one', 'none', 'nothing'

In English, when we use such expressions as *no one*, *nobody*, *none*, *nothing*, no other marker is needed to convey the negative meaning:

1 *Nobody has written.*
2 *Nothing has happened.*
3 *None (of them) has replied.*
4 *No one is a prophet in his/her own country* (proverb).

In standard French, however, the negative particle **ne** (or **n'**) must be used as well:

1 Personne *n'*a écrit.
2 Rien *n'*est arrivé.
3 Aucun *n'*a répondu.
4 Nul *n'*est prophète en son pays.

Note that **pas**, which normally forms the second part of the negation, must not be used, since the words **personne, nul, rien, aucun**, have taken its place.

Insight

In standard French, the negative particle **ne**, used without **pas** after **rien** (*nothing*) and **personne** (*nobody*), e.g. **'Rien n'est arrivé'** ('*Nothing has happened*'), **'Personne n'est venu'** ('*Nobody came*'), is often omitted in familiar language. This does not apply with the pronouns **nul** (*no one*) and **aucun** (*none*), which are considered too highbrow!

Activity 7

Translate the following sentences, using the support of the articles of the **Déclaration**. Please note that, in a few cases, some minor grammatical or vocabulary adjustments may need to be made.

1 No one can be compelled to do what is not forbidden.
2 Social distinctions can only be based upon common usefulness.
3 No one can be forced to do what the law does not demand.

4 All citizens can speak and write freely.
5 Any citizen makes himself guilty by resisting.
6 Any unnecessary harshness must be severely punished.
7 The natural rights of man are the rights to freedom, safety and resistance to oppression.
8 Those limits can only be determined by law.

Activity 8
In the **Déclaration**, there are a few verbs in the subjunctive. Make a list of them and, for each, say whether they are in the present or the perfect.

5 Using the present participle to lighten your style

The present participle can be used in several distinct ways.

a On its own, it is often used to replace whole subordinate clauses beginning with qui:

Nous avons vu la vieille femme qui *lisait* le journal.	*We saw the old woman who was reading the paper.*
Nous avons vu la vieille femme *lisant* le journal.	*We saw the old woman reading the paper.*

In this role, as can be seen from the above example, the present participle is invariable and should be distinguished from the corresponding adjective which agrees with the noun phrase as appropriate:

Lisez les informations suivantes.	*Read the following information.*

b Preceded by en (it is then called a gerund), it can convey the idea of *by* (*dint of*), *through* or *whilst* + *-ing*.

C'est en *forgeant* qu'on devient forgeron (proverb).	*Practice makes perfect (lit. it is through forging that one becomes a blacksmith).*
***En travaillant* dur, vous deviendrez riche.**	*By working hard, you will become rich.*

c It is used to indicate that the action it represents occurs at the same time as another action.

Ils sont partis *en chantant*.	*They went away (while) singing.*

Note the difference between:

Je l'ai vu *parlant* à un ami.	*I saw him talking to a friend (when he was …)*
Je l'ai vu *en parlant* à un ami.	*I saw him while (I was) talking to a friend.*

Sometimes, the present participle can also be used to replace *as/since/given that*:

***Étant* votre invité(e), je ferai ce que vous demandez.**	*As (or since) I am your guest, I will do what you ask.*

Activity 9

There are several present participles in the **Déclaration**. List each of them and give the infinitive of the verb they come from. There is one example of the present participle used as an adjective. Note it down, if you can find it.

6 Refine your use of the subjunctive

We have already mentioned in Unit 1 the role of the subjunctive as a mood serving to express possibility, fear, doubt, desire, etc. We have also examined (in Unit 9) the formation of its two main tenses, the present and the perfect.

There are a number of expressions which, when used, automatically require the subjunctive. Many of these use the impersonal construction: il est + adjective + **que** + verb (*it is … that …*). Some of them are listed below:

Il est peu probable que (*it is unlikely that*); **il n'est pas certain que** (*it is not certain that*); **il est douteux que** (*it is doubtful that*); **il faut que** *or* **il est nécessaire que** (*it is necessary that*); **il est essentiel que** (*it is essential that*); **il est important que** (*it is important that*); **il est**

urgent que (*it is urgent that*); il est souhaitable que (*it is desirable that*); il est recommandé que (*it is recommended that*); il est impératif que (*it is imperative that*); il est vital que (*it is vital that*).

As you can see from the above expressions, the ideas of possibility, desirability, urgency, etc. are present. This clearly places the action of the verbs which follows them outside the domain of the indicative mood (which deals with reality), and into the domain of the subjunctive (which deals with hypothesis):

Ils feront leur travail.	*They will do their work (it's a fact!).*
Il est nécessaire qu'ils *fassent* leur travail.	*It is necessary that they should do their work (but it may not happen!).*

The subjunctive must also be used when the following expressions (or similar ones) are present:

à condition que (*provided that*); **afin que** (*in order that*); **à moins que** (*unless*); **avant que** (*before* + verb phrase); **de peur que/de crainte que** (*for fear that*); **de sorte que** (*so that/in order that)*; **en attendant que** *or* **jusqu'à ce que** (*until* + verb phrase); **pour que** (*so that* + verb phrase); **quoique** (*although*); **sans que** (*without* + verb phrase).

Nous resterons ici en attendant qu'il *finisse* la réparation.	*We shall wait here until he finishes the repairs.*
Il vous pardonne à condition que vous vous *excusiez!*	*He forgives you provided you apologize! (note that this verb is reflexive).*
Je t'ai appelée pour que tu *viennes* dîner avec nous.	*I (have) called you so that you may come and have dinner with us.*

It should, however, be noted that because the subjunctive is considered as stylistically heavy, it is often replaced in conversation by simpler forms, with little or no loss of meaning.

Il faut que nous *partions.*	*We must go.*
Il (nous) faut *partir.* (infinitive used as replacement with pronoun to clarify)	

Nous attendrons que vous *arriviez.* **Nous attendrons votre *arrivée.*** (noun used as replacement)	*We will wait until you arrive.*

Finally, there are a few idiomatic phrases in which the subjunctive verb is used virtually on its own, without any of the verbs or expressions usually associated with it.

Dieu *soit* loué!	*Thank God/May God be praised!*
***Périsse* le tyran!**	*May the tyrant perish!*

Although the subjunctive is not as popular as it deserves to be, it may be a good idea for you to make a note of other expressions leading to its use.

Insight

We often replace the subjunctive either with an infinitive or an imperative: '**Il faut téléphoner**' or '**Téléphonons**', instead of '**Il faut que nous téléphonions**' ('*We must telephone*'); or with a noun: '**Nous attendons votre arrivée**' instead of '**Nous attendons que vous arriviez**' ('*We are awaiting your arrival*').

Reading 2

Presidential address

The following represents a New Year address to the nation from the President of the French Republic. Read it several times in preparation for the language activities which follow.

Françaises, Français

Lorsque j'ai été élu par vous, j'ai fait un certain nombre de promesses que je tiens à honorer. Deux d'entre elles avaient trait à la santé et à la sécurité, et en particulier à la lutte contre le cancer et l'insécurité routière. J'ai tenu ces promesses et, bien qu'il y ait encore beaucoup à faire dans ces deux domaines, les résultats sont déjà visibles.

Une autre de mes promesses concernait la lutte contre la pauvreté et l'exclusion. Lorsque nos ancêtres écrivirent la *Déclaration des Droits de l'Homme et du Citoyen*, ils voulurent tourner une page historique, abandonner pour toujours les inégalités et les privilèges caractérisant l'Ancien Régime. En un mot, ils s'efforcèrent de créer une société basée sur la liberté, l'égalité et la fraternité. Beaucoup de pays suivirent leur exemple et décidèrent d'adopter ces mêmes principes démocratiques. Nous pouvons, je crois, en être fiers. Cependant, quoique la liberté soit, chez nous, un fait acquis, il n'en est malheureusement pas de même pour l'égalité. Les derniers chiffres de l'INSEE indiquent clairement qu'un trop grand nombre de nos concitoyens vivent encore au-dessous du seuil de pauvreté. Il y a en France 100.000 sans-abri. J'ai demandé à mon gouvernement qu'il prenne les mesures nécessaires pour que tous les citoyens puissent jouir des mêmes droits. Pour ce faire, nous avons amélioré le quotidien de milliers de nos compatriotes. Mon gouvernement a également créé des milliers d'emplois pour les jeunes en situation de précarité, et relevé le SMIC et le RMI. Nous avons, en outre, revalorisé la rémunération des chômeurs en cours de formation. Des crédits spéciaux ont aussi été débloqués pour augmenter l'accès aux soins pour les plus démunis.

Je suis conscient du fait que le chômage des jeunes et la montée de la criminalité ne sont pas totalement étrangers l'un à l'autre. C'est pourquoi, comme je l'avais promis, j'ai demandé à mon gouvernement de débloquer les crédits pour que puissent être développés des centres d'accueil et de conseil pour les jeunes et les sans-emploi.

Étant également conscients du fait que la pauvreté engendre la maladie, nous avons doublé l'enveloppe consacrée aux soins pour les personnes en situation de précarité.

De plus, la création de logements d'urgence a été poursuivie pour que des SDF ne périssent plus de froid comme ce fut encore le cas cet hiver. Je salue au passage les immenses efforts fournis dans ce domaine par nos diverses organisations caritatives.

En outre, des mesures ont été prises pour lutter contre l'illettrisme, lui-même source de détresse, puisqu'il empêche ceux qui en souffrent de profiter pleinement des prestations qui leur sont accessibles.

Dans cette vaste gamme de mesures nous n'avons pas oublié les citoyens du troisième âge qui ont, eux aussi, droit à une vie décente. Les prestations ont donc été relevées pour les personnes de plus de soixante ans aux revenus modestes afin qu'elles puissent faire face aux dépenses quotidiennes.

La France est un pays riche où chaque citoyen mérite une vie digne et décente. Je sais qu'il y a encore beaucoup à faire pour réduire les inégalités sociales et combler le fossé qui existe entre les riches et les pauvres, mais avec votre aide mon gouvernement y parviendra, restant ainsi fidèle aux grands principes de 1789 qui ont fait de notre pays un modèle et un exemple pour le reste du monde.

Mes chers concitoyens, je vous présente mes vœux pour une bonne et heureuse Nouvelle Année.

Vive la République,

Vive la France.

Insight

The French word for thousand is **mille.** It is invariable and must be used with a precise number e.g. **dix mille trois cents personnes** (*ten thousand three hundred people/persons*). For *one thousand*, you can also use the word **un millier**. If you want to say *thousands of* …, you must use **des milliers de** …, and not **des mille de** …).

QUICK VOCAB

une promesse *a promise. The verb is* **promettre.**
avoir trait à ... *to bear a relation to (of events)*
la pauvreté *poverty*
tourner une page *to turn over a new leaf*
l'Ancien Régime *the Ancien Regime (the Monarchy)*
fier *proud*
l'INSEE *A government body which conducts research into people's attitudes, habits, etc. Stands for* **Institut National de la Statistique et des Études Économiques.**
le concitoyen *fellow citizen*
le seuil de pauvreté *the poverty threshold/line*
un sans-abri *a homeless person.* **Être sans abri** *means to be homeless;* **un abri** *is a shelter.*
le quotidien *daily routine. As a noun, it can also mean daily paper.*
relever *Here: to increase*
le SMIC *minimum wage. Stands for* **le Salaire Minimum Interprofessionnel de Croissance.** *It is index-linked and, in 2009, amounted to a monthly wage of €1,337 for 151 hours of work.*
le RMI *An allowance to enable poorly paid working couples to meet their living costs. It is based on the number of adults and children involved. It stands for* **Revenu Minimum d'Insertion.**
débloquer des crédits *to make credits available (lit. to unblock ...)*
les sans-emploi *the unemployed*
une enveloppe *Here: a sum set aside by the government for a specific purpose. It can also mean an envelope.*
la précarité *precariousness*
un(e) SDF *a homeless person. The acronym stands for* **Sans Domicile Fixe** *(of no fixed abode).*
caritative *(fem.) caring (applied to an organization which cares for the needy)*
en outre *besides (in addition/moreover)*
l'illettrisme *illiteracy*
le troisième âge *the third age (refers to people over sixty)*
digne *dignified*
combler le fossé *to fill the gap;* **un fossé** *is a ditch*
parvenir *Here: to succeed.* **Parvenir à** *can also mean to manage (to do ...) or to reach (a goal).*

Insight

To translate *when*, the French have two words: **quand** and **lorsque.** The latter belongs to a more elevated style than the former. In addition, note that *the day when*, *the year when*, *the time when*, etc., are translated as: **le jour où, l'année où, le moment où**, etc.

Comprehension 2

1 What were the first two promises which the President refers to in his speech and what does he say about them?
2 What, according to him, were the aims of the people who wrote the Déclaration?
3 Can you clarify the reference to 'many other countries'?
4 What do the latest INSEE statistics show?
5 In terms of employment what have been the improvements made?
6 Why has he asked his government to make money available to develop welcome and advice centres for young and unemployed people?
7 Why has his government made money available to combat illiteracy?
8 Has something been done for citizens over 60 years of age? Clarify.
9 What does the President acknowledge at the end of his speech?
10 What value does the President attach to the 'great principles of 1789'?

Activity 10

In the speech there are several examples of subjunctives. Make a list of each of them and give the verb or expression which prompted their use.

Activity 11

There are, in the speech, five examples of the past definite. Note them down and, for each, give the infinitive. Can you justify their presence in this oral presentation?

7 How to say 'having done', 'having been', etc.

In English, it is possible to use the above construction to situate an action further back than another expressed in one of the traditional past tenses:

1 *Having finished their meal, they got up.*
2 *Having called a taxi, she would go and do her shopping* (here: *would = used to*).
3 *Having arrived first, he had waited for the others.*

The same construction can be used to the same end in French, but we must remember that not all verbs form their compound tenses with avoir!

1 Ayant fini leur repas, ils se levèrent/se sont levés.
2 Ayant appelé un taxi, elle allait faire ses achats.
3 Étant arrivé le premier, il avait attendu les autres.

Activity 12
The sentences below are each divided into two sections. Use the technique shown above to create a time gap between the actions expressed by the verbs. In each case, logic should dictate the order of the two sections.

1 je téléphonai – je partis immédiatement.
2 elle l'examina – elle lui ordonna de rester au lit.
3 ils avaient arrêté le voleur – ils l'avaient mis en prison.
4 tu es plus intelligent que moi – tu as pu résoudre ce problème.
5 ils sont partis avant nous – ils sont arrivés les premiers.
6 nous sommes sortis de l'appartement – nous avons fait une petite promenade.
7 vous avez réussi à vos examens – vous pouvez prendre des vacances.

Insight

The formal demonstrative pronouns **ceci** (*this*) and **cela** (*that*) are both replaced in familiar French by the informal ça. Instead of: '**Vous préférez ceci ou cela?**' ('*Do you prefer this or that?*') you can say: '**Vous préférez ça ou ça?**' (pointing helps!).

Dialogue

If you have the recording, listen to the dialogue at least twice. The second time, try to follow the exchange as it develops in preparation for the activities relating to it.

With the help of Pierre Castel, with whom he is spending a few days, Marc Swift has found some houses which may appeal to his parents, who are still thinking of buying a second home in France. Marc is very taken with Villeneuve, but he wants to know more about the social atmosphere of the area and, as ever, he goes straight to the point.

CD2, TR 5, 06:49

Marc Je pense que mes parents aimeront cette région. Le climat y est très agréable. Mais est-ce qu'il y a des problèmes au niveau social?

Pierre Pas plus qu'ailleurs! Il y a quelques vols de temps en temps, mais rien de très grave. Croyez-moi, Villeneuve est une ville bourgeoise et calme, une ville où il y a beaucoup de retraités.

Marc J'ai tout de même remarqué qu'il y avait pas mal d'Arabes aux terrasses des cafés.

Pierre Vous êtes raciste?

Marc Non, pas du tout! Je me demandais pourquoi, c'est tout!

Pierre La raison est simple: vous savez que depuis longtemps la France a une réputation de terre d'accueil. À la fin de la guerre d'Algérie, en 1963, les Algériens qui étaient restés fidèles à la France ont été rapatriés parce qu'on craignait des représailles de la part du FLN.

Marc Le FLN?

Pierre Oui, le Front de Libération National qui voulait l'indépendance de l'Algérie. Alors en 63–64, nous avons accueilli à Villeneuve plus de 2.500 réfugiés venant du Maghreb.

Marc Du …?

Pierre Du Maghreb, de l'Afrique du Nord si vous préférez.

Marc Ah, je vois. Mais, ça fait beaucoup pour une ville de 25.000 habitants.

Pierre C'est vrai, admettons-le! Mais Villeneuve avait l'habitude! À la fin de la guerre d'Indochine, en 54, nous avions accueilli environ le même nombre de réfugiés indochinois, et pour les mêmes raisons d'ailleurs.

Marc Et tous ces réfugiés se sont bien adaptés?

Pierre Au début, il y a eu quelques frictions entre les gens du coin et les nouveaux arrivants, surtout à cause des indemnités que, selon certains, le gouvernement distribuait trop généreusement aux réfugiés, mais ces gens avaient tout perdu, ils arrivaient sans rien et ils avaient combattu aux côtés des troupes françaises contre le FLN.

Marc Et ces gens-là se sont bien intégrés?

Pierre En général oui, surtout les jeunes. Mais beaucoup d'entre eux ont voulu garder leurs coutumes, et quelques Villeneuvois ont vu ça d'un mauvais œil. Ils voulaient donc que les nouveaux arrivants adoptent notre manière de vivre, mais ce n'était pas raisonnable. Dans l'ensemble, aujourd'hui, les choses se sont calmées. Il y a bien encore quelques vieux qui votent pour le Front National. Oublions-les!

Marc Et le chômage? Vous m'aviez dit que la situation économique n'était pas brillante ici!

Pierre Non, si je me souviens bien, je vous avais dit que l'économie de la région, autrefois agricole, avait beaucoup souffert de la concurrence étrangère. Mais récemment le gouvernement a fait des efforts considérables pour aider les sans-emploi à créer de nouvelles entreprises. Disons qu'aujourd'hui, la région se situe dans la moyenne générale au niveau du chômage.

Marc J'ai vu qu'il y avait des SDF qui faisaient la manche dans la grand'rue. En général, c'est mauvais signe!

Pierre Ne dramatisons pas! Ici encore, le gouvernement a mis sur pied des initiatives pour éliminer la pauvreté et l'exclusion, mais il y a toujours, comme partout, des paresseux qui ne veulent pas travailler.

Marc Et la drogue?

Pierre Pour ce qui est de la drogue, tranquillisez-vous. Ce n'est pas un problème chez nous!

Marc Alors, si je comprends bien, Villeneuve est un paradis.

Pierre N'exagérons pas, mais vos parents pourraient tomber plus mal, avouez-le! Les prix sont raisonnables, la nourriture est excellente, comme vous avez pu le remarquer, l'air est sain, et ici, les gens vivent plus longtemps qu'ailleurs!
Marc Vous devriez vous embaucher au syndicat d'initiative!
Pierre J'y ai pensé!

QUICK VOCAB

au niveau social *from the social point of view (lit. at the social level).*
ailleurs *elsewhere.* **D'ailleurs** *usually means besides.*
pas mal de ... *quite a few/a fair number of ...*
l'accueil (masc.) *welcome. A little earlier, Pierre used the expression* **terre d'accueil** *haven (lit. land of welcome).*
le Maghreb *the countries on the Northern coast of Africa (Tunisia, Algeria, Morocco, which had previously been French colonies). People from these areas are called* **les Maghrébins.**
ça fait beaucoup *that's quite a lot* (lit. *that makes much)*
les gens du coin *the people from the area* (lit. *... of the corner)*
s'intégrer *to fit in/become integrated*
voir d'un mauvais œil *to frown upon something (lit. to see from a bad eye)*
le Front National *the National Front. In France the* **Front National***'s rating is much higher than the equivalent BNP in Britain, since the last time its leader, Jean-Marie Le Pen, stood as presidential candidate, he polled around 17% of the national vote.*
selon *or* **d'après certains** *according to some (people)*
souffrir *to suffer. Sometimes to endure/bear.*
faire la manche *to beg (because beggars often used to tug at the sleeves of passers-by)*
mettre sur pied *to set up (a company)* (lit. *to put on foot)*
un paresseux *a lazy/idle person. The noun (laziness) is* **la paresse.**
se tranquilliser *to stop worrying*
mal tomber *to do badly.* **(Ils) pourraient tomber plus mal!** *They could do worse!*
avouer *to confess. The noun is* **un aveu.**
s'embaucher (fam.) *to go and get a job. In the same context,* **débaucher** *means to clock off/leave work at the end of the day. It can also mean to lead astray (morally).*
le syndicat d'initiative *the tourist office. Often called* **l'office du tourisme** (*or* **S.I.** *or even* **ESSI**) *nowadays. Marc is amused by the way Pierre is trying to 'sell' Villeneuve to him, hence the quip.*

Insight

There are two French words to translate *to know:* **savoir** and **connaître. Savoir** is used when the meaning is *to have learnt;* **connaître** is used when the idea is *to have come across something or someone.* Compare: **'Vous savez votre leçon?'** ('*Do you know your lesson?*') and **'Vous connaissez Marc?'** ('*Do you know Marc?*').

General de Gaulle, having publicly shouted in June 1958 **Vive l'Algérie française** during a visit to that country, thereby signifying that Algeria would remain French, changed his mind and, in January 1961, ordered **un référendum sur l'autodétermination**, to allow Algerians to choose whether they wanted to become independent or to remain French. The principle of independence was approved by 70% of Algerian voters. This sparked a vicious terrorist campaign and a **coup** (*revolution*) in Algiers (April 1961), organized by a small group of generals, who wanted Algeria to remain French. This sad episode in the history of France came to a close in 1962 with **les accords d'Évian** (*the Evian agreement*).

Comprehension 3

Having studied the text carefully, try to answer the following questions in English. Please note that, as usual, they are not in sequence.

1 Pierre says that Villeneuve is used to welcoming refugees. Explain.
2 What is the situation as regards crime and drug-taking in the town?
3 What, according to Pierre, are the four big advantages which Villeneuve has to offer?
4 Why was the government generous with Algerian refugees?
5 Did the total number of refugees in 1954 and 1963–4 represent a significant proportion of the total local population? Clarify.
6 What has recently been done by the government to alleviate the unemployment problem?
7 From the social point of view, what sort of a town is Villeneuve?

Activity 13
Now that you know the text well, try to answer the following questions in French. With a little effort and few adjustments, you should be able to identify the information you need.

1 Marc pense que ses parents aimeront la région de Villeneuve. Pourquoi?
2 Qu'est-ce que Marc a remarqué à Villeneuve?
3 Pourquoi les Algériens fidèles à la France ont-ils été 'rapatriés' en 1963?
4 Qu'est-ce qui s'est passé en 1954?
5 Qu'est-ce que le Maghreb?
6 Est-ce que la drogue est un problème à Villeneuve?
7 Quel a été le principal facteur de frictions entre les Villeneuvois et les rapatriés du Maghreb?
8 Est-ce qu'il y a beaucoup de criminalité à Villeneuve? Expliquez.

8 More on the imperative

We have already examined the formation and the use of the imperative, which is the mood used to give orders, warnings and advice. As you will remember, the imperative has only three persons and no subject pronouns (Unit 9):

***Fermons* les fenêtres, il fait froid!**	*Let us close the windows, it (the weather) is cold!*
***Attendez* une minute!**	*Wait a minute!*
***Mange* ta soupe!**	*Eat your soup! (familiar sing. form)*

There are however a few more things to say about the imperative:

1 If the verb which you wish to put in the positive form of the imperative (*do!*) is a reflexive/pronominal verb (indicating that the performer of the action is also the one affected by it), the reflexive pronouns (**toi, nous** and **vous**) will be placed after the verb and joined to it by a hyphen:

se lever (*to get up*) → lève-**toi**, levons-**nous**, levez-**vous**
se dépêcher (*to hurry*) → dépêche-**toi**, dépêchons-**nous**, dépêchez-**vous**

2 In the negative (*do not!*), the pronoun goes before the verb and toi becomes te:

se cacher (*to hide oneself*) →	Ne **te** cache pas, ne **nous** cachons pas, ne **vous** cachez pas
se déranger (*to disturb oneself*) →	Ne **te** dérange pas, ne **nous** dérangeons pas, ne **vous** dérangez pas

3 The same happens if the verb, without being a reflexive, is constructed with one of the following pronouns: **me, te, le, la, lui, nous, vous, les, leur** (*me* or *to me*, *you* or *to you* (fam.), *him/her/it* or *to him/her/it, us* or *to us*, *you* or *to you* (pol. sing. or plur.), *them* or *to them)*.

Please remember that the pronouns not preceded by *to* generally represent a direct object. Those preceded by *to* normally represent an indirect object. For a fuller explanation of those two categories, please consult your grammar book.

Donnez-*lui* la main.	*Give (to) him/her your hand.*
Ne *lui* donnez pas la main.	*Do not give (to) him/her your hand.*
Vendons-*leur* la maison.	*Let us sell (to) them the house.*
Ne *leur* vendons pas la maison.	*Let us not sell (to) them the house.*

Please note that the *to* indicating an indirect object, while essential in French, is not normally used in English (hence the brackets around *to*), unless the word order is changed as shown below:

Do not give him/her your hand.	→ *Do not give your hand to him/her.*
Let us sell him/her the house.	→ *Let us sell the house to him/her.*

Activity 14

In the conversation between Pierre and Marc, there are a few verbs in the imperative. Make a list of them, and, for each, give the infinitive.

Soyez réalistes, demandez l'impossible! *Be realistic, ask for the impossible!* This was one of the most famous slogans shouted by students during the May 68 'revolution' which, according to the government, was merely **une tempête dans un verre d'eau** (*a storm in a teacup*).

Les Français ont le cœur à gauche, mais le portefeuille à droite. *French people's heart is on the left, but their wallet is on the right.* This means that they have left-wing ideals but right-wing views about money.

Insight

When using a reflexive verb in the imperative (positive) you need the pronouns **-toi**, -**nous**, and -**vous** after the verb: **lève-toi, levons-nous, levez-vous** (*get yourself up* (fam.), *let's get up*, *get up* (polite sing. or plural). The negative forms are: **ne te lève pas, ne nous levons pas, ne vous levez pas.**

TEST YOURSELF

1 What is the difference in meaning between **ils sont allés** and **ils allaient**, both meaning *they went*?

2 Is the French national (military) service still in force today?

3 Who, until 2002, benefited from **un sursis** in a military context?

4 What are the two debating chambers which make up the French legislative system?

5 Why would the '**Déclaration des droits de l'homme et du citoyen**' written in August 1789 not be considered politically correct today?

6 How would you say in French *no one/nobody has arrived* and why are these expressions at variance with their English equivalent?

7 What is the difference in meaning between: '**Je l'ai vu parlant à un ami**' and '**Je l'ai vu en parlant à un ami**'?

8 Complete the French grammatical rule: when two verbs follow each other ...

9 What tense should be used after **de peur que, pour que** and **afin que**?

10 Who is likely to benefit from a visit to a **syndicat d'initiative** or **S.I.**?

Key to the exercises

In this section you will find that some information has been put in brackets. This will either:

1 clarify the reason why a particular answer was chosen,

or:

2 give useful additional information which does not form part of the expected answer (in the Comprehension sections).

UNIT 1

Comprehension 1 1 Because it is more privileged than its neighbours from the point of view of the climate and the economy.
2 Because the frontier between France and Belgium is an open one (i.e. without natural obstacles).
3 Anticlockwise from the top: the North Sea, the English Channel, the Atlantic Ocean and the Mediterranean.
4 Spain. 5 (Gently rolling) hills. 6 Clockwise from the top: Belgium, Luxembourg, Germany, Switzerland, Italy and Spain. 7 Four: Maritime (Normandy and Brittany), Parisian (similar to the previous one), Continental (Eastern areas), Mediterranean (the South).

Activity 1 1 True. 2 False: as we have seen there are no natural obstacles (mountains or rivers) between France and Belgium.
3 True. 4 False: la Beauce is a plain (known as the granary of France because of its vast wheat fields).
5 False: whereas it is true that the Alps are 'young' in geological terms, the Massif Central belongs to the oldest mountain formation (it dates from the Hercynian period).
6 False: all of them are.

Activity 2 A3; B5; C2; D1; E4.

Activity 3 1 Nouns ending in -sion (not just -ion) are feminine. 2 Feminine, as are all abstract nouns ending in -té. 3 Nouns ending in -age are generally masculine. 4 Nouns ending in -isme are always masculine. 5 Feminine, as all nouns ending in -tion are feminine.

Comprehension 2 1 It enables agricultural products (fruit, vegetables, cereals and above all vineyards, which are an economic treasure) to be grown successfully. 2 On average, France produces between 60 and 75 million hectolitres of wine a year, but only a (small) proportion of this is of superior quality; the rest goes by the name of ordinary or table wine. 3 It is economic activity related to agricultural production. It plays a very important role in the national economy and brings in billions of euros for the government. 4 Competition from other EU member states and from low-income countries (and this threatens the existence of smaller, non-specialized farms). 5 France must import most of the crude oil it needs and this damages its balance of payments, but the country has plentiful natural reserves of uranium.

Activity 4 1 La France est riche et superbement/très bien située en Europe, ce qui explique son succès économique. 2 L'agriculture est encore/toujours très importante pour l'économie nationale. 3 Le pays doit importer bon nombre/beaucoup de produits de l'étranger. 4 Les sols et le climat sont excellents. 5 Le vin rapporte des milliards d'euros à l'économie française. 6 Les importations étrangères menacent la balance des paiements et l'existence de bon nombre de petites fermes.

Activity 5 1 d' (a vowel follows). 2 de (a consonant follows). 3 de (plural adjective precedes the noun). 4 d' (it should be **de** + plural adjective, as in 3, but a vowel follows). 5 des (consonant and no preceding adjective).

Activity 6 1 du. 2 du. 3 du. 4 de l'. 5 de la. 6 du. 7 du. 8 du. 9 de l'. 10 de l'.

Activity 7 1 False: his father is British, but his mother is French. 2 False: they met on the day of Claudine's birthday, which was also the day of President Kennedy's assassination. 3 False: Claudine is a teacher, but John works in a bank as a bank clerk. 4 False: for the last six years he has been working in a big British company which specializes in sport and leisure equipment. 5 True. 6 False: he is completely bilingual. 7 True (it knows no bounds).

Activity 8 1 Vous avez encore de la famille dans le nord? Vous avez toujours vos parents? 2 Do you still have relatives in the North? (Don't forget that in France the term **la famille** is used for the nuclear as well as the extended family.) Do you still have your parents/Are your parents still alive?

Activity 9 1 Are your parents still (living) in the North? 2 He is still in the café/He is always in the café. 3 The postman always rings twice. 4 He is late again. 5 Is she still living in Bordeaux?

Activity 10 1 J'habite (je suis) dans cette région depuis ma naissance. 2 Je suis en France depuis deux semaines/quinze jours. *or* Il y a deux semaines/quinze jours que je suis en France. 3 Je suis au café depuis dix minutes. *or* Il y a dix minutes que je suis au café. 4 Il y a dix ans que je viens en France. *or* Je viens en France depuis dix ans. 5 Il y a trois ans que j'occupe mon emploi/mon poste actuel ('false friend'). *or* J'occupe mon emploi actuel depuis trois ans. 6 J'ai habité un appartement (pendant) six ans, mais maintenant j'habite une petite maison à la campagne.

Activity 11 a 4; b 2; c 5; d 3 (present); e 4 or 1.

Activity 12 allons; choisissons; peut; aimons; a; préfère; adore; veut; passe; dis; est; moque.

Activité 13 1 choisissant, choisi; 2 pouvant, pu; 3 ayant, eu; 4 voulant, voulu; 5 disant, dit.

Activity 14 1 a 3rd group; b été. 2 a 3rd group; b vécu. 3 a 3rd group; b parti. 4 a 1st group; b marché. 5 a 3rd group; b voulu. 6 a 3rd group; b pris. 7 a 3rd group; b revenu.

Test yourself

1 Because if you draw straight lines to join the extreme points of the country, you end up with an almost perfect six-sided geometrical figure. 2 Because, in most cases, they give indications on the gender of the nouns concerned, therefore helping you to avoid agreement errors. 3 No. For the first day of the month the ordinal number is used: **le premier**; but, thereafter, it's the cardinal number: **le deux, le trois,** etc. which is used. 4 One is 'of the' and the other is 'some'. 5 **Encore** can mean 'again' or 'still'; **toujours** can mean 'always' or 'still'. 6 **Depuis** can mean 'since' if followed by a past date or event, and 'for' if followed by an expression indicating duration. 7 **DOM** have exactly the same status as one of the 95 metropolitan **départements,** whereas **TOM** have a more flexible status and enjoy greater autonomy. 8 In formal French **on** means 'someone'/ 'somebody' when the gender of the person is not known. In familiar French it is used to replace the subject pronoun **nous** and is followed by the verb in the 3rd person singular. 9 The conditional mood indicates the possibility that an action might take (or might have taken) place if certain conditions were (or had been) met; the imperative conveys commands, orders and recommendations. 10 The indicative deals with reality in the past, present or future, whereas the subjunctive is used to express doubt, fears and events which might/might not happen.

UNIT 2

Comprehension 1 1 The Dufrênes are 'old' friends of his family. As he is in the area, he wondered if he could pay them a quick visit (**passer les voir**) to say hello. 2 He has been in Poitiers on business for two days and he will be leaving tomorrow morning. 3 He is staying at the hotel Métropole, opposite the station; he is due to see a customer at three o'clock this afternoon, but he should have finished work by four at the latest. 4 She is called Élise; she has gone to Paris for a meeting and will be back in two days. 5 He is inviting Marc for a pre-dinner drink (**apéritif**) and a meal; he will go and pick him up at his hotel at 5.30 p.m. 6 Daniel has invited him to stay the night at his home. Marc turns the offer down, because he is due to catch the TGV to Paris at 6 a.m. 7 No, the two of them will cook 'a little something' for their guest.

Activity 1 1 Je suis ici depuis six jours pour affaires (*or* il y a six jours que je suis ici pour affaires). 2 Je ne veux pas vous déranger. 3 Je reste ici jusqu'à demain après-midi à quatre heures. 4 Je suis libre ce soir. 5 Je devrais téléphoner à cinq heures et demie au plus tard. 6 C'est très gentil, mais ... 7 Écoutez/Écoute, je viens vous/te chercher à l'hôtel! (*polite/familiar*).

Activity 2 2 b: Daniel is listening at this very moment. 3 b: Daniel asks where Marc is at this very moment. 4 c: Marc has been in Poitiers for two days. 5 c: Marc is staying in Poitiers until tomorrow. 6 c: if Marc has been staying at the hotel for two days, but it could also be b, if he is there right now. 7 e: the evening is still several hours away. 8 e: the meeting with the customer is going to happen in the near future. It could also be d, if the time is very near three o'clock. 9 e: they will have a drink this evening (i.e. several hours from now). 10 e: as well, for the same reason as 9. 11 e: Élise will be coming back in two days. 12 e: the night is still a long way away. 13 e: Marc will be going back on the TGV tomorrow morning.

Activity 3 1 à. 2 au. 3 en. 4 à. 5 en. 6 au. 7 aux (*also* **dans les**).

Activity 4 1 Wrong: it should be **de.** 2 Wrong: it is **du** (because **Honduras** begins with an aspirated **h**). 3 Wrong twice: **de la** should be **du** (**Maroc** ends with a consonant), and **au Paris** should be **à** Paris (city). 4 Correct. 5 Wrong: Hollande is a country, ending in -e and beginning with an aspirated **h**, so it should be **en.** 6 Correct. 7 Correct: **Espagne** is a (feminine) country and it begins with a vowel. 8 Wrong: **Pakistan** is a (masculine) country, so it should be **au.** 9 Wrong: **Russie** is feminine (ends in **-e** and is not one of the exceptions), so it must be **en.** 10 Wrong: **Suisse** is feminine, so it is **en** which is required.

Activity 5 A: 1 à Monsieur Dufrêne. 2 pour toi. 3 à l'appareil. 4 en ce moment. 5 à Poitiers. 6 pour affaires. 7 coup de fil. 8 pour quelques jours. 9 à l'hôtel. 10 au Métropole. 11 en face de la gare. 12 à trois heures. 13 vers quatre heures. 14 au plus tard. 15 à cinq heures et demie. 16 avec nous. 17 pas du tout. 18 à Paris. 19 pour une réunion. 20 de travail. 21 dans deux jours. 22 chez nous. 23 pour Paris. 24 à six heures. 25 à ton hôtel. 26 après le dîner. 27 à bientôt. 28 au revoir. B: 1 pour vous dire. 2 à voir. 3 à manger.

Activity 6 1 Allô, je voudrais parler à ... s'il vous plaît. 2 Une seconde, je vous le (la) passe. 3 Allô, ici ... J'écoute. 4 ... à l'appareil. 5 Je vous passe un coup de fil.

Activity 7 1 Allô. Ici ... Qu'est-ce que je peux faire pour vous? 2 Je suis désolé(e), mais ... 3 Ah, oui, c'était à une réunion d'affaires. Quelle surprise! 4 C'est vrai. Où êtes-vous en ce moment? 5 À l'hôtel? 6 C'est très gentil et je suis libre en ce moment. Écoutez, je prends la voiture et je suis (= *immediacy*)/je serai là dans cinq minutes!

Activity 8 1 S'il vous plaît (please). 2 Si ça ne vous dérangeait pas (if you don't mind). 3 C'est très gentil (that's very kind). 4 Je ne veux pas vous déranger (I don't want to disturb you). 5 Merci et à bientôt (thank you; see you soon).

Activity 9 1 lui. 2 toi (familiar form prompted by **tu**). 3 vous (plural prompted by **partez**). 4 eux (one male, one female). 5 elle. 6 vous. 7 elles (feminine plural). 8 soi (impersonal; if familiar it would be **nous**). 9 elle.

Activity 10 1 They left/went with him. 2 You are going to keep this secret to yourself. 3 Go, I will get back (home) without you. 4 She arrived before them. 5 He does not agree with her. 6 You must always have your passport with (or on) you. 7 Those students have their whole life ahead of them. 8 One must always look forward/ahead. 9 I bought (some) flowers for her.

Comprehension 2 1 Chez nous (in our country). 2 His last trip to Paris (he did not see many stylish/elegant Parisian women).

3 They should try hard/make a real effort to integrate and to speak the language (it's a matter of respect towards French culture). 4 People have become more open and more tolerant. 5 He says there are now excellent chefs in Britain who present television programmes (to encourage people to cook). 6 It is better to make love than war. 7 He says: 'we must be modest on that point'. He is not sure/convinced that the French deserve that very subjective reputation any longer, but he admits that they can be romantic when the occasion arises. 8 They go weak at the knees/lose their head. 9 Farmers' demonstrations, roadblocks and sit-ins.

Activity 11 A3; B5; C6; D2; E10; F7; G12; H4; I1; J11; K9; L13; M8.

Comprehension 3 1 The news that Concorde was to be retired. 2 It has ended up in a museum after a little less than thirty years of faithful service. 3 The Russians built an aircraft which was a copy of Concorde, and it was ironically christened Concordski. 4 It was capable of flying at Mach 2 (twice the speed of sound) and put New York less than three and a half hours from Paris. It was a dream for businessmen in a hurry who could travel in comfort and arrive 'fresh as daisies' at their destination. 5 From the start it was beset with problems: its development costs, which were far higher than those of the initial budget, the small number of passengers it could carry compared with jumbo jets, the stringent rules imposed by the American authorities about noise and pollution levels, but it was probably the accident which occurred in 2000 which signed its death warrant.

Activity 12 1 Né dans les ateliers aéronautiques de Toulouse. 2 Il a été, pendant toute sa vie active, un fleuron de la technologie française. 3 Plus qu'un avion, Concorde était un symbole du génie français, des capacités technologiques de nos ingénieurs et techniciens. 4 Bien sûr, il a eu de problèmes, notre Concorde. 5 Sa silhouette restera pour toujours gravée dans nos mémoires.

Test yourself

1 The present tense can be used to refer to:

- ▶ Something that happens regularly
- ▶ Something that is happening right now
- ▶ Something that has happened up to now and is likely to continue
- ▶ Something just about to happen
- ▶ Something which will happen in the not too distant future.

2 To refer, in familiar spoken French, to something the gender of which is unclear. 3 Travellers' tales, literature, films and the media. 4 The south of France. 5 Words or groups of words used to express relationship (space, time, purpose, etc.) between related parts of a sentence. 6 When **le** and **les** are not articles but object pronouns. 7 When the name of the town contains the article **le**. 8 They can be used with a verb as well as a noun/pronoun. 9 When used to address a complete stranger who is not a member of a close-knit community. 10 The first one, because there is a mismatch between the pronoun **tu** and the adjective **votre**: it should be **tu** and **ton**.

UNIT 3

Activity 1 1 étais; 2 avaient; 3 allais; 4 arrivions; 5 devions; 6 tombaient; 7 faisait; 8 courions, 9 sonnait; 10 faisait; 11 inspectait; 12 étaient; 13 envoyait; 14 avions; 15 détestions, 16 finissait; 17 sortions; 18 rentrions; 19 était; 20 mangions.

Comprehension 1 1 20; 2 12–14; 3 10–11; 4 4; 5 7–9; 6 2–3; 7 15.

Activity 2 1 For the first time, the Eagle lowered his head (in defeat). 2 The emperor was retreating slowly. 3 The army was in total disarray (it was impossible to make out the flanks from the centre). 4 Buglers could be seen frozen to death at their posts. 5 It was snowing. It kept on snowing. 6 The icy north wind kept on howling (whistling).

Activity 3 1 neiger (1st group); 2 être (3rd); 3 baisser (1st); 4 revenir (3rd); 5 fondre (3rd); 6 connaître (3rd); 7 distinguer (1st); 8 s'abriter (1st); 9 voir (3rd); 10 pleuvoir (3rd); 11 marcher (1st); 12 siffler (1st); 13 avoir (3rd); 14 aller (1st).

Activity 4 Present participles: laissant (laisser); collant (coller). Reflexive: s'abritaient.

Activity 5 neige (x5); est; baisse; revient; fond; connaît; distingue; s'abritent; voit; pleuvent; marchent; siffle; a; va.

Comprehension 2 1 False: he says **ma femme et moi étions gérants** … 2 False: his response to Marc's question is 'reasonably well, mustn't complain'. 3 False: he says **la population diminuait constamment.** 4 True. 5 False: his argument is that people are not obliged to consume those products and if he does not sell them, someone else will. 6 True. 7 True.

Activity 6 1 étions (être – 3rd group); 2 devenait (devenir – 3rd); 3 voulaient (vouloir – 3rd); 4 étaient (être – 3rd); 5 diminuait (diminuer – 1st); 6 réussissait (réussir – 2nd); 7 venaient (venir – 3rd); 8 bavardait (bavarder – 1st); 9 jouait (jouer – 1st); 10 était (être – 3rd); 11 jouait (jouer – 1st); Note that **on était venus** is a pluperfect, not an imperfect.

Activity 7 1 C'est bien calme en ville ce matin! 2 Vous travaillez dans quelle branche? 3 Par rapport au reste de l'économie, c'est une industrie qui marche bien (*or* qui est en expansion). 4 Vous travaillez ici depuis longtemps? 5 Avant de venir à Reims, je travaillais dans un petit village. 6 Qu'est-ce qui vous a poussés à venir ici? 7 On arrivait (*or* nous arrivions) juste à joindre les deux bouts. 8 Le travail marche bien ici? Faut pas se plaindre. 9 Le sport est bon pour la santé. 10 Je veux bien vous croire.

Activity 8 suis venu; avez commencé; a poussé; a vu; a pris; avez … eu; ont … changé.

Activity 9 1 one/somebody: on bavardait, on jouait; on dit. 2 we: on réussissait; on était venus; on a vu; on a pris.

Comprehension 3 1 Artists and writers used to meet there to exchange ideas, talk about philosophy, etc. 2 Customers would talk about the events of the day or the week, discuss politics (albeit at a superficial level), communicate, air their problems, get some advice (from the owner or other customers). 3 Nowadays, most people go straight home to watch television and have a drink. They buy their alcohol at the supermarket. 4 They have unrestricted access to alcohol (bought in by their parents). 5 They are offering their customers simple dishes such as sandwiches, steak and chips. 6 Because, in addition to pizzerias and McDonald's restaurants, there are many small shops (such as bakers and confectioners) that are now doing the same thing. 7 He is amazed and says he would never have guessed (**chapeau!** I take my hat off to you!). 8 He is a farmer (peasant) who destroyed a McDonald's restaurant in 1999. His nickname is 'Robin of the Fields' (an adaptation of 'Robin Hood'), and many French people agree with him about fast food outlets.

Activity 10 1 J'admets qu'il a fallu s'adapter. 2 Il y a des tas de gens qui rentrent directement à la maison (*or* chez eux). 3 Ma femme cuisine des trucs simples; ça nous aide un peu. 4 (Il) faut dire qu'il y a pas mal de Français qui sont d'accord avec José Bové. 5 Si vous voulez mon avis, c'est dangereux surtout pour les moins de dix-huit ans. 6 Autrefois, les clients venaient prendre un verre à midi ou le soir. 7 Il faut regarder les choses en face, aujourd'hui tout ça c'est fini.

Activity 11 1 ces; 2 ce; 3 cette; 4 cette; 5 cette; 6 ce; 7 ce; 8 cette; 9 cette; 10 cette.

Activity 12 1 cet; 2 ce; 3 ce; 4 ce; 5 cet; 6 cet; 7 cet; 8 ce; 9 ce; 10 ce.

Activity 13 1 wrong; 2 wrong; 3 correct; 4 wrong (**cet haricot** is wrong but very frequently heard); 5 wrong; 6 wrong; 7 correct.

Activity 14 1 wrong: **celles**; 2 correct; 3 correct; 4 wrong: **celle**; 5 wrong: **celle**; 6 wrong: **celui**; 7 wrong: **celles** (because **voisines** is feminine).

Activity 15 1 False: a sweet white wine (or Champagne) should be served; 2 True; 3 False: a dry white wine or rosé should be served; 4 True; 5 False: it should be drunk chilled (**frappé**); 6 False: it's the reverse; 7 False: no wine should be served with salad (the vinegary dressing would destroy the taste).

Activity 16

1	**2**
Mushroom soup	No wine.
Seafood platter	A dry white wine (e.g. Bordeaux, Bergerac).
Duck with orange	A well-rounded or full-bodied red (Bourgogne, Loire).
Vegetables	The same as for the duck.
Salad	No wine.
Cheese board	A full-bodied red (Côtes du Rhône, Bordeaux).
Apple tart	A sweet white wine (Bergerac, Bordeaux).
Coffee	Brandy, Armagnac, a liqueur.

Test yourself

1 The four main uses of the imperfect tense are:

- To translate the English 'used to'
- To indicate that an action was in progress in the past when another happened
- To describe enduring features characteristic of something or someone in the past
- To express a condition which holds good for the present but would also apply in the future.

2 It is the capital of the Champagne area where the famous sparkling wine is produced. 3 Because they have traditionally been places where literary and artistic figures met to discuss music,

painting, philosophy, poetry, etc. 4 A simple tense is a one-word tense such as the present, the future, the imperfect... A compound tense uses an auxiliary verb before the main verb. 5 They are **avoir** (to have) or **être** (to be). 6 For verbs of movement, including **naître** (to be born) and **mourir** (to die) and reflexive you must use **être**. For all the others, use **avoir**. 7 When the next word begins with a vowel or a mute **h** (see Appendix 6 for explanation of the mute/aspirated **h**). 8 None (as the dressing would obliterate the taste of the wine). 9 Because, so long as it is **frappé** (chilled), it can be served with any food or as an **apéritif**. 10 A (chilled) sweet white wine (or champagne, of course).

UNIT 4

Activity 1 1 In principle, schooling is compulsory in France from six to 18. 2 Around 15 per cent of pupils leave secondary education without any qualifications. 3 According to recent statistics, nearly half the pupils leave school at 16 to look for employment. 4 In secondary schools, the average student timetable is 27 hours per week. 5 Nearly half the students who complete their studies in a **LEP** (technical school) go on to a **lycée** to try and obtain a technical **baccalauréat**. 6 Approximately 50 per cent of the students who gain the **baccalauréat** go to university to continue their studies. 7 In this last category, more than 60 per cent give up their studies at the end of the first year. (Note: **près de** indicates that the benchmark figure has not been reached, whereas **environ** or **à peu près** can indicate a value either under or above the benchmark.)

Activity 2 1 Non, il est en train de la finir (**traduction** is feminine, as the -tion ending indicates). 2 Non, il était en train de l'expliquer (he was in the process of explaining it). 3 Non, ils sont en train de sortir (the action is not yet completed). 4 Non, il sera en train de le visiter (the action will still be in progress when we get there).

Comprehension 1 1 No, he is wrong: Jean-Michel is going on a language course and an industrial placement. 2 He did well. He was awarded a good pass (**la mention bien**). 3 He has just had a meeting with the tutor in charge of (international) exchanges, who confirmed that he had obtained a place on the scheme. 4 He will attend a six-week intensive language course to improve (rather than perfect) his general and technical English and his knowledge of British institutions. After that, he will spend six months, from January to June, (working) in a British firm. 5 No, they will have nothing to pay (according to him). He has been awarded a grant by his regional authority and the EU will pay his university enrolment fees as part of a student exchange agreement. 6 Because it is the lecturers in the host university who will look after that side of things. 7 The company may decide to up his salary (which initially will be fairly modest).

Activity 3 a 1 Immediate past: tu viens de finir; je viens d'avoir; tu viens de travailler; je viens … d'avoir; il vient de … confirmer; je viens d'obtenir. 2 Immediate future: tu vas faire; je vais aller; tu vas prendre; je vais aller; je vais partir; tu vas faire; je vais aller; je vais suivre; je vais passer; (ils) vont financer; (la CE) va payer; ça va être; (ils) vont s'occuper; tu vas être payé; je vais pas gagner; ça va s'améliorer; tu vas nous envoyer.

b 1 → 2: tu vas finir; je vais avoir; tu vas travailler; je vais avoir; il va … confirmer; je vais obtenir. 2 → 1: tu viens de faire; je viens d'aller; tu viens de prendre; je viens d'aller; je viens de partir; tu viens de faire; je viens d'aller; je viens de suivre; je viens de passer; (ils) viennent de financer; (la CE) vient de payer; ça vient d'être; (ils) viennent de s'occuper; tu viens d'être payé; je viens pas de gagner; ça vient de s'améliorer; tu viens de nous envoyer.

Activity 4 M'sieur (instead of Monsieur); ça va! (i/o je vais bien); ça a marché? (i/o les choses se sont bien passées?); pas mal (i/o bien); c'est pas vrai (i/o ce n'est pas vrai); ils ont rien (i/o ils n'ont rien); c'est tes parents (i/o ce sont tes parents); c'est les profs (i/o ce sont les professeurs); tu vas être payé …? (i/o est-ce que tu vas être payé?); je vais pas gagner beaucoup (i/o je ne vais pas gagner beaucoup d'argent).

Activity 5 1 Mais pourquoi veux-tu aller là-bas? (giving the impression it is totally unreasonable to want to go). 2 Tu sais bien que les Rosbifs sont francophobes (a mildly derogatory term and a sweeping generalization). 3 Tu donneras mes amitiés à Sa Très Gracieuse Majesté (an ironic suggestion unlikely to come true). 4 Bon courage! (this could also be seen as ironic = jolly good luck to you!). 5 N'oublie pas ton parapluie! (typical preconceived idea, according to which it always rains in Britain).

Activity 6 In the dialogue: meeting; Rosbifs; businessman; cool; fair-play; OK. On the postcard: job; manager; week-end. (As a rule, nouns borrowed from English are masculine (see Appendices 2 and 5).)

Activity 7 1 **je vient** should be **je viens** (first person ending); 2 **envoi** should be **envoie** (it is the first group verb **envoyer,** not the noun); 3 **plus** should be **plu** (invariable past participle of **pleuvoir,** 'to rain', nothing to do with 'more'); 4 **dis** should be **dit** (**on** requires the third person singular); 5 **sympatiques** should be spelt with an **h**: **sympathiques**).

Activity 8 1 Because he agreed to do so; to tell him everything is going fine; to stress that since he arrived it has only rained twice. 2 He has finished his language course at the university; he has just started his industrial placement. 3 It is taking place in a local firm; the salary is not wonderful; the work is interesting. 4 The fact that the British hate the French (Jean-Michel says that the people of the area are very friendly). 5 He is going to work hard and, if his manager is pleased with him, he may get a salary increase.

Activity 9 1 grande, petite (both **maison** and **ville** are feminine); 2 correct; 3 vieille (**femme** is feminine singular); 4 nouveaux, charmants (**voisins** is masculine plural); 5 douce (**voix** is feminine singular); 6 grosse, noire (**voiture** is feminine singular); 7 curieuse (**idée** is feminine singular).

Activity 10 1 Wrong: it should be **une vieille femme;** 2 Wrong: **américaine** must be placed after the noun (adjective indicating geographical origin), and l' should be replaced by **la**, since there is no longer any clash of vowels; 3 Correct (adjectives indicating political belief come after the noun); 4 Wrong: **catholique** must be placed after **église** (adjective denoting religious creed) and **la** must be replaced by l', because of the vowel clash; 5 Wrong: **intelligente** must be placed after the noun (intellectual trait); 6 Correct (adjectives of nationality are placed after the noun); 7 Wrong: **grosse** must come before the noun (adjective indicating size).

Activity 11 1 Elle a rarement besoin de moi; 2 Généralement vous travaillerez dans mon bureau. *or* Vous travaillerez généralement dans mon bureau. (adverbs of time or frequency are more flexible as regards position); 3 Quelquefois tu as pris des décisions sans me consulter. *or* Tu as quelquefois pris ... (same rule as for 2); 4 Les enfants ont beaucoup grandi (the adverb is normally placed between the auxiliary and the past participle); 5 Ils avaient un peu bu (same rule as for 4); 6 Nous sommes légèrement blessés (adverbs normally precede the adjective they modify); 7 Il est follement amoureux de toi (same rule as for 6).

Activity 12 1 Mon prof' (professeur), Monsieur Mercier, est anglophobe. 2 Je vais suivre un cours pour améliorer mon français. 3 Jean-Michel a trouvé un stage industriel dans une entreprise (firme) britannique. 4 Ils vont augmenter leurs chances de trouver un bon emploi (job). 5 Pas de problème, c'est le responsable des échanges qui va s'occuper de ça. 6 Nous allons prendre nos vacances en septembre. 7 Elle vient juste d'avoir un meeting avec le technicien. 8 Les étudiants vont aller travailler en Grande-Bretagne dans le cadre du programme européen. 9 On dit que les Français sont xénophobes, mais je suis sûr(e) que c'est pas vrai! (In some of these sentences, note the difference in the use of lower case and capital letters between French and English!)

Activity 13 1 Right. 2 Wrong: it should be **où sont les tiens** (since **amis** is masculine plural). 3 Wrong: it should be **le tien** (since **passeport** is masculine singular). 4 Right. 5 Wrong: it should be **la mienne** (since **fille** is feminine singular). 6 Wrong: the gender is right but the correct form is **le tien** (since the verb **reste** is in the 2nd person singular). 7 Wrong: **difficultés** is feminine plural, so the pronoun required is **les siennes**.

Activity 14 1 la tienne; 2 la nôtre; 3 le tien; 4 les vôtres; 5 le mien; 6 les nôtres; 7 la vôtre; 8 les leurs; 9 la mienne; 10 le sien.

Activity 15 1 La route est bloquée par les fermiers. 2 L'usine va être fermée par le directeur. 3 Le magasin a été vendu par les propriétaires. 4 Une réunion est demandée par les parents. 5 Les arbres viennent d'être arrachés par le vent. 6 La lettre va être signée par le responsable. 7 Elles ont été arrêtées par la police. 8 Un visa a été exigé par les autorités.

Activity 16 1 Le directeur a licencié le personnel. 2 Un loubard a volé la voiture. 3 Le professeur va la punir. 4 Les voisins les ont avertis. 5 Des Parisiens ont acheté la maison. 6 Un gros camion bloque la circulation.

Activity 17 1 Correct (**argent** is masculine singular). 2 Wrong: it should be **refusés** (**visas** is masculine plural, not feminine plural). 3 Correct (**ils** is masculine plural). 4 Wrong: **votés** should be **votées**, since **lois** is feminine plural). 5 Wrong: **elles** is feminine plural therefore **soignés** should be **soignées**). 6 Wrong: **gangsters** (an English word) is masculine plural so **arrêtées** should be **arrêtés**.

Test yourself

1 With the present of **aller** + the infinitive of the main verb. 2 To indicate that an action will take place very shortly. 3 With the present tense of **venir** + **de** + the infinitive of the main verb. 4 To indicate that an action has just taken place. 5 To be in the process of doing something. 6 It changes the style from formal to familiar. 7 Adjectives expressing age, duration and size normally go before the noun. Those expressing nationality and colour go after the noun as do adjectives derived from verbs. 8 The corresponding masculine singular forms **bel**, **nouvel**, **vieil** and **fol** are used when

the noun which follows begins with a vowel of a mute **h**. 9 The adverb usually goes after simple (= one word) tenses. In the case of compound tenses (auxiliary + verb), the adverb goes between the two. There are, however, exceptions. 10 In French, possessive adjectives agree in gender and number with the thing or being 'owned'. Compare: his son, his daughter, his friends and **son fils, sa fille, ses amis.**

UNIT 5

Activity 1 1 cité (in this context: housing estate; also city); 2 voiture (car); 3 maison (house/home); 4 bizarre (strange/odd); 5 fou (mad).

Activity 2 1 j; 2 l; 3 e; 4 g; 5 b; 6 h; 7 n; 8 d; 9 i; 10 m; 11 o; 12 f; 13 k; 14 a; 15 c.

Comprehension 1 1 He asked him if he had done well in his examinations. 2 Because he had worked well all year and his results, without being brilliant, had been acceptable. 3 He lost his cool and could not remember even the simplest things; he had skipped some subjects when revising. 4 Because he had told the class countless times not to skip subjects when revising. 5 He was ill in the second term and he did not have time to revise everything. 6 He feels sure they are going to be disappointed (**déçus** is a false friend). 7 He could retake the failed exams in September, or repeat the year. 8 He says that he will do neither and that he has had enough of studying (the expression **alors là, pas question** indicates the strength of his feelings). 9 He wants to get a job, earn money and enjoy life as his friends do. 10 He says: 'You are the all same! But, for heaven's sake, there are other things in life apart from money!'

Activity 3 1 Est-ce que ces examens se sont bien passés? (**Ces examens se sont-ils bien passés?** would belong to a more elevated register.) 2 J'avais pensé que cela marcherait. 3 Oui, mais ce/cela n'est pas une excuse. 4 Je n'avais pas eu le temps de réviser. 5 Ce sont tes parents qui vont être déçus, n'est-ce pas? 6 Est-ce que tu vas te représenter en septembre? (**Vas-tu te représenter ...**, although perfectly acceptable, would belong to the elevated rather than the standard style.) 7 Je n'y ai pas encore pensé. 8 Il n'y a pas que l'argent dans la vie!

Activity 4 1 dis-moi (in familiar style, **dis-donc** would be more likely). 2 que vas-tu faire? (in standard French, **qu'est-ce que tu vas faire?** would be the expected form). Both of the above are perfectly acceptable, so long as you abide by the rule governing the use of **tu** as opposed to **vous**.

Activity 5 1 Je vous avais prévenus; 2 Je vous l'avais dit et répété cent fois; 3 Vous êtes tous les mêmes. The **vous** form in the first two expressions refers to Olivier and his classmates. In the third one, it refers to young people in general.

Activity 6 The two expressions are: **nom d'un chien!** (literally 'in the name of a dog'), and **nom d'une pipe!** ('in the name of a pipe'). Both mean 'for heaven's sake!' The innocuous **chien** and **pipe** are used to replace **Dieu** (God). Another similar humorous euphemism is **nom d'un petit bonhomme!** ('in the name of a small man!'). All three belong to the familiar register.

Activity 7 1 We sent an e-mail (d.o.). 2 I gave the beggar (i.o.) two euros (d.o.). 3 She brought her friends (i.o.) some flowers (d.o.). 4 He returned the book (d.o.) to the bookshop (i.o.). 5 They gave the owner (i.o.) the keys (d.o.). 6 The director wrote the employees (i.o.) a letter (d.o.). 7 The police permitted him (i.o.) to leave. 8 You have contacted the shop (d.o.). 9 I have lent my neighbour (i.o.) a ladder (d.o.). 10 His master sold him (d.o.) to a slave trader (i.o.).

Activity 8 1 Nous avons envoyé un courriel/email. 2 J'ai donné deux euros au mendiant. 3 Elle a apporté des fleurs à ses amis/amies. 4 Il a ramené le livre à la librairie. 5 Ils (Elles) ont donné les clés au propriétaire. 6 Le directeur a écrit une lettre aux employés. 7 La police lui a permis de partir. 8 Vous avez contacté le magasin. 9 J'ai prêté une échelle à mon voisin/ma voisine. 10 Son maître l'a vendu à un marchand d'esclaves.

Activity 9 1 **appelée** should be **appelé:** the person speaking is obviously male since he says 'my wife'. 2 **Vendue** should be **vendu:** the direct object **maison** (**ils ont vendu quoi? leur maison**) occurs after the past participle and comes too late for the agreement to be made. 3 **Sali** should be **salis:** since it is a reflexive construction with **être,** the past participle has to agree with the masculine plural subject. 4 **ouverte** should be **ouvert:** as in 2, the answer to the question **quoi?** comes too late for the past participle to agree. 5 **arrivé** should be **arrivée** since the verb used is **être** and the subject is feminine. 6 **descendue** should be **descendu;** since the verb is **être,** the past participle agrees with **frère,** like an adjective. 7 **endormis** should be **endormies** (reflexive form using **être**). 8 **furieux** should be **furieuse,** since here again the main verb is **être** albeit in the conditional perfect. 9 **changée** should be **changé:** there is no direct object in this sentence. 10 **revenu** should be **revenus** (masc. plur.), or **revenues** (fem. plur.), since the subject is **nous** and the verb **être.**

Activity 10 1 tombée; 2 lavés; 3 pleuré; 4 vu; 5 arrivés; 6 oublié; 7 perdu, cherchée; 8 achetée; 9 perdus.

Activity 11 1 Non, pas vraiment. Y avait pas mal de candidats brillants. Je suis sûre que j'ai aucune chance! 2 Oui, mais j'ai paniqué. Je sais que c'est pas une excuse, mais ils m'ont demandé des trucs que j'avais pas préparés. 3 Oui, je sais, mais c'est la vie! 4 Je sais pas. J'y ai pas encore pensé. 5 Alors là, pas question! Je vais profiter de la vie.

Activity 12 monter = E; acheter = A; rester = E; tomber = E; manger = A; vendre = A; descendre = E; regarder = A; aller = E; prendre = A; sortir = E; pouvoir = A.

Activity 13 Nous étions partis de la maison à six heures du matin. Nous avions pensé qu'il n'y aurait pas beaucoup de circulation sur l'autoroute. Avant le départ, nous avions téléphoné à nos amis pour leur annoncer l'heure de notre arrivée. Nous avions fait à peine une dizaine de kilomètres quand nous sommes tombés en panne: Jacques avait oublié de faire le plein d'essence! Heureusement, nous avions emmené notre téléphone portable. J'ai appelé notre garagiste. Il est venu nous dépanner tout de suite!

(Note that **partis** is in the masculine plural because one of the people involved is a man.)

Comprehension 2 1 That the role of young people in France had changed drastically since 1968 and that, from the end of the sixties onwards, they assumed considerable economic importance in French society. 2 From 68 onwards, parents who belonged to the baby-boom generation decided to give their children more freedom and independence, and to treat them like adults. They were allowed to express their views, first around the dinner table, then in public and finally in the media. 3 The baby-boomers, who had known a period of deprivation immediately after the war, wanted to give their children what their own parents had not been able to afford; they also wanted to 'get some peace' (to stop the children pestering them). So, they began giving more and more pocket money to their 'little darlings'. 4 It enabled teenagers to spend a significant amount of money on magazines, records and, in the case of girls, beauty products and cosmetics. 5 No, according to the expert, it also involved their younger counterparts, the pre-teens. 6 Gradually, the children who until then had not been allowed to speak up became not just consumers, but decision-makers capable of influencing their elders.

Activity 14

RP That is true, and it did not take long for marketing people (experts) to realize the commercial potential of this new market.

SE Absolutely. We must not forget that in the seventies, the under-20s represented roughly a third of the population of France. So, the top brands launched products specially designed for this category of customers. The eighties and nineties saw the explosion of branded (designer) goods specifically aimed at young people. As their (pocket) money and their purchasing power increased, young consumers became more demanding and asked for designer goods that Nike, Adidas, Diesel, to name but a few, were only too happy to make available (present) to them. Peer pressure played its part (helped) and we have now come to a point where, if a product is not branded, young people do not want it!

RP Thank you for these clarifications, Professor.

Test yourself

1 They use markers (abbreviations, asterisks, etc.). If no marker is present, it means that the word is acceptable in all circumstances. 2 Because these words can shock or cause offence to some people. 3 It never does. 4 Reflexive verbs indicate that the action performed falls back on the performer (e.g. to shave oneself); reciprocal verbs indicate that the performer and the recipient do the same action to each other e.g. to fight (with each other). 5 On some of the blue motorway signs. It means you will have to pay a toll for using a given section of the network. 6 It is **j'ai été malade**, because, in compound tenses where the main verb is **être,** the auxiliary used is **avoir.** 7 They are masculine except for **la star** and, of course, for nouns referring to females (e.g. **la script-girl**). 8 The period when the birth rate was at its highest in France (between the end of the Second World War and the 1956 0s). 9 To indicate that a past action had been completed at a given time or when another one occurred. 10 By 20 May at least ten million people were demonstrating in the streets. During that month, 800 million working hours were lost. The May events led to the departure of General de Gaulle from politics in 1969.

UNIT 6

Comprehension 1 1 As soon as dawn breaks at the hour when darkness gives way to light (lit. whitens the countryside). 2 He says 'I know you are waiting for me (expecting me)', and 'I cannot remain away from you any longer'. 3 'I will walk through the forest and across the mountain.' 4 Line 7: 'alone, unknown, with back bent and hands crossed'. 5 Lines 5 and 6: 'I will walk, deep in thought' (lit. 'with my eyes fixed on my thoughts'), 'without paying any attention to the outside world, or noticing (hearing) any noise'; 9 and 10: 'I will look neither at the gold of the setting sun (lit. the falling evening), or at the distant ships sailing down to Harfleur'. 6 Lines 1 and 9: **dès l'aube** and **l'or du soir qui tombe** indicate that the journey will take all day. 7 The words: **je mettrai sur ta tombe …** ('I will put on your grave …').

Activity 1 1 je partirai (partir, partant); j'irai (aller, allant); je marcherai (marcher, marchant); sera (être, étant); regarderai (regarder, regardant); j'arriverai (arriver, arrivant); je mettrai (mettre, mettant). 2 descendant (descendre).

Activity 2 1 blanchit: whitens (blanchir); vois-tu: you see (voir); je sais: I know (savoir); tu m'attends: you're waiting for me (attendre); tombe: falls (tomber). 2 Because Hugo wants to give an impression of permanence, rather than suggest something which will only be true tomorrow.

Activity 3 1 seront; 2 fera; 3 aura; 4 dureront; 5 voilera; 6 baisseront; 7 pleuvra; 8 verrons; 9 persistera; 10 reprendront.

Activity 4 1 nous allons voir; 2 il va y avoir; 3 vont souffler; 4 va se renforcer; 5 va persister. They have been used to break the monotony of an all-future forecast, to give a feeling of greater immediacy (particularly in the case of 1 and 3) and to avoid the repetition of the same verb twice in succession (in the case of 2 and 5).

Activity 5 1 In the South West tomorrow, it will be cloudy in the course of the morning and the temperature will fall slightly in the early afternoon. 2 On the Atlantic Coast, there will be fairly strong winds and it will rain in the course of the evening and night. 3 In the Midi-Pyrénées region, the wind will become stronger. 4 In the Languedoc-Roussillon area, the clouds will persist and the rain will return in the course of the day. 5 The Provence-Côte d'Azur area will have excellent weather. 6 In the Rhône valley, the good weather will continue at least until Monday. 7 In Eastern France, the weekend weather will be spring-like with a great deal of sunshine; however, it will be a little chilly in the mornings. 8 In the North, Normandy and the Paris region, there will be a great deal of sunshine and blue skies. 9 In Corsica, the weather will be fine as in Provence-Côte d'Azur. 10 There will be some scattered showers but the rain will not last.

Activity 6 Les prévisions pour ce week-end sont excellentes. Nous allons avoir un temps printanier sur toute la France, avec beaucoup de soleil et de ciel bleu. Les températures matinales seront fraîches, de 8 à 10 degrés, mais elles augmenteront dans le courant de la matinée, et dans l'après-midi elles atteindront 26 degrés dans le sud (*or* le Midi). Demain, les températures descendront jusqu'à 6 ou 8 degrés pendant la nuit, mais elles remonteront rapidement dimanche matin et nous aurons une autre journée ensoleillée. Lundi, il y aura pas mal de soleil dans la plupart des régions, sauf dans l'est, où on verra quelques averses éparses (quelques petits passages pluvieux) dans le courant de la matinée, mais elles (ils) ne dureront pas. Dans le nord, il y aura quelques petits nuages mais ils ne persisteront pas très longtemps. Le beau temps continuera jusqu'à mardi. Mardi, les températures baisseront et il pleuvra sur tout le pays, sauf dans la vallée du Rhône et la Provence où le soleil continuera (se maintiendra) au moins jusqu'à jeudi. Bon week-end!

Activity 7 1 Tu iras jouer quand tu auras fini de manger. 2 Vous m'enverrez un email dès que vous aurez eu des nouvelles. 3 Quand il sera rentré à la maison, je parlerai de cette affaire avec lui. 4 Lorsque vous aurez payé la facture, vous pourrez prendre la voiture. 5 Après que vous aurez fermé le bureau, vous laisserez les clés à la réception.

Activity 8 a 1 Personne n'a vu l'accident. 2 Tout est clair. 3 Nul n'est prophète en son pays. 4 Chacun pour soi! 5 Il y a quelqu'un à la porte. 6 Tout est perdu. 7 Chacun de vous va signer cette lettre. b 1 Aucun n'a fini son travail (with **aucun, nul, personne, rien …** the negative particle **ne/n'** is needed, but **pas** must not be used). 2 Correct (although **plus d'une** suggests a plural, it is **a** which is normally used). 3 Wrong: here, **ont** should be **a**, since **pas un** means 'not one'. 4 Correct: **tout** means everything; the verb must therefore be in the 3rd person singular. 5 Wrong: **quelqu'un** is a singular so the verb should be **a**, not **ont**.

Activity 9 2 Quand rentrerez-vous? (E) Vous rentrerez quand? (F) 3 Où est-ce que nous allons? (S) On va où? (F): **on** replaces **nous.** 4 Pourquoi cries-tu? (E) Pourquoi est-ce que tu cries? (S) 5 Quand va-t-il venir? (E) Quand est-ce qu'il va venir? (S) 6 Qui est-ce? (S) = same as elevated. C'est qui/qui c'est? (F) 7 De quoi parlez-vous? (E) De quoi est-ce que vous parlez? (S) 8 Allons-nous attendre encore longtemps? (E) On va encore attendre longtemps? (F): use of **on** for **nous.**

Activity 10 1 Nous avions déclaré que nous étions ruinés. 2. Pierre a répondu qu'il était occupé. 3 Le patron m'a dit que j'avais bien travaillé. 4 La secrétaire a ajouté qu'elle enverrait les documents ce soir. 5 Le professeur s'est exclamé que demain il serait trop tard.

Comprehension 2 1 He has booked a room in a small hotel surrounded by pine trees and lavender (fields), in the South of France. 2 They will go and spend a few days with Daniel's parents. 3 No. To Daniel's statement: 'they will have had enough of us' she replies 'and we of them'! 4 Audrey wants to go to Greece with her boyfriend. 5 Last year, she said she would never go on holiday with them again, because they were old fashioned and not fun to be with at all (boring); she did not talk to them for a whole week. 6 Because if they go there, her husband will be working all the time, repairing the roof, retiling the kitchen ... What will she do during that time? 7 She can take the car, go and visit her friend Évelyne and chat with her (without a man around). 8 She would prefer to spend a few days alone with her husband, read, have some peace and quiet, go for walks, chill out, because it's been a long year and, come September, she will have a whole series of meetings in Paris. 9 The forthcoming presidential election (Élise is involved in politics). 10 She says he is talking rubbish.

Activity 11 a *Familiar vocabulary and expressions:* pas de problème; copain; c'est bien beau; ringards; marrants; décroché les dents; fauchée; ben; copine; décompresser; dis-donc; un petit ami; n'importe quoi! *Familiar questions:* le paradis pour toi, non?; on restera combien de temps avec eux? Tu crois qu'Audrey viendra ...? Elle a dit ça? Et nous, alors? *Other non-standard structures:* on pourrait descendre; ça serait trop beau; on restera …?; après ça; on était trop ringards; pas marrants du tout; on sera plus tranquilles; on verra; on ira passer …; si on va là-bas; je suis pas mariée … b *Elevated/standard expressions:* ce que nous ferons (*i/o* ce qu'on fera); qu'est-ce que nous ferons? (*i/o* qu'est-ce qu'on fera/on fera quoi?); ce que tu voudras (*i/o* comme tu voudras); j'ai toute une série de réunions.

Comprehension 3 1 To please keep their questions short, because there are many calls (coming in) this morning. 2 No, he had arrived in the studio earlier, to take part in 'direct questions', a programme which takes place between 8.20 and 8.30 a.m. 3 She said that at holiday time there are always massive traffic jams around Lyons and that it takes local people three to five times longer to make their usual journey. She wondered whether the government could not find a solution to this problem. 4 They were the staggering of school holidays and the setting up of the **Bison Futé** information system. 5 He said that building more motorways might be a solution, but this could not be done overnight and in any case, the government had no wish to pave France over with concrete (or more accurately tarmac). 6 She asked him if he thought that repression was the answer to the problem of road accidents. 7 He wanted to remind listeners that during his election campaign, the President had clearly said that his two key priorities would be the fight against carnage (lit. violence) on the roads and the fight against cancer. 8 He feels that the answer lies not in repression but in the 'education' of drivers (particularly young ones). 9 The police have now adopted a policy of zero tolerance against the majority of law-breaking incidents; the number of penalty points has been increased for speeding and drink-driving (there will be another 22,000 police and gendarmes on the roads for the holiday rush). 10 A few years ago, his young son was killed on his way to school by a driver who had been drinking and was speeding through the town like a madman. He had been given two years. Christian thinks that was a scandal. 11 This year, the number of road casualties has fallen below 8,000. 12 'And now, the weather!' (The morning phone-in is always followed by the weather forecast.)

Activity 12 -tion: question; solution; situation; opération; actions; infractions; éducation; constatation; limitations; agglomérations (nouns with this ending are all feminine, no exceptions). **-ance/-ence:** vacances; patience; violence; tolérance; conscience (nouns with this ending are feminine; one exception: le silence). **-ssion:** émission; répression (nouns with this ending are all feminine, no exceptions). **-té:** actualité; sécurité; majorité; priorités (abstract nouns with this ending are feminine). **-ment:** gouvernement; commencement (nouns with this ending are masculine; one exception: la jument (the mare)). **-age:** embouteillages (masculine). In this category there are six exceptions: la cage (cage); l'image (image); la nage (swimming); la page (the sheet/page); la plage (the beach); la rage (rage/rabies). Note that the word **invité** is a past participle used as a noun, and does not fit into the -té category, which relates to abstract concepts.

Activité 13

Automobilistes attention!

Le gouvernement vient d'introduire une nouvelle législation pour réduire le problème de l'alcool au volant. Comme vous le savez, il cause chaque année plus de quarante pour cent de tous les accidents mortels de la route!

Si vous conduisez, dites 'non' à l'alcool! Si vous voulez boire, demandez à un ami ou à votre partenaire de conduire.

Ne vous laissez pas tenter par un hôte généreux mais malavisé. Dites 'non' à l'alcool!

La Ligue Antialcoolique

Activité 14 1 Les questions sont extrêmement nombreuses. 2 Les conducteurs sont de plus en plus impatients./Les conducteurs sont de moins en moins patients. 3 Il est plus difficile de voyager en juillet qu'en septembre./Il est moins difficile de voyager en septembre qu'en juillet./Il est moins facile de voyager en juillet qu'en septembre./Il n'est pas aussi difficile de voyager en septembre qu'en juillet./Il n'est pas aussi facile de voyager en juillet qu'en septembre. 4 Les itinéraires bis sont plus tranquilles que les autoroutes./Les autoroutes sont moins tranquilles que les itinéraires bis./Les autoroutes ne sont pas aussi tranquilles que les itinéraires bis. 5 Le nombre des accidents de la route est plus bas que l'année dernière./Le nombre des accidents de la route est moins haut que l'année dernière./Le nombre des accidents de la route n'est pas aussi haut que l'année dernière. 6 La police devient de plus en plus sévère avec les mauvais conducteurs. 7 Les Français sont moins disciplinés que les autres Européens./Les Français sont plus indisciplinés que les autres Européens./Les Français ne sont pas aussi disciplinés que les autres Européens.

Test yourself

1 They are the same. 2 The tense is the future perfect. It is formed by using the appropriate auxiliary (**être** or **avoir**) with the past participle of the main verb. It is used to indicate that an action will have taken place in the future by the time another action occurs. 3 It means to enjoy a long weekend by taking advantage of a few extra days' holiday. 4 No, it means traffic jam. 5 When the speaker or writer refers to things or beings whose identity is unclear or unknown. 6 It's an insult which means a dangerous driver or road hog. 7 It's a government-sponsored service which supplies motorists with traffic information and travel advice at holiday time. 8 Because, despite its age (it was published in 1954), it gives an amusing and very accurate analysis of the French temperament and idiosyncrasies. 9 Because depending on the context it can mean 'more' or 'no more'. 10 **De plus en plus** and **de moins en moins** respectively.

UNIT 7

Activity 1 1 que; 2 qui; 3 quoi; 4 où; 5 dont; 6 que; 7 qui.

Activity 2 1 à qui; 2 pour qui; 3 dont/de qui; 4 pour qui; 5 sans qui.

Activity 3 1 téléphonerais; 2 passerait; 3 prendraient; 4 boirait; 5 irions; 6 appellerais; 7 pourrais.

Activity 4 1 aurais voulu; 2 serait venue; 3 auriez pu; 4 aurait dû; 5 auraient été; 6 aurions mangé.

Activity 5

a Present conditional	*b Conditional perfect*
1 pourriez	auriez pu
2 voudrais	aurais voulu
3 seraient	auraient été
4 voudriez	auriez voulu
5 faudrait	aurait fallu

There is one conditional perfect in the conversation: **vous auriez dû** … It is used to remind Claudine that she should have notified the consulate of her change of address before now!

Activity 6 1 False: it has already expired. 2 True. 3 False: she says she will put the list in the post. 4 False: she moved house two years ago. 5 True. 6 False: the secretary will put them in the post today (this very day). 7 True. 8 False: it will take at least four weeks ('a good month'). 9 True. 10 True.

Activity 7 1 Je voudrais renouveler mon passeport qui vient d'expirer. 2 Est-ce que vous êtes déjà immatriculée à ce consulat? Oui. 3 Je vous envoie la liste des documents à fournir. 4 Nous avons déménagé il y a deux ans. 5 Par courrier, à cause de mes horaires de travail. 6 Aujourd'hui même. 7 En principe, nous préférons la première solution (les démarches en personne). 8 Il faudra compter un bon mois. 9 Un conseil: renvoyez-les en recommandé (c'est plus sûr). 10 J'ai complètement oublié, je suis désolée.

Activity 8 1 vous désirez? 2 je vous prie; s'il vous plaît. 3 désolé(e). 4 bien sûr; bon; d'accord. 5 ce n'est pas grave. 6 une seconde; un moment. 7 pardon? 8 bien; bon. 9 je vous remercie; merci, à vous aussi. 10 use of the conditional: vous pouvez → vous pourriez; je veux → je voudrais, etc.

Activity 9 1 pourriez (pouvoir); 2 voudrais (vouloir); 3 seraient (être); 4 voudriez (vouloir); 5 faudrait (falloir).

Activity 10 1 a is fine; b is far too formal. A one-word formula (**Cordialement** or **Amicalement**) would suffice. 2 a is again fine; b is also appropriate; **mes sentiments respectueux** could be replaced by **l'assurance de mon profond respect.** 3 a is correct; b is also perfectly acceptable for the purpose. 4 a is acceptable, although these days **Madame, Monsieur** is seen as less likely to offend a female employee than **Messieurs;** b is far too familiar. The polite formula of 3 would be fine.

Activity 11 1 They must measure 35 by 45 mm, be identical, recent; taken full face against a white background, and the person must be bare-headed. 2 Either the expired passport or, if the person has never had a passport, the national identity card. 3 No, the instructions clearly state that it is the full birth certificate which is required. 4 A contract of employment with six monthly payslips; proof of residence/address (rent book, invoice/bill ...) 5 Height and colour of eyes. 6 Either cash (in euros or sterling), or by credit card. 7 Ten years. 8 Children under 15 can be put on the parents' passport.

Activity 12 1 Because her working hours coincide with the opening hours of the consulate office, she cannot go in person. 2 Because the rate of exchange is calculated on the day of issue of the passport (the rate of exchange on that day will be used to calculate the amount due). 3 A telephone number where he/she can be contacted during working hours. 4 For the return of the application documents and the passport. 5 It is a disclaimer, which states that the consulate accepts no responsibility for problems relating to mail deliveries.

Activity 13 1 SWIFT; 2 Marc; 3 masculin; 4 britannique; 5 25 février 1970; 6 Londres; 7 célibataire; 8 directeur marketing;

9 75 Belmont Terrace Londres EC1 4UP; 10 père: SWIFT John; 11 mère: SWIFT Claudine; 12 LESCAZE; 13 185 Wilson Street, Londres, EC2A 2BX; 14 père: employé de banque; mère: enseignante.

Activity 14 1 Je suis désolé(e) mais votre passeport est périmé. 2 Je n'ai pas votre présente adresse. 3 Suite à ma visite dans votre bureau, j'aimerais vous remercier de vos conseils. 4 Ma mère désire (*or* voudrait) renouveler sa carte d'identité. 5 Pourriez-vous (*or* voudriez-vous bien) épeler votre prénom, s'il vous plaît? 6 Nous allons déménager dans deux mois. 7 Un moment, je vérifie votre demande. 8 Il est désolé, mais vous n'êtes pas sur sa liste.

Activity 15 1 est; 2 fait; 3 j'avais su; 4 aurions visité; 5 pourrions.

Activity 16 1 Wrong: **si nous aurions** should be **si nous avions.** 2 Correct. 3 Wrong: **nous restions** should be **nous resterions** (present conditional). 4 Correct: **nous passons** instead of the expected **nous passerons** indicates the immediacy of the action. 5 Correct. 6 Correct: **nous pouvons** indicates the fact that the action is imminent; **nous pourrons,** which is equally possible, would situate it a little further into the future. 7 Correct. 8 Wrong: **si j'aurais su** should be **si j'avais su; j'aurais pas venu** should be **je (ne) serais pas venu**(e).

Activity 17 1 doit (probability); 2 savez; peux; 3 faire; 4 laisse; 5 doit (it could also be **peut**, if her solvency is in question); 6 veux (it could be **je dois** if the idea of 'must' rather than 'want' is appropriate).

Test yourself

1 No, the direct object pronoun **que** cannot be omitted; so you must say: **l'homme que j'ai vu.** 2 To express what would happen, now or later, if certain conditions were met; to express a wish, a desire which may not come to fruition; to express a polite request. 3 The first is a polite request. It means: I would like to speak to the director; the second is a demand. It means: I want to

speak to the director. 4 Its Cartesian spirit: the content must be clearly structured to help the reader understand what is required or needs to be done. 5 They must be of the prescribed size, identical, recent, on a white background, full face and bare-headed.
6 **Monsieur, Madame, Messieurs** or **Mesdames** as appropriate.
7 To replace **oui** in response to a negative question; to express doubt; to express a condition. 8 **Pouvoir** indicates ability or permission whereas **savoir** indicates capability (through learning) or knowledge. 9 The fact that, if certain conditions had been met, a given action would have been possible. Unfortunately, that did not materialize. 10 It can, as its English equivalent (must), indicate obligation or great probability.

UNIT 8

Activity 1 1 False: there are important variations in population density (caused by geographical and economic differences).
2 False: for several years there has been a very small increase (this is not in contradiction with later information, but may be due to a slight increase in immigration figures). 3 True. 4 False: it is also due to the fact that women go out to work. 5 False: they are now fully-fledged citizens, and equal to men in all areas of life. 6 False: they do but, despite the legislation, their salaries are lower than those of their male counterparts and lag behind in the promotions 'hit-parade' (league tables). 7 False: it also includes people who are actively seeking employment. 8 False: it's the services sector. (The secondary sector is concerned with industrial activity.)

Activity 2 environ; en moyenne; en partie; à peu près; grosso modo; près de; approximativement.

Activity 3 1 En moyenne les salaires des cols bleus sont à la traîne de ceux des gens qui travaillent dans le (secteur) tertiaire. 2 Depuis mai 68, bon nombre de femmes travaillent à l'extérieur, pour améliorer les revenus de la famille. 3 Malgré la législation introduite après (*or* au lendemain de) mai 68, les salaires des femmes sont, en moyenne, plus bas que ceux de leurs homologues masculins, pour un travail égal (*or* à travail égal).

4 Dans tous les pays industrialisés, le secteur tertiaire se développe significativement (*or* d'une façon significative), au détriment des deux autres secteurs. 5 Actuellement, la population active de l'Hexagone compte approximativement 28 millions de personnes. 6 En ce moment, il y a en France environ 2 millions de travailleurs qui sont sans emploi.

Activity 4 1 Ils (elles) voulaient aller au cinéma, mais en fait ils (elles) sont resté(e)s à la maison et ont regardé la télévision. 2 Vous êtes un col bleu. En fait, vous ne devriez pas être là (*or* ici). 3 Vous avez aimé le film? En effet! 4 Est-ce que je pourrais voir votre passeport (s'il vous plaît)? En fait, je l'ai laissé chez moi/à la maison. 5 Les gens pensent que nos produits sont chers, mais en fait ils sont très compétitifs.

Activity 5 1 inactif; 2 imbuvable; 3 indestructible; 4 illégitime; 5 immoral; 6 impersonnel; 7 irrationnel; 8 insupportable.

Activity 6 1 recouper; 2 redécorer; 3 refaire; 4 remonter; 5 replacer; 6 reprendre; 7 revivre. Note the difference between **replacer** (to put something back where you found it) and **remplacer** (to replace with something/someone else).

Activity 7 1 avertissement (masc.); 2 changement (masc.); 3 construction (fem.); 4 lavage (masc.) *or* lavement (masc.); 5 modification (fem.); 6 nettoyage (masc.); 7 opération (fem.); 8 ouverture (fem.); 9 préparation (fem.).

Activity 8 1 consommateur (masc.); 2 croissance (fem.); 3 équipement (masc.); 4 expression (fem.); 5 finition (fem.); 6 fournisseur (masc.); 7 productivité (fem.); 8 protection (fem.); 9 représentant (masc.); 10 livraison (fem.).

Comprehension 1 1 He said that Marc could do worse. The Lot-et-Garonne is still a good place to buy property. 2 When people (of the area) were young, they moved to big cities to seek their fortune, but now that they have retired, they tend to come back to their roots. 3 A few years ago, prices were still reasonable;

now things have changed, like everywhere else, and prices have a tendency to rocket (or go through the roof). 4 Jean-Claude says that there are still a number of market gardeners and farmers in the area; twice a week there is a market in the town centre where the local farmers come and sell their fruit and vegetables. 5 They irritate her beyond measure, because they have no intention of buying the product they want from her. Once they have all the information they need, they go to the hypermarket to buy the product. (The expressions **ça m'énerve, casser les pieds** and **ça me tue** attest to her irritation.) 6 The personnel do not have the technical competence; they are salesmen and women, not specialists. 7 He says that small retailers tried to get together to bulk-buy, but without much success because they could not compete against the reductions hypermarkets are able to offer their customers. 8 Michèle is young (that is why these things irritate her), whereas Jean-Claude will be retiring in three months. 'I don't care what happens when I'm gone', he says.

Activity 9 On the whole, Michèle's register is familiar. She uses **vous** instead of **nous**, as if she was switching places with Marc: **vous avez des clients** (for **il y a des clients**); **des tas** (for **beaucoup**); **vous casser les pieds** (for **vous ennuyer**); **ils ont aucune envie** (for **ils n'ont aucune envie**); **une fois que** (for **quand/lorsque**); **ça** (for **cela**); **ça me tue** (for **cela me déprime**); **le personnel ... a pas ...** (for **le personnel ... n'a pas ...**); **ça ne va pas plus loin** (for **cela ne va pas plus loin**); **y a** (for **il y a**).

Activity 10 1 On a essayé de s'organiser (nous avons ... de nous ...), mais sans grand succès. 2 N'oublions pas que ... 3 Ceci dit, on a (nous avons) essayé de lutter contre la concurrence. 4 La meilleure solution serait de demander un rendez-vous. 5 Je vais chercher fortune à Paris. 6 On va (*or* nous allons) au restaurant deux fois par semaine. 7 Les gens ont beaucoup changé. Maintenant ils ont tendance à aller dans les hypermarchés (les grandes surfaces) pour faire leurs achats. 8 Pourquoi est-ce que les clients ne viennent pas dans votre magasin? 9 Ce qui m'irrite le plus (ce qui me tue), c'est que pas mal (*or* beaucoup) de petits magasins ont dû fermer leurs portes.

Comprehension 2 1 Working conditions, salaries and the retirement issue. 2 The international economic climate is not conducive to wage increase demands of up to 15 per cent, considering that this year the rate of inflation is 2 per cent. 3 To the first group he says: 'you can expect from me neither weakness nor sympathy' and to the second he advocates patience and moderation. 4 He says that hundreds of thousands of schoolchildren and students will see their examinations postponed or cancelled because of the strike. 'Is it reasonable', he asks, 'to gamble with the future of our young people in what is for them a crucial period?' 5 The government will study the demands, as it does regularly, and will, as far as possible, try to satisfy them. 6 He pledges to meet with the representatives of the various trade unions involved, to work out (set up) a programme likely to satisfy them. 7 The period of contribution has been extended to 40 years (without a payment increase). 8 It is what people would call **un discours musclé**. The tone is both tough (**n'attendez de moi ni faiblesse ni sympathie; est-il raisonnable ...? Je ne le crois pas!; il faut se rappeler que toute réforme est coûteuse; nous devons faire de notre mieux ...**), and conciliatory (**le gouvernement essaiera dans la mesure du possible d'y donner satisfaction**). The Prime Minister is putting forward proposals for meetings and discussions with the various trade unions. He promises to listen to the demands and, as far as circumstances will allow, to take measures to satisfy them. He also reminds his listeners that the government has kept its promises as far as financially possible.

Activity 11 1 avoir eu; 2 avoir été; 3 s'être trouvé; 4 avoir voulu; 5 être devenu (because **devenir**, like **venir**, **revenir**, etc. takes être as its auxiliary).

Activity 12 1 Quand je rentrerai (à la maison), il sera en train de laver sa voiture. 2 Je viens juste de téléphoner à Marc. Il est en train de préparer le document. 3 Si tout va bien, demain à cette heure-ci, je serai en train de signer le contrat. 4 Quand je suis arrivé(e), ils (elles) étaient en train de finir leur déjeuner. 5 On savait (nous savions) qu'il serait en train de décorer sa chambre.

Test yourself

1 It's a range (of products). 2 It's the first one. In French the comma is the equivalent of the English decimal point. 3 It's the name of a hypermarket. 4 **En fait** means 'in fact' or 'as a matter of fact' and **en effet** means 'indeed!'. 5 The first one means 'to close one's door' and the second means 'to close down/cease trading'. 6 Après moi, le déluge! 7 Because it is a 'false friend'! It means likeable/nice/friendly. 8 The prefix in- becomes im- before b or p; it becomes il- before l; and it changes to ir- before r. 9 With the present infinitive of **avoir** or **être**, as appropriate, and the past participle of the main verb (e.g. **avoir fini; être allé**). 10 The present infinitive is used to indicate an action which is to take place now or later, and the perfect infinitive indicates an action which is to have taken place by a given time. Compare: **Tu dois partir à midi** (You must go at 12 p.m.) and **Tu dois être parti à midi** (You must be gone by 12 p.m.).

UNIT 9

Activity 1 1 que j'aie payé; 2 que nous ayons fini; 3 qu'il soit rentré; 4 qu'ils aient réussi; 5 que vous ayez pu; 6 que nous ayons eu; 7 qu'elle soit partie.

Activity 2 1 indicative; 2 subjunctive; 3 subjunctive; 4 indicative; 5 subjunctive; 6 indicative; 7 indicative; 8 subjunctive; 9 subjunctive; 10 subjunctive.

Activity 3 1 Il (nous) faut fermer le magasin. 2 J'aimerais pouvoir voyager avec toi. 3 Nous voulons attendre ton arrivée. 4 Il est essentiel pour vous de finir ce travail. 5 J'exige (de lui) le remboursement de cet argent. 6 Ils ont peur du refus du consulat. 7 Ils aimeraient avoir votre accord.

Activity 4 1 Il est encore possible que le message arrive. 2 Il faut que nous changions de l'argent. 3 Il serait impossible que nous refusions. 4 Combien de temps faudra-t-il que j'attende? 5 Il faut que nous réservions une place au restaurant. 6 Je ne crois pas que je puisse réussir. (This last sentence, in which the subject is the same in the two clauses (je and je), does not usually need the subjunctive.)

Activity 5 1 s; 2 h; 3 r; 4 p; 5 g; 6 n; 7 l; 8 d; 9 a; 10 c; 11 u; 12 e; 13 o; 14 f; 15 m; 16 k; 17 q; 18 j; 19 t; 20 i; 21 b.

Activity 6

Ingrédients:

Un litre et demi de bouillon. Trois oignons moyens. Soixante grammes de beurre. Quatre-vingts grammes de farine. Une cuillère à café de sucre.

Préparation: douze minutes. Cuisson: vingt minutes.

Épluchez les oignons et coupez-les en tranches. Mettez-les dans une casserole, ajoutez le beurre et le sucre et faites dorer. Saupoudrez de farine. Ajoutez le bouillon, faites bouillir, puis faites cuire à feu doux de quinze à vingt minutes. Ajoutez le sel et le poivre (*or* salez et poivrez). Couvrez le fond d'une soupière avec de fines tranches de pain (*or* des tranches de pain fines). Versez la soupe sur le pain. Si vous le désirez (*or* Si désiré) ajoutez du (fromage de) gruyère râpé. Servez chaud.

Comprehension 1 1 It is a charming little town with a population of 25,000, situated in the département of Lot-et-Garonne, in verdant countryside and amidst gently undulating hills; a river, the Lot, flows through the town. 2 It lies 60 kilometres south of Bergerac, and half way between Bordeaux (to the west) and Toulouse (to the east). 3 Although it is called Villeneuve, it is a very old town. It used to be a walled (fortified) town, but nowadays most of the ramparts have disappeared; one of its bridges dates back to the 13th century, a time when the English still occupied Aquitaine. 4 Holidaymakers, retired people, and foreigners who dream of settling in France, because of the climate and the gently rolling landscape. 5 Formerly, thanks to its climate and its rich soils, the region was predominantly agricultural and was famous for its fruit and vegetables. Although it is still renowned for its **pruneaux**, agricultural activity has declined, partly because of foreign competition, but there are still some farms and market gardens in the area. 6 There is no mention of the (violent) storms which sometimes occur in the area. Presumably the omission is due to the fact that the local tourist office does not want to scare visitors away. 7 The **pruneaux d'Agen** are in fact produced around Villeneuve and, in spite of the competition of imports from California, the local prunes are well known and much appreciated by connoisseurs. The plums are picked in September and dried in special ovens in which temperature and moisture are rigorously controlled. (A few years ago there was a humourous slogan, about Villeneuve being the only town in the world where people worked for 'prunes', i.e. for nothing.)

Activity 7 1 True; 2 True; 3 True; 4 False: it is Bergerac which is renowned for its wines. (Although prunes are produced in the Villeneuve area, its reputation has been usurped by Agen, the main town of the département.) 5 False: the reference applies to Bordeaux and Toulouse, not Villeneuve. 6 This is no longer true, partly because of foreign competition, but there is still some farming and market gardening in the area. 7 False: the market takes place twice a week, on Tuesdays and Saturdays.

Activity 8 1 fem. (ending in -tion); 2 masc. (ending in -ment); 3 masc. (English word); 4 fem. (ending in -ence); 5 masc. (all nouns for months are masculine); 6 fem. (ending in -ture); 7 fem. (ending in -té).

Activity 9 agréablement (agréable); anciennement (ancien); internationalement (international); largement (large); essentiellement (essentiel); principalement (principal); rigoureusement (rigoureux); sérieusement (sérieux); actuellement (actuel); fraîchement (frais); vraiment (vrai).

Activity 10 1 Villeneuve est une charmante petite ville. 2 La région est renommée/célèbre pour ses légumes et ses fruits.

3 Anciennement/Autrefois Villeneuve était une ville fortifiée. 4 Les gens du coin vous diront que la ville attire de nombreux touristes. 5 La production est rigoureusement contrôlée. 6 Les fruits et les légumes de la région sont très appréciés. 7 Au treizième siècle, les Anglais occupaient encore l'Aquitaine.

Activity 11 1 Les œufs se vendent à la douzaine. 2 Les pruneaux se récoltent en septembre. 3 L'espagnol s'apprend facilement. 4 Ce signal se verra de loin. 5 Ces produits peuvent s'acheter au supermarché.

Activity 12 1 Nous avons pris nos parapluies car il pleuvait et nous sommes allés nous promener. 2 Elle voulait nous accompagner, mais elle avait beaucoup de travail, donc elle est restée à la maison. 3 Je pense donc je suis.

Comprehension 2 1 Because she is is a bit homesick. 2 He suggests that Marc should go to an estate agent's (that's the most logical solution). 3 This free paper carries a good many adverts about properties for sale. This would give Marc an idea about prices. 4 He suggests that Marc's parents should exercise caution if they wish to buy a property, because unfortunately, in Villeneuve as elsewhere, there are dishonest people. 5 Because it was situated on a hill, to the south of the town; the view was superb and the price seemed reasonable. 6 Renovating the property cost them an arm and a leg and this year they have decided to sell up and to go back to England. 7 He points out that she left France so long ago that she may be out of her depth (in such matters).

Activity 13 afin que (+ S); pour que (+ S); parce que (+ I); vu que (+ I); de sorte que (+ S).

Activity 14 1 Tu viens de Paris? Oui, j'en viens. 2 Vous êtes revenues de Marseille? Nous n'y sommes pas allées! 3 Vous avez parlé de cette affaire? Oui, nous en avons parlé. 4 Vous habitez dans la région? Oui, nous y habitons. 5 Tu viens d'Espagne? Oui, j'en viens et j'y retourne!

Activity 15 Il n'est pas le propriétaire du magasin, il n'en est que le gérant; non, pas pour l'instant, mais ils y pensent; il y en a une bonne douzaine à Villeneuve; vous pourrez done y aller: on trouve pas mal de propriétés à vendre; il y a malheureusement des gens malhonnêtes, ici comme partout; je vais vous en chercher une de sorte que vous puissiez y jeter un coup d'œil. (Note that in the expression **la remise en état, en** is not a pronoun, but a preposition followed by a noun.)

Activity 16 The first property is recent, in excellent condition. No DIY skills appear to be needed at this stage. The house has (mains) gas central heating, a lounge and a reception room; the kitchen is fully equipped. The garden is sizeable, secluded and planted with trees. The price is high, compared with the others, considering there are only three bedrooms.

The second one sounds like a bargain at just under half the price of the first. It is stone-built, and has a basement and four bedrooms, a games room, a laundry room, gas central heating (mains). The garden is also secluded and is bigger than that of the first property. The fact that it is near the town centre could be a plus (or a minus).

The third property seems like a real bargain; it has four bedrooms but has development potential. The expression **à rénover** should set alarm bells ringing, unless you are a very keen DIY enthusiast, ready to 'rough it' for a while. The attractive features are the view over the Lot valley and a large plot of land. It sounds like a challenge. The price seems very reasonable, almost too good to be true!

The last property does not give a great deal of information, except as regards the habitable floor space, which is greater than that of property number 3 (and bigger than the garden!). The garden is mature but fairly small (possibly 10 m × 13 m). The price is reasonable for the area, and the plus point is the view over the river.

Our ranking would be: 3, 2, 4, 1, which corresponds to the price range.

Test yourself

1 To express possibility, doubt, fear, hope, longing or command. 2 No. They all have the same endings, except for the two auxiliaries **avoir** and **être**. 3 No. If the action expresses a reality rather that a vague possibility or doubt (see 1 above), it will be followed by the indicative. Compare: 'Je suis sûr qu'elle viendra' ('I'm sure she will come' – indicative) and 'Je ne suis pas sûr qu'elle vienne' ('I don't think she will come' – subjunctive). 4 By using an infinitive, a noun, or the imperative tense. 5 They are truffles and farmers use dogs or pigs to find them. 6 Adjectives in **-ent** (e.g. **violent**) and **-ant** (e.g. **courant**). They form their adverbs of manner in -emment (e.g. **violemment**) and **-amment** (e.g. **couramment**) respectively. 7 It is situated in the south west, on the river Lot, half way between Bordeaux and Toulouse and 60 kilometres south of Bergerac. 8 Because some sections of the ancient fortified walls are still visible and there are two towers which used to control entry into the town. 9 No. Because of its soil and climate, it was essentially an agricultural area, but its activities have declined because of foreign imports. 10 Dried prunes, incorrectly called les **pruneaux d'Agen,** (sometimes preserved in alcohol).

UNIT 10

Activity 1 1 je réduisis; 2 je rougis; 3 je déclarai; 4 je suivis; 5 j'émigrai; 6 je me réfugiai; 7 je vendis; 8 je couvris.

Activity 2 naquit; durent; fut; allèrent; acheta; fit; décida; effectua; prépara; dut; acheta; fut; aidèrent; prospéra; devinrent; résolut; sut; put; valut; entretint.

Activity 3 No model is given for this activity.

Activity 4 a durent quitter; allèrent s'installer; dut faire; sut rendre; put donner. b il décida d'aller; il fut obligé d'emprunter; il résolut de faire. c il fut muté, il fut obligé (both of which are in the passive mood).

Comprehension 1 1 The representatives of the people, who had set themselves up as a National Assembly. 2 To set out, in a solemn declaration, the natural, inalienable and sacred rights of human beings. 3 Disregard (wilful ignorance), neglect and contempt concerning human rights. 4 The upholding of the Constitution and the happiness of all.

Activity 5 A article 10; B article 5; C article 4; D article 1; E article 7; F article 9; G article 7.

Activity 6 1 constamment (constantly) constant; 2 strictement (strictly) strict; 3 évidemment × 2 (evidently/obviously) évident; 4 antérieurement (previously/beforehand) antérieur; 5 légalement × 2 (legally) légal; 6 sévèrement (severely) sévère; 7 librement (freely) libre.

Activity 7 1 Personne ne peut être obligé de faire ce qui n'est pas défendu/interdit. 2 Les distinctions sociales ne peuvent être fondées/basées que sur l'utilité commune. 3 Nul ne peut être contraint à faire ce que la loi n'ordonne/n'exige pas. 4 Tous les citoyens peuvent parler et écrire librement. 5 Tout citoyen se rend coupable par la résistance. 6 Toute rigueur excessive doit être sévèrement réprimée/punie. 7 Les droits naturels de l'homme sont les droits à la liberté, la sûreté et la résistance à l'oppression. 8 Ces limites ne peuvent être déterminées que par la loi.

Activity 8 1 leur rappelle (present subjunctive); 2 soient (present subjunctive); 3 tournent (present subjunctive); 4 ait été (perfect subjunctive); 5 trouble (present subjunctive).

Activity 9 considérant (considérer); pouvant (pouvoir); étant (être) × 2. The present participle used as an adjective is **suivants**.

Comprehension 2 1 They were the fight against insecurity and health, in particular the fight against cancer and the fight against danger (lit. insecurity) on the roads. He says that he kept his promises and that the results are already visible, but that there is still a great deal to be done in both areas. 2 They wanted to write a new page in history, and to abandon for ever the inequalities and privileges characteristic of the Ancien Régime. In a word, they strove to create a society based on freedom, equality and fraternity. 3 Many other countries decided to follow their example and to adopt the same democratic principles (something for France to be proud of). 4 Too many French citizens live below the poverty line. There are, in France, 100,000 people who are currently homeless. 5 Thousands of jobs have been created for disadvantaged young people, and the minimum wage and the starting salary have been increased, as has the allowance given to unemployed people during training. 6 Because he says he is conscious of the fact that there may be a link between youth unemployment and the rise in crime. 7 Because illiteracy, which is in itself a cause of poverty (lit. distress), prevents those who suffer from it from benefiting fully from the help to which they are entitled. 8 Allowances have been increased for over-sixties on low incomes, to enable them to meet their daily expenditure. 9 That France is a rich country in which every citizen deserves to live with dignity and decency, but that there is still much to be done to reduce social inequalities and to close the gap that exists between the rich and the poor. 10 Those principles have made France a model and an example for the rest of the world to follow.

Activity 10 1 il y ait (bien que); la liberté soit (quoique); il prenne (j'ai demandé); puissent × 2 (pour que); puissent (afin que); vive × 2 (set phrase).

Activity 11 1 écrivirent (écrire); 2 voulurent (vouloir); 3 s'efforcèrent (s'efforcer – reflexive); 4 suivirent (suivre); 5 décidèrent (décider). The situation is formal and, in the first part, the President gives a historical account of the aims of the founders of French democracy.

Activity 12 1 Ayant téléphoné, je partis immédiatement. 2 L'ayant examiné, elle lui ordonna de rester au lit. 3 Ayant arrêté le voleur, ils l'avaient mis en prison. 4 Étant plus intelligent que moi, tu as pu résoudre ce problème. 5 Étant partis avant nous, ils sont arrivés les premiers. 6 Étant sortis de l'appartement, nous avons fait une petite promenade. 7 Ayant réussi à vos examens, vous pouvez prendre des vacances. (Note: to create a similar time gap between the two actions you can use the preposition **après** followed by the perfect infinitive in sentences 1, 2, 3, 5, 6 and 7 (but not in 4), i.e. **avoir/être** + past participle, e.g. **après avoir téléphoné**).

Comprehension 3 1 In 1963–4, Villeneuve welcomed over 2,500 refugees from North Africa. In 1954, at the end of the war in Indo-China, a similar number of Vietnamese refugees arrived in the town. 2 He acknowledges that there are a few thefts from time to time but he says that Villeneuve is a quiet town where drugs are not a problem. 3 Prices are reasonable, the food is excellent, the air is clean and people live longer than elsewhere. 4 Because, having fought alongside French troops, they had to be repatriated for fear of reprisals from the FLN and they arrived in France with nothing (they had to flee, leaving everything behind). 5 On both occasions the influx of refugees was over 2,500, which represented approximately ten per cent of the total local population. 6 It has recently made considerable efforts to help the unemployed set up new businesses. 7 Following the arrival of North African refugees in Villeneuve, there was some friction between them and the local community, but things have now quietened down. It is a peaceful middle-class town with a large number of retired people, where unemployment is at about the national average. There are a few layabouts, like everywhere else, but no major social problems.

Activity 13 1 Parce que le climat est agréable, et que c'est une ville bourgeoise, calme et sans problèmes. 2 Il a remarqué (*false friend*) qu'il y avait pas mal d'Arabes aux terrasses des cafés, et des SDF qui faisaient la manche dans la grand'rue. 3 Parce qu'on craignait (contre eux) des représailles de la part du FLN, car ils avaient combattu aux côtés des troupes françaises (pendant la guerre d'Algérie). 4 Villeneuve a accueilli à peu près 2.500 réfugiés indochinois pour les mêmes raisons (politiques) que dans le cas des Algériens. 5 Le Maghreb est le nom que l'on donne aux trois pays d'Afrique du Nord (Algérie, Tunisie, Maroc), qui étaient autrefois des colonies françaises (et qui sont aujourd'hui indépendants). 6 Non, pas du tout. 7 Les indemnités que le gouvernement distribuait/donnait aux réfugiés (trop généreusement selon certains). 8 Non, il y a quelques vols de temps en temps mais rien de très grave.

Activity 14 1 Croyez-moi (croire); 2 admettons-le (admettre); 3 Oublions-les (oublier); 4 Disons (dire); 5 Ne dramatisons pas (dramatiser); 6 Tranquillisez-vous (se tranquilliser – reflexive); 7 N'exagérons pas (exagérer); 8 avouez-le (avouer).

Test yourself

1 The first indicates that the action took place once; the second that it used to happen regularly. 2 No. It was abolished in 2002. 3 Students successfully following a course in higher education. 4 The **Assemblée Nationale** and the **Sénat**. 5 Because the wording refers to men and not to both sexes. 6 **Nul/personne n'est arrivé**. In standard French, such expressions incorporate the particle **ne** to reinforce the negative meaning. 7 The first one means 'I saw him (as he was) speaking to a friend' and the second 'I saw him as I was speaking to a friend'. 8 The second one is in the infinitive the first is **avoir** or **être**. 9 The subjunctive, because they imply conjecture, fear, uncertainty. 10 A stranger to the area (visitor/tourist), since the expression means the same as **office du tourisme** (tourist office).

Appendices

1 False friends

When learning a foreign language, we sometimes get the feeling that some words and phrases seem familiar, because they sound or look like expressions that exist in our own language. This feeling should not be dismissed out of hand, since it will help us make good progress, but it should be treated with care. Keep your eyes open: quite often in conversation, the general context, the situation and people's facial expressions will give you useful clues and warn you to be careful.

'False friends' are usually words (or expressions) which look similar or even identical in the two languages, but have a totally different meaning. A famous example is the French expression **un éléphant blanc**. Literally, it means *a white elephant*, but whereas in English it is used to refer to something worthless, in French, it means *one in a million*. So, if someone (usually a man) is told: **Vous êtes un éléphant blanc**, he should feel flattered, not insulted!

Whenever you encounter **des faux amis** (*false friends*), you should make a special effort to remember them, since they are – in the beginning at least – likely to 'trip you up'.

Below is a list of French words/expressions which you have to be particularly wary of:

- **attendre** means *to wait* not *to attend* which is **être présent** (**à** ...)
- **content** (adj.) means *pleased*, rather than *content*
- **costume** (masc.) means *a suit* (although **un costume de bain** can mean *a swimsuit*)

- **course** (fem.) is *a race* or *an errand; a course* is **un cycle d'études** or **un cours**
- **déçu** (past part.) means *disappointed; deceived* is **trompé**
- **demander** means *to ask* (*to demand* is **exiger**)
- **drogue** (fem.) means a *noxious substance* (alcohol, tobacco, cocaine, heroin, etc.). A drug as prescribed by a doctor is **un médicament** or **un remède.**
- **énervant** means *irritating* or *annoying*, rather than *debilitating/enervating*
- **étranger** (masc.) can mean *a stranger* or *a foreigner*
- **formidable** (adj.) normally means *wonderful, smashing* as in **un type formidable** (*a great guy*)
- **hasard** (masc.) means *chance*, rather than *hazard,* which in French is translated by **un risque, un danger,** or **un péril**
- **inhabité***:* here, the prefix in- means *un-* or *not …;* **habité** means *lived in*, so **inhabité** means *uninhabited* or *empty*
- **intoxiqué** means *affected by some harmful substance* (bad food, fumes/gas …). *Intoxicated* is **ivre** or more familiarly **saoûl** (pronounced like **sous**).
- **jogging** (masc.) means *the act of jogging* and also *the suit you wear for jogging*!
- **merci** (adv.) means *thank you.* Sometimes it can mean *mercy* as in John Keats' poem **'La Belle Dame sans Merci'** (definitely not *'the beautiful woman who did not say thank you'*!).
- **pourpre** (adj.) means *crimson* and not *purple,* which is **violet**
- **récipient** (masc.) is *a container. The recipient* of a letter or parcel is **le destinataire.**
- **regarder** means *to look at; to regard* would be **considérer**
- **reporter** as a verb means *to postpone. To report* is **rapporter.** Note, however, that **un reporter** (from English) is *a newspaper reporter.*
- **résumer** means *to sum up* and not *to resume*, which is **reprendre**
- **slip** (masc.) when referring to a garment means *briefs/ underpants/knickers* (for men or women). Note, however, that **un slip de bain** is *bathing trunks* for a man. *A slip (underskirt)* is **une combinaison.**

- **sympathique** means *friendly, amicable. Sympathetic* would be **compréhensif** or **compatissant.**
- **terrible** (adj.) can mean *awfully good* as well as *dreadful.* In this case, you will have to rely on other clues (like facial expressions) to find out the exact meaning. **J'ai vu un film terrible!** *(I saw/I've seen a smashing film!)*
- **trafic** (masc.) means *traffic* when referring to the volume of traffic specifically related to lorries, trains, boats. For the normal movement of vehicles on the roads, the word is **la circulation** which also means *blood circulation*
- **veste** (fem.) is *a jacket*; *a vest* is **un tricot de corps**

For the above and many similar words, you must learn to rely on the 'linguistic context' (tone of voice, facial expressions, what precedes or follows …) to give you clues about the meaning.

As your learning progresses you will encounter many more of these treacherous 'false friends'. Whenever you come across one, make a note of it, write down its meaning, try to remember it, and make a point of using it as soon as appropriate.

---

2 Franglais

Because of the economic, political and artistic influence of Britain and the United States on French life, a great many English words and expressions are used in everyday communication, in spite of the desperate attempts of the French authorities to halt what they see as a linguistic invasion. A special government commission, **le Haut Comité pour la Défense de la Langue Française,** was set up many years ago to try to preserve 'the purity of the French language'. It failed dismally. More recently, legislation was introduced to curb the use of English words in official publications/documents.

Some of the reasons for the use of Franglais stem from the fact that certain inventions (computers), technical fields (cinema, space research), economic activities (business and marketing), etc. came from the United States or Britain. French business specialists, having gone to study at Harvard or at other prestigious business schools, brought back with them words like *merchandising*, *break-even*, *sourcing*, initially coined in a language much more flexible and capable than French of creating new words with the greatest of ease.

Young people also played their part, by borrowing words and expressions from the American and British youth culture (films, songs …). So, even now, the dictates of the French government tend to be ignored in everyday communication, to the great dismay of purists.

A helpful pointer

As already mentioned, there are thousands of English words in everyday use in France. Virtually all nouns borrowed from English are masculine. Their presence, as stated above, is particularly noticeable in certain fields of activity:

1 Business: **le business, le brain storming, le break-even, le holding, le leader, le management, le marketing, le meeting, le merchandising, le sourcing …**
2 Amenities/Places: **le building, le bungalow, le club, le drugstore, le parking, le hall, le loft, le mobile home, le snack (-bar) …**
3 Machines/Tools: **le cutter, le freezer, le hovercraft, le mixer, le rotavator, le roundbaler, le scanner …**
4 Sport: **le corner, le crack (*champion!*), le cricket, le foot(-ball), le goal (score), le golf, le hand-ball, le match, le penalty, le spoiler, le surf(-ing), le sweepstake …**

The above are nouns, but you will also encounter some verbs: **dribbler** (*to dribble – basketball*), **scotcher** (*to repair with sticky tape*), **shooter** (*to shoot*), as well as some adjectives: **cool** (*relaxed*), **hard** (*hardcore*) …

Sometimes the meaning is not faithful to the original, and could even be grossly misleading: **le ball-trap** (*clay pigeon shooting!*),

le catch (*wrestling*), **le footing** (*jogging*), **le jogging** (*activity* or *jogging suit*) …

Knowing which English words are commonly used in French will be helpful to increase your vocabulary, so long as you heed the following advice:

1 Do not over-use English words;
2 Avoid using Franglais when writing formal letters;
3 Be aware that, although the words come from English or American, they have often been adapted to comply with the pronunciation rules of French (**roundbaler** sounds like the unlikely association of the English words '*room-ba-lair*'!

As pointed out before, nouns borrowed from English are nearly always masculine. There are, however, a few exceptions:

la star (*famous person* – male or female), **une interview** (-), and, of course, the names of women performing a particular job: **la continuity-girl, la script-girl, la call-girl** …

---

3 Vocabulary development

There are a very large number of words which, because of the 'Latin connection', appear in both English and French, often (but not always) with the same meaning. They are known as 'cognates'. Being aware of this has two advantages for you:

1 The first is that, for a given category, you will, with a fair degree of accuracy, be able to guess the form (and the meaning) of the French word corresponding to the English one. But beware: in language, you can never be absolutely sure that 'rules' will work 100% of the time;
2 The second is that, for many categories, you will be able to 'predict' whether the word is masculine or feminine.

Rule 1: English nouns ending in *-tion* (not just *-ion*), have an equivalent or near-equivalent in French, and the French noun is feminine:

administration, concentration, déclaration, composition, dévotion, fraction, formation, génération, indication, modération, nation, perfection, vérification ... (beware, however, of **caution** which in French means *a bond on a house*).

The same rule applies to nouns ending in *-sion* or *-ssion*:

confusion, décision, excursion, fusion, intrusion, version; admission, concession, confession, fission, profession, session ...

Rule 2: English nouns ending in *-ism* have French equivalents or near-equivalents ending in **-isme**, which are masculine:

antagonisme, communisme, conservatisme, dynamisme, fanatisme, socialisme, terrorisme, vandalisme, charisme.

Rule 3: English abstract nouns ending in *-ty* have a French equivalent or near-equivalent in **-té**, and they are feminine:

activité, beauté, capacité, faisabilité, familiarité, futilité, généralité, impartialité, moralité, normalité, qualité, sénilité, totalité, vanité, vulgarité, vérité ...

Beware, however of **férocité** which is usually *ferociousness* in English and **fatalité**, a 'false friend', which means *fate* and refers to something which was bound to happen!

Rule 4: English nouns ending in *-ment* usually (but not always) have near-equivalents in French, and they are masculine:

appartement, développement, document, fragment, gouvernement, ligament, moment, monument, mouvement, tourment ...

Rule 5: English nouns ending in *-ture* have an equivalent or near-equivalent in French, and they are feminine:

architecture, culture, facture, fracture, fourniture, investiture, lecture, posture, structure, torture …

Beware: **lecture** means *reading* as a leisure activity, **facture** means *a bill*, **fourniture** means *supply*.

Rule 6: A good many French nouns ending in *-age* are masculine:

courage, garage, message, passage, voyage (which indicates travel by any means, and not just by boat), **page** (which means *a pageboy*)

Beware, however, of the following, which are feminine: **la cage** (*cage*), **l'image** (*image/picture*), **la nage** (*swimming*), **la page** (*page in a book*), **la plage** (*beach*), **la rage** (*rage/rabies*).

In language as elsewhere, daring often pays off, but be cautious all the same!

---

4 Grammar

One of the things that learners of a foreign language find off-putting about grammar is that it uses 'technical jargon' whose relevance is not immediately obvious. If you want to access information from a dictionary, however, you will find that this jargon is used – often in abbreviated form – in the definition. For most of the categories defined below, the abbreviations have been included as they appear in dictionaries. This should make your search for the correct word easier and more accurate. Let us take a simple example: Suppose that you are looking for the word fast, to translate the sentence *the cars are very fast* into French.

For *fast*, the dictionary will give several possibilities, among which:

1 *fast* (n.) **le jeûne** (the act of not eating – note the accent on the u)
2 *fast* (adj.) **rapide**
3 *fast* (adv.) **vite, rapidement**

Which one should you choose?

Obviously, the noun (1) makes no sense in this context, so you can eliminate it immediately. But what about (2) and (3)?

We have seen that an adverb can modify a verb, so you may be tempted, but you also know that, after *to be*, *to become*, *to seem/to appear*, *to remain/stay*, it is not acceptable to use an adverb (3). So you are left with **les voitures sont rapides**, which is correct!

Adjectives (adj.) are single words or groups of words, which we insert in a **noun phrase** to give precise details about (some of) its characteristics:

le *gros* chat *noir*	*the **big black** cat* (**chat** is masculine)
la *grosse* voiture *noire*	*the **big black** car* (**voiture** is feminine)

We have already mentioned two important differences between the way adjectives behave in the two languages:

1 In French not all adjectives are placed before the noun (adjectives of colour, for instance, are placed after it).
2 French adjectives agree with the noun they qualify, whereas in English they do not.

Adverbs (adv.) are used to modify the meaning of:

1 A verb (*except* être, devenir, etc. as seen above):

ils parlent *fort*	*they speak **loudly***

2 Another *adverb*:

ils parlent *très* fort	*they speak **very** loudly*

3 An *adjective*:

ils sont *très* forts	*they are **very** strong/clever*

Clauses are units of language often composed of a subject, a verb and an object. There are three categories of clauses:

1 Independent clauses:

Venez me voir.	*Come and see me.*

2 Main clauses:

***Venez me voir* | afin que** (main clause) **je vous paie.**	*Come and see me so that I can pay you.*

3 Subordinate clauses:

Venez me voir ***| afin que je vous paie.*** (subordinate clause)	*Come and see me so that I can pay you.*

Conjunctions (conj.) are words designed to link:

1 Two clauses of equal status as in:

Les enfants ont mangé leur dîner *et* ils sont allés au lit.	*The children ate their dinner and **went to bed**.*

In this case they are (logically) called co-ordinating conjunctions (et, mais, ou ...).

2 Two clauses of unequal status, the 'lesser' clause being introduced by a subordinating conjunction:

Les enfants sont allés au lit *parce qu'* ils étaient fatigués.	*The children went to bed* ***because*** *they were tired.*

The conjunction introduces additional information (here, the reason why the children went to bed). **Parce que, afin que, pour que ...** are subordinating conjunctions.

For a comprehensive list of the two types of conjunctions, you should refer to your grammar.

Determiners (det.) are words placed before a **noun** to give information about gender (masc. or fem.) and number (one or more than one), or to indicate which noun we want to focus on (this one rather than that one). In the following examples, the determiners are shown in ***bold italics***.

le **président** (-); ***la*** **facture** (*the invoice/bill*); ***un*** **jour** (*a/one day*); ***cette*** **carte postale** (*this postcard*); ***quelques*** **amis** (*some friends*), etc.

Moods are groups of tenses which will enable the speaker/writer and the reader/listener to make a clear distinction between reality (indicative mood), the result of a condition (conditional mood), orders (imperative mood), fear/doubt/improbability and also commands (subjunctive mood). Within each mood, the various tenses are then used to situate actions along the past–present–future timeline.

Nous *irons* en vacances.	*We will go on holiday. (reality = indicative mood)*
Si nous avions de l'argent nous *irions* en vacances.	*If we had money, we would go on holiday. (action linked to a condition = conditional mood)*

Il est possible que nous *allions* en vacances. *It is possible that we will go on holiday. (possibility = subjunctive mood)*

As you can see, each of these moods plays an important role in conveying specific shades of meaning.

Nouns or **noun phrases** (n. or n. p.): Nouns are words that name things, beings or ideas: they are divided into two categories, common nouns and proper nouns.

In the sentence below, the nouns are in italic:

Dans le *magasin* de *Monsieur Dumas*, j'ai acheté des *pommes*, des *poires* et *des oranges*, et j'ai vu *Robert*. *In Mr Dumas' shop, I bought apples, pears, and oranges, and I saw Robert.*

Monsieur Dumas and Robert are proper nouns; the others are common nouns.

The expression 'noun phrase' refers to a group of words normally associated with the noun, as in:

Le beaujolais nouveau | *The Beaujolais nouveau has arrived.*
(noun phrase)
est arrivé.
(verb phrase)

Bear in mind, however, that a noun phrase can also be a subject pronoun on its own. So, **le beaujolais nouveau** can be replaced by **il**, which then becomes the noun phrase.

Note that noun phrases are often divided into two broad subcategories:

1 Subject. This refers to a noun phrase which clarifies *who* or *what* is doing the action indicated by the verb.

2 Object. This applies to a noun phrase identifying the 'recipient' of an action.

Both types are shown in the sentence below:

Les agents de police | (subject noun phrase) **ont arrêté | les trois fugitifs.** (verb phrase) (object noun phrase)	*The police officers (have) arrested the three fugitives.*

Prepositions (prep.) are words or phrases indicating a relationship (time, space, purpose …) between two (or more) noun phrases or clauses:

La boîte aux lettres est derrière toi!	*The letter box is **behind** you!*
Vous êtes avec moi ou contre moi?	*Are you **with** me or **against** me?*

Pronouns (pr.) are elements of speech which we use to replace noun phrases which have been mentioned before. This eliminates unnecessary repetition and enables our speech to be neater, quicker and more fluid:

1 Jean aime le théâtre. Jean va au théâtre tous les soirs.	*John loves the theatre. John goes to the theatre every night.*
2 Jean aime le théâtre; *il y* va tous les soirs.	*John loves the theatre; he goes (there) every night.*

It is clear that Example 2 is more elegant than Example 1.

There are many sorts of pronouns. Here are just a few:

1 Subject pronouns, identifying the performer of the action: **je, tu, il, elle** … (*I, you, he/she, it …*);
2 Object pronouns, indicating the recipient of the action: **me, te, le, la** … (*me, you, him, her, it …*);

3 Relative pronouns, referring to beings or things mentioned in the main clause: **qui, que, dont, où** … (*who*, *which*, *whom*, *where*);
4 Demonstrative pronouns, used to point out a being or thing mentioned earlier: **celui-ci, celle-ci** … (*this one/that one* …);
5 Prepositional pronouns, used after prepositions such as *with*, *for*, *on* …: **moi, toi, lui, elle** … (*me*, *you*, *him*, *her* …).

Sentences (s. or sent.) are complete units capable of functioning on their own, made up of a number of elements and ending with a full stop, an exclamation or question mark, or similar marker (in the case of a written text) or a pause (in speech):

Jean aime le théâtre. *Il y* va tous les soirs.	*John loves the theatre. He goes (there) every night.*

The example above is composed of two sentences separated by a full stop. Each is referred as an independent clause (a self-standing unit).

The pattern of the above sentence is simple but sentences can be longer, more intricate and composed of several **clauses**.

The sentence we saw earlier:

Jean aime le théâtre | et | il y va tous les soirs.

has now been modified and is composed of two units of equal status, linked by **et**. Both could again be separated by a full stop and still make sense. In this new structure they are called main clauses. **Et, ou, mais, car, donc** are co-ordinating conjunctions.

We will now modify 'our' sentence as follows:

Jean aime le théâtre | qui est près de chez lui | et | où il va tous les soirs.
main clause — subordinate clause 1 — subordinate clause 2

In this case, two subordinate clauses giving additional information are attached to the main clause by a link word (here: the relative pronouns **qui** and **où**). In this structure, the subordinate clauses could not function on their own. They are subordinated to the main clause, hence their name.

As we have seen, subordinating conjunctions are numerous and varied: some require the indicative, and some demand the subjunctive, as do those used in the sentence below:

J'ai téléphoné au consulat | pour que tu puisses avoir ton passeport
main clause subordinate clause 1
la semaine prochaine, | afin que nous partions le plus tôt possible.
subordinate clause 2
I telephoned the consulate for you to have your passport next week so that we can leave/go as soon as possible.

Stem or **root:** The stem is the part of a word onto which will be grafted a prefix, a suffix or (for a verb) an ending.

This enables us to create new word forms, to expand our vocabulary or, in the case of verbs, to indicate the performer and to situate the action in a particular time zone. In the following words the stem is shown in bold italics:

Passage (-), ***prépar*ation** (-), **re*pris*** (*retaken*), ***descend*ons** (*let's go down*), **nous *manger*ions** (*we would eat*), etc.

Beware: the same word may have different stems, depending on the form you wish to create!

Tenses are constructs which enable the speaker or writer to situate actions in a given time zone (past, present, future), and to indicate who/what the performer of a given action was/is/will be …

In French there are two types:

1 Simple (one-word) tenses, formed by grafting an ending to a stem:

Ils rentrer*ont* ce soir.	*They will get back this evening.*

2 Compound tenses which are constructed by adding the past participle of the main verb to an auxiliary (**avoir** or **être**):

Le train *est parti* il y a dix minutes.	*The train left ten minutes ago.*
Nos amis *ont téléphoné*.	*Our friends (have) telephoned.*

The above list is not exhaustive and you will find much more in-depth information in your grammar, if you already own one. If not, you should consider purchasing one, as well as a good dictionary, to refine your knowledge and your performance.

Verbs or **verb phrase** (vb. or vb. p): Verbs are words used to express an action, a feeling or a state:

Le soleil *brille*.	*The sun shines/is shining.* (action)
Les enfants *sont* heureux.	*The children are happy.* (state)
Il *aime* la musique classique.	*He likes classical music.* (feeling)

---

5 The gender of nouns

In your earlier French studies, you no doubt wondered why **une table, une porte, une voiture** (*a table*, *a door*, *a car*) should be feminine, and why **un sac, un jardin, un ordinateur** (*a bag*, *a garden*, *a computer*) should be masculine. The reason lies in antiquity. During and after the Roman invasions, Latin had a very strong influence on the French language, particularly on the gender of nouns: roughly speaking, masculine and neuter Latin nouns became masculine in French, and feminine ones became feminine. Admittedly, for those who have not studied Latin, the above information is of limited help! However you should not lose heart.

It is always possible to make some simple rules to help yourself. Here are a few examples:

1 Most nouns referring to fruit are feminine:

la pomme (*apple*); **la poire** (*pear*); **la cerise** (*cherry*); **la pêche** (*peach*) …

Beware, however; there are some exceptions:

le raisin (*grape*); **le melon** (*melon*); **le citron** (*lemon*); **le pamplemousse** (*grapefruit*); **l'ananas** (*pineapple*) …

2 Nouns for countries ending in **-e** are feminine:

la Belgique; l'Allemagne; la Suisse; l'Italie; l'Espagne; l'Angleterre

If the ending is not **-e**, the noun for the country is masculine:

le Maroc (*Morocco*); **le Brésil** (*Brazil*); **le Guatémala** (*Guatemala*) …

3 Nouns referring to trees are usually masculine:

le chêne (*oak*); **le platane** (*plane tree*); **le peuplier** (*poplar*); **le pin** (*pine*) …

4 Nouns ending in **-er** or **-eur** indicating a person, an object or a machine doing a specific job are masculine:

l'ouvrier (*worker*); **le boucher** (*butcher*); **le boulanger** (*baker*); **le travailleur** (*worker*); **le programmeur** (*computer programmer*)

le levier (*lever*); **le bouclier** (*shield*); **le moteur** (*engine*); **le tracteur** (*tractor*); **l'ascenseur** (*lift*) …

5 Nearly all nouns borrowed from English are masculine:

le catch (*wrestling*); **le marketing** (-); **le parking** (*car park*); **le rock** (*rock 'n' roll*); **le stress** (-) …

One notable exception: **la star** (*celebrity – male or female*).

6 Nouns made from adjectives are feminine:

beau *(beautiful)* → **la beauté**
chaud *(hot)* → **la chaleur**
doux *(soft)* → **la douceur**
froid *(cold)* → **la froideur**
haut *(high)* → **la hauteur**
nouveau *(new)* → **la nouveauté**
tendre *(tender)* → **la tendresse**

For a more exhaustive list of rules and exceptions regarding this topic, you should consult a good grammar.

Generally, there is no need for learners to worry unduly about genders. With very few exceptions, making a word masculine instead of feminine (or vice versa) will not cause a major problem, since, as mentioned before, the listener will work out what you must have meant.

Note, however, that very occasionally some confusion may occur:

> **le vase** (*vase*) – **la vase** (*silt*); **le page** (*page boy*) – **la page** (*page in a book*)

So, **les fleurs sont dans *la* vase** may raise a smile, as would **je vais faire *une* tour**, since **le tour** means *trip*, and **la tour** means *tower*.

The most important side effect of the masculine/feminine split is that it affects the shape of the adjectives involved. If we take the example of the nouns **tour, vase** and **page** (mentioned above), we can see the effect of the noun's gender on the adjectives **fini** (*finished*), **vieux** (*old*) and **blanc** (*white/blank*):

Le tour est fini. *The tour is over.*
La tour est finie. *The tower is finished.*
Le vase est vieux. *The vase is old.*

La vase est vieille.	*The silt is old.*
Le page est blanc.	*The page boy is white.*
La page est blanche.	*The page is white/blank.*

The more you learn, the easier it is to develop a 'feel', a sort of 'sixth sense' for what is right. So, be alert to anything you see or hear, trust your instinct, and train your brain to do some detective work for you!

---

6 The sounds of French

Although it has been said earlier that French people like an English accent, it will be rewarding for you to try and reproduce the sounds of French as faithfully as you can. Generally there will be few problems.

The main things to remember are as follows:

In French, vowels like **a, e, i, o, u** are 'pure', or 'steady state': this means that the position of the tongue and jaw does not alter at all while the vowel sound is made. This is the case for the Standard British English vowel sounds found in *beef* or *coo*.

By contrast, in the words *mine* or *coast*, the tongue and jaws change position during the articulation of the vowel; such vowel sounds are called *glides*, and they do not exist in standard French. To clarify this point further, let's examine the vowel sound in the word **beau** used in both languages. In Standard English, the vowel starts with *o* and the mouth closes for an *u* sound. In French, the tongue and jaw will remain in the same position from the beginning to the end of the vowel sound. This means that when saying French vowels, you will have to curb your natural tendency to close your mouth, so that the word **gros** (*big/fat*) does not sound like *grow*, the word **lait** (*milk*) does not sound like *lay*.

In addition to pure vowels, French has four nasalized vowels, found on their own or within words. They are usually spelt **ain/ein**,

an/en, on, un. To produce them, the air coming from your lungs must go through both the oral and the nasal cavities.

Nasalized sounds are now creeping into the English language owing to the introduction of words like **croiss*ant***, **patr*on*** (*boss* – fam.), Verdun (the scene of a famous World War I battle), etc.

Aspiration or no aspiration?

In English, if a word begins with the letters *p*, *t* and *k* (or *c* followed by *a*, *o*, *u*), a very short puff of air called aspiration, represented below by a superscript ʰ, occurs before the start of the vowel. In French there is no such aspiration! To eliminate this problem, use the following trick: Place a piece of paper flat against your lips and say the English words *pʰick*, *tʰap*, *cʰash*. The paper should move away from your lips after the *p*, *t*, *k* sounds. Now, practise saying the French words **pas** (*not*), **ta** (*your*), **car** (*coach*). The paper should not move away from your lips. If it does, try again until it stops!

One 'l' or two?

You may be surprised to learn that, in English, there are two *l* sounds. One, found in word-initial positions before a vowel, as in *lip*, *loop*, etc., is called a 'clear *l*'. The other, found after a vowel as in *peel*, *pool*, etc., is called a 'dark *l*'.

In French, the l, in both positions, has the value of a 'clear l'. Therefore, the l sounds in **lippe** (*lower lip/pout*), **loupe** (*magnifying glass*), **pile** (*pile/battery*) and **poule** (*hen*) are the same.

Note that the French examples above have been chosen to be as close as possible to the English *lip*, *loop*, *peel* and *pool*.

What about 'r'?

Traditionally the sound **r** seems to pose enormous problems to British learners of French because, in standard English, the sound is articulated with the point of the tongue pushed towards the top teeth, and the air going sideways. In French the **r** is pronounced at the back of the mouth, a narrow passage being left between the back of the tongue and the roof of the mouth. It is similar to a gentle gargling sound. One small trick may help you to master this troublesome item: place the end of a cotton bud on the tip of your tongue to hold it down against your bottom teeth, and raise the back of your tongue as high as you can without discomfort. You should achieve something resembling a gargling or a purring sound. This will do nicely as a French **r**. But remember: even if in a word you say the **r** the English way, you will not be misunderstood.

There is another small matter relating to the pronunciation of the **r** in French. In standard British English (not in regional pronunciation or American English), the **r** is not sounded after a vowel: *car*, *door*, *for*, etc. unless another vowel follows, e.g. *after an hour*, *for a few dollars more*, etc. In French, the **r** is normally sounded except in the following cases:

1 At the end of -er verbs: **marcher, regarder, manger**, etc.
2 At the end of nouns indicating fruit trees: **le pommier** (*apple tree*), **le cerisier** (*cherry tree*), **le prunier** (*plum tree*), etc.
3 At the end of nouns indicating a person's profession: **le boulanger** (*baker*), **le boucher** (*butcher*), **le charpentier** (*carpenter*), etc.

In a few nouns and adjectives ending in **-er**, such as **cher** (*dear*), **la mer** (*the sea*), **le fer** (*iron*), **le ver** (*worm*), the **r** is sounded.

Remember: in Standard British English, the **r** which follows the vowel is not sounded in words like *party*, *carp*, *form*, *norm*. In the corresponding French words **partie, carpe, forme, norme** it is!

The relation between spelling and sound

Vowels

1 a is sounded like the *a* in *car* but shorter;
2 i is pronounced like the vowel in *see* but shorter;

3 With some exceptions, if **e** is part of the word-final group **er** (particularly in categories 1 to 3 above), or if it is spelt **é**, it is normally pronounced a bit like the *y* in *city*. If it is spelt **è** or **ê**, or if it is before a double consonant, as in **cette** (*this/that* fem.) or **belle** (*beautiful*), it will be pronounced like the *e* in *net*. If there is no accent on the **e** and if it is not followed by a <u>double</u> consonant, it will be pronounced like the *e* in the word *the*, as in *the car*.

Note: If **e** appears as the last letter in a word and is not written **é**, **è** or **ê**, it will be missed out in Northern French and, in the South, it will be pronounced like the **e** in *the* (+ consonant), as in *the car*.

4 **u** after a consonant is pronounced like the *ee* in *see*, but with rounded lips;
5 **ou** is pronounced as *oo* in *food* or *mood* … but shorter;
6 **eu** followed by a consonant which is sounded is pronounced like the *i* in *fir*. If it is the word's final letter as in **peu** (*little*), **feu** (*fire*), or is followed by a silent consonant as in **deux** (*two*), **jeux** (*games*), etc. it will sound like Inspecteur Clouseau of Pink Panther fame, when he says: '*can I use your pheune?*';
7 **ai/ei** are normally pronounced like the *e* in *set*, *bet*, etc.
8 **o** followed by a silent consonant as in **nos** (*our* plur.) or **gros** (*fat*, masc. mentioned before) is a steady state vowel, not a glide!

Consonants

Apart from problems about the aspiration of **p, t, k** and the pronunciation of clear and dark **l**, consonants tend to have a similar value in the two languages.

Note, however, the following oddity: although the expressions 'aspirated' and 'mute **h**' are used in French, the sound **h** is no longer pronounced, whereas in English there is still a difference between the **h** found in *hatred*, *house* or *high* and that found in *honour*, *hour*, *heir*; the former is pronounced and said to be aspirated, the latter is not pronounced, and called mute. In French, words like **haut, haine, heure, honneur** are all pronounced as if the **h** was not there, and yet in the first two the **h** is aspirated, and in the last two it is not. So, why worry? Because there is a catch!

Although the aspirated **h** is not pronounced in French, it acts like a ghost consonant which can influence the word that occurs immediately before it:

le hibou or **un beau/vieux hibou** (*the owl* or *a beautiful/old owl* – the **h** is aspirated);

l'hôtel or **un bel/vieil hôtel** (*the hotel* or *a beautiful/old hotel* – the **h** is mute)

As can be seen from the above two examples, although the **h** has no reality as regards the sound, it determines a change in some of the words which precede it, in particular the adjectives **vieux, beau, nouveau, fou, mou** (*soft*), and the article **le** or **la.**

To find out if a word begins with an aspirated or a mute **h,** you can use the dictionary: after each word entry, there are slanting lines // or square brackets [ ], which contain the phonetic transcription of the item. The presence of an apostrophe or asterisk immediately after the first slanting line or bracket tells you that the **h** is aspirated; the preceding word will therefore not be affected (see the first example above). If, however, there is no apostrophe present, the **h** is mute. So, the modifications indicated in the second example above are needed.

c and *g*

These two letters are a little troublesome, but their pattern of change follows a common principle:

1 If **c** is followed by **e** or **i,** it is pronounced as in English in the same context: **cité** (*city*), **ce** (*this/that*);
2 If followed by **a, o, u,** it will be pronounced **k** as in English in the same context: **cage** (*cage*), **cou** (*neck*), **curé** (*vicar*);
3 If **g** is followed by **e** or **i,** it is pronounced as the **ge** in **rouge;**
4 If **g** is followed by **a, o,** or **u,** it will be pronounced **g,** as in the English words *gate, golf, good.*

Digraphs

As seen before, some consonants will have similar values in the two languages.

Beware, however, of the following associations:

1 ch normally pronounced as the *sh* in *shoe*, *shape*, etc. In a very small number of words, it is pronounced *k* as in English: **Christ** (*Christ*), **chorale** (*choral*), **charisme** (*charisma*), etc.
2 ph pronounced *f* as in English: **pharmacie** (*pharmacy/chemist's*), **physique** (*physics/physique*).
3 ps or **pt** at the beginning of a word: in French, both the **p** and the **s** or **t** are sounded as in **psychologie** (*psychology*), **ptérodactyle** (*pterodactyl*), etc. This may explain why the popular French brand of lemonade called **Pschitt** was never marketed in English-speaking countries!
4 For the letters **gn**, occurring together in the same word, there are two possibilities:

a A pronunciation similar to that of the *ni* in *onion*: **montagne** (*mountain*), **campagne** (*countryside/campaign*). It is the most common pronunciation.
b The other, resembling that of the group *gn* in *ignore* or *signature*. It is only found in a few learned words such as **agnostique** (*agnostic*), **magnum** (*magnum*).

5 The *th* sounds found in words like *this*, *that*, *thin*, *thick* do not exist in French. So they will be difficult to master by learners of English. When the letters **t + h** occur together, they are simply sounded as **t: thème** (*theme*), **théâtre** (*theatre*), etc.

It is obviously rewarding to speak as accurately as possible, but you should not forget:

1 Those listening to you will exercise their judgement to find out what must have been said;
2 An English accent is often considered by French people as attractive and even sexy.

Stress in French

Having studied the sounds of French, we should now focus on another important point. It concerns the way in which stress is used. In language, stress is usually defined as 'the degree of force with which a part of a word (a syllable) is pronounced relative to other parts'.

A syllable is a section of word generally composed of one or more consonant(s) and one vowel unit. People, even without technical knowledge of linguistics, are normally able to determine how many syllables there are in a given word. For instance, in English:

pre|pa|ra|tion has four syllables
1 2 3 4

ra|tio|na|li|za|tion| has six.
1 2 3 4 5 6

The equivalent words in French have the same number of syllables. Do not, however, be tempted to say them in the same way!

English is a word stress language. This means that words of two (or more) syllables are marked by one (or more) stress(es). In the English examples below, the stressed syllable is indicated in bold italics:

*decla**ra**tion, **ad**mirable, con**sis**tent, **po**licy, en**vi**ronment*

Every time the word appears in a sentence, the stress will fall on the same syllables which, in the sentence below, are shown in bold italics:

*I find your decla**ra**tion **ad**mirable, and con**sis**tent with our **po**licy on the en**vi**ronment.*

All the main words listed above also exist in French, but the equivalent sentence will only normally bear one stress, which will fall on the last syllable of the sense group (a group of words, which – like an independent clause – make complete sense on their own). However, because of the comma and the conjunction et the sentence could be divided into two sense groups. This would result in two stresses being used as shown below. The stressed syllables are underlined:

Je trouve votre déclaration admi<u>ra</u>ble, et consistante avec notre politique sur l'environne<u>men</u>t.

As a consequence, the rhythm of the two languages is quite different, regardless of the value of the sounds used.

It is to be noted, however, that on the radio and television, it is quite common for speakers to stress the first syllable of words of two syllables or more and to disregard the traditional rule stated above:

Je <u>trou</u>ve votre déclaration <u>ad</u>mirable, et <u>con</u>sistante avec notre <u>po</u>litique sur l'<u>en</u>vironnement.

This is done for effect, and you do not have to imitate it.

Intonation (changes in the pitch of the voice)

For the purpose of this book, the intonation patterns of the two languages can be considered as similar.

If you have the recordings that accompany the book, listen to them carefully as well as to any other French-language material you come across. Try to reproduce the sounds as faithfully as you can and above all don't feel silly when practising!

Bon courage!

Self-assessment record form

Throughout the book, a number of activities have been designated part of your self-assessment programme. The grid below will enable you to record your marks for the self-assessment work completed. You should note down the marks you have scored for each exercise, enter the grand total at the bottom and calculate the percentage you have reached. The grades are listed overleaf. Good luck!

Unit number	*Activity number*	*Page*	*Maximum points available*	*Points awarded*	*Running total*
1	6	10	50		
2	Comp. 3	55	50		
3	1	61	100		
4	9	102	50		
4	14	108	100		
5	Comp. 1	123	100		
6	3	147	100		
7	6	184	100		
7	15	195	50		
8	8	212	50		
8	11	224	50		
9	2	232	50		
9	11	246	50		
10	2	263	100		
				Total:	

The total should be divided by ten and checked against the percentages and corresponding grades shown below.

70 + = excellent
60–9 = very good
50–9 = good
40–9 = fair
Below 40 = greater focus needed

French–English vocabulary

This vocabulary contains the words and expressions you will need to complete the activities of each unit. The vocabulary introduced in the lists which follow the texts has not been repeated. Words which are easily understandable from their shape or the context have also been left out, except when they are likely to mislead ('false friends'). In general, basic items which you are likely to have encountered during earlier studies have not been included. Irregular past participles have been included in brackets after the infinitive of the relevant verb.

Abbreviations used to avoid ambiguity: adj. = adjective; f. = feminine; fam. = familiar; impers. = impersonal verb; m. = masculine; n. = noun; pl. = plural; refl. = reflexive verb; sbdy = somebody; sl. = slang; sthg = something; vb. = verb

abandonner *to abandon*
absolument *absolutely*
accepter *to accept*
accès *(m.) access*
acheminement *(m.) transport (goods/mail)*
acheter *to buy/purchase*
acte *(m.) act*
admettre (admis) *to admit*
adresser *to address*
affaires *(f. pl.) business*
alcool *(m.) alcohol*
améliorer *to improve*
aménagement *(m.) conversion (property)*
aménager *to convert/do up*
ami *(m.) friend*
amical *friendly/cordial*
amie *(f.) friend (female)*
amour *(m.) love*
amoureux *in love*
an *(m.) year*
année *(f.) year (span)*
anniversaire *(m.) birthday/anniversary*
appareil *(m.) apparatus*
appeler *to call*
apprécier *to appreciate*
approcher *to get close*
approvisionner *to supply*
approvisionner *(refl.) to get supplies*
appuyer *to support (a claim)/lean on*
après *after*
après-guerre *(m.) post-war period*
arboré *planted with trees*
arbre *(m.) tree*
arracher *to pull out/uproot*
arrêt *(m.) stop*

arrêter *to stop/halt*
assurance *(f.) assurance/insurance*
attendre (attendu) *to wait*
attirer *to attract*
au cas par cas *case-by-case*
au courant *aware*
au juste *precisely*
au revoir *goodbye/see you later*
aucun *none*
augmentation *(f.) increase*
augmenter *to increase/augment*
aujourd'hui *today*
automne *(m.) autumn*
automobiliste *(m./f.) driver (car)*
autorité *(f.) authority*
avertir *to warn*
avertissement *(m.) warning*
avoir raison *to be right*
avoir tort *to be wrong*

besoin *(m.) need*
blanc *white*
blessé *wounded*
bloquer *to block*
boire (bu) *to drink*
bonheur *(m.) happiness*
boulanger *(m.) baker*
boulangerie *(f.) baker's shop*
boulet *(m.) cannon ball*
boulot *(m., fam.) job*
bourgeois *(adj./n.) middle-class (person)*
bouteille *(f.) bottle*
boutique *(f.) shop*
branche *(f.) branch*
britannique *British*
Britannique *(m./f.) Briton*
brûler *to burn*
buanderie *(f.) laundry room*
bulletin *(m.) bulletin/payslip*
bureau *(m.) office/desk*
but *(m.) aim*
buvable *drinkable*

cabinet *(m.) cabinet/office (lawyer, etc.)*
cadet *younger (person)*
cadre *(m.) framework*
camion *(m.) lorry*
campagne *(f.) countryside/ campaign*
caritatif *caring (organization)*
carré *(adj.) square*
carrière *(f.) career*
carte *(f.) card/map*
cas *(m.) case*
casser *to break/to lower (price)*
casserole *(f.) pan*
cause *(f.) cause/reason*
célèbre *famous*
célibataire *(n./adj.) single (unmarried)*
cent *hundred*
centrale *(f.) (purchasing) centre*
cependant *however*
certain *sure*
certainement *certainly*
certains *(m. pl.) some (people)*
cesser *to stop/cease*
chacun *each one*
chambre *(f.) bedroom*
change *(m.) exchange (money)*
changement *(m.) change/ alteration*
changer *to change/alter*
charmant *charming*
château *(m.) castle*
chaud *hot*

chauffard *(m.) road hog/bad driver*
chef *(m.) chief/head*
cher *(adj.) dear*
chercher *to search for/seek*
chez ... *at ...'s (house)*
choisir *to choose*
chômeur *(m.) unemployed/jobless*
ci-inclus *enclosed*
circonstances *(f. pl.) circumstances*
circulation *(f.) traffic/circulation*
citoyen *(m.) citizen*
clairon *(m.) clarion/bugle*
client *(m.) customer/client*
cloche *(f.) bell*
clos *closed/enclosed*
coin *(m.) corner*
col *(m.) collar*
col bleu *(m.) blue collar*
colère *(f.) anger*
collège *(m.) secondary school*
coller *to stick/glue*
colline *(f.) hill*
combattre (combattu) *to combat/fight*
combler *to fill (a gap)*
compagnie *(f.) company*
complet *complete/full*
comprendre (compris) *to understand/include*
compte *(m.) account*
compter *to count*
concitoyen *(m.) fellow citizen*
concurrence *(f.) competition (business)*
concurrent *(m.) competitor (business)*
conducteur *(m.) driver*
conduire (conduit) *to drive*
conduire *(refl.) to behave*
confronter *to confront*
congés *(m. pl.) holidays*
conjoncture *(f.) economic climate*
connaître (connu) *to know*
conquête *(f.) conquest*
conscient *conscious*
conseil *(m.) advice*
consommateur *(m.) consumer*
consommation *(f.) consumption*
consommer *to consume (goods)*
construction *(f.) building/construction*
construire (construit) *to build/construct*
consulaire *consular*
consulat *(m.) consulate*
contrat *(m.) contract*
contre *against*
convaincre (convaincu) *to convince*
copain *(m., fam.) (boy) friend*
copie *(f.) copy*
copine *(f., fam.) (girl) friend*
corps *(m.) body*
cotisation *(f.) subscription/dues*
coup d'œil *(m.) glance (fam.)*
couper *to cut*
coupure *(f.) cut*
couramment *currently*
courant *current/common*
courir (couru) *to run*
courrier *(m.) mail (letters)*
coût *(m.) cost*
craindre (craint) *to fear*
crise *(f.) crisis*
croire (cru) *to believe*
croissance *(f.) growth*
croître (crû) *to grow/increase*

croyable *credible/believable*
cueillir *to pick (fruit/flowers)*
cuisiner *to cook*
cuisson *(f.) cooking (action)*
cuivre *(m.) copper (metal)*

d'accord! *agreed!*
d'après *according to*
décéder *to die (formal)*
décennie *(f.) decade*
déchets *(m. pl) waste/refuse*
décider *to decide*
décideur *(m.) decision maker*
décision *(f.) decision*
décliner *to refuse (liability)*
décompresser *to let off steam/relax*
décorer *to decorate*
découper *to cut out*
décrocher *to unhook*
défendre (défendu) *to defend/forbid*
dehors *outside/out*
déjeuner *to lunch/breakfast*
délivrance *(f.) issue (of document)*
délivrer *to issue/free*
déluge *(m.) flood*
demain *tomorrow*
demande *(f.) request/application*
demander *to ask/request*
démarche *(f.) approach*
déménager *to move house*
démonter *to dismantle/take apart*
dépanner *to fix (repair)*
déplacement *(m.) travel (business)*
déplacer *to displace/move*
depuis *since*
déranger *to disturb*
dernier *last/latter*
derrière *behind*
désastreux *disastrous*
descendre (descendu) *to go down/descend*
déséquilibrer *to unbalance*
désespoir *(m.) despair*
désolé *desolate/sorry*
déstresser (se) *to unstress/relax*
détail *(m.) detail/retail*
détester *to hate/loathe*
détruire *to destroy*
deuxième *(adj.) second (2nd)*
devant *before/in front of*
développer *to develop*
devenir (devenu) *to become*
devoir *(m.) duty*
devoir (dû) *to have to/must*
dieu *(m.) god*
difficulté *(f.) difficulty*
diminuer *to reduce/dwindle*
dire (dit) *to say*
dis-donc! *I say!*
disparaître (disparu) *to disappear*
distinguer *to distinguish/make out*
divers *various*
domaine *(m.) field/domain*
domicile *(m.) domicile (address)*
domicilié *(adj.) resident*
donner *to give*
dont *of/from whom*
dormir *to sleep*
doute *(m.) doubt*
douter *to doubt*
doux *mild/soft*
drapeau *(m.) flag*
dureté *(f.) harshness*

échange *(m.) exchange*
échanger *to exchange*
échelle *(f.) ladder/scale*
écouter *to listen*

écrivain *(m.) writer*
effectifs *(m. pl.) pay roll, number of employees*
effectuer *to accomplish*
efforcer *(refl.) to strive/try*
église *(f.) church*
élevage *(m.) rearing (cattle)*
élève *(m./fem.) student*
élire (élu) *to elect*
éloignement *(m.) distance (from a place)*
embaucher *to take on (for jobs)*
embouteillage *(m.) traffic jam*
émission *(f.) broadcast/emission*
empêchement *(m.) difficulty*
emploi *(m.) employment*
emprunter *to borrow*
en cas *in case*
en ce moment *at the moment*
en dépit de *in spite of*
en effet *indeed*
en état d'ivresse *drunk*
en fait *in fact*
en gros *wholesale*
en moyenne *on average*
en outre *besides*
en somme *all in all*
en train de *in the process of*
encore *still/again*
endormir *(refl.) to go to sleep*
énerver *to irritate/annoy*
enfant *(m./f.) child*
engagement *(m.) undertaking*
engager *(refl.)* **à** *to undertake to*
énorme *enormous*
enseignant *(m.) teacher/professor*
ensoleillé *sunny*
ensuite *then*
entier *whole/complete*
entre *between*
entrer *to go in/enter*
enveloppe *(f.) envelope/allocation (money)*
envie *(f.) jealousy/envy*
environ *approximately*
environnement *(m.) environment*
envoyer *to send*
épeler *to spell*
équiper *to equip/fit (equipment)*
essayer *to try/attempt*
essence *(f.) petrol/essence*
est *(m.) east*
établissement *(m.) establishment*
étaler *to spread (out)*
été *(m.) summer*
étranger *(adj./n.) strange(r)/foreigner*
étude *(f.) study*
étudier *to study*
européen *European*
évaluation *(f.) evaluation/assessment*
évaluer *to evaluate/weigh up*
événement *(m.) event*
éventuel *possible/likely*
évoluer *to evolve/develop*
évolution *(f.) evolution*
exagérer *to exaggerate*
examen *(m.) examination*
excès *(m.) excess*
exiger *to demand*
expédier *to despatch*
explication *(f.) explanation*
expliquer *to explain*
expression *(f.) expression*
exprimer *to express*

face *(f.) face (of building, mountain, etc.)*
faible *weak*

faiblesse *(f.) weakness*
faire (fait) *to do/make*
faire face à *to confront*
fait *(m.) fact*
falloir *(***fallu** *– impers.) to be necessary*
familial *(adj.) family*
famille *(f.) family*
fatigue *(f.) tiredness*
faucher *to mow down*
faux *(adj.) false*
félicitations *(f. pl.) congratulations*
femme *(f.) woman/wife*
fenêtre *(f.) window*
ferme *(f.) farm*
fermer *to close/shut*
fermier *(m.) farmer/peasant*
fille *(f.) girl/daughter*
fils *(m.) son*
fin *fine/thin*
fin *(f.) end*
financier *financial*
finir *to finish/end/complete*
finition *(f.) finish (quality)*
fixe *fixed*
flamber *to flare up*
fleuve *(m.) river (large)*
flocon *(m.) flake*
fois *(f.) time (stage occurred)*
follement *madly*
fond *(m.) bottom/background*
fonder *to found*
fondre *to swoop/pounce*
forêt *(f.) forest*
formation *(f.) training*
fossé *(m.) ditch/gulf/gap*
fou *mad*
fournir *to supply*
fournisseur *(m.) supplier*
foyer *(m.) home/family unit/hearth*
fraîchement *recently (picked)*
frais *cool/fresh*
frais *(m. pl.) costs/expenses*
franchement *frankly*
frapper *to strike (a blow)*
frites *(f.) chips (UK); fries (US)*
froid *(adj./n.) cold*
fromage *(m.) cheese*
fumer *to smoke*
furieux *furious*
futé *cunning/crafty (fam.)*

gamme *(f.) range (products)*
garagiste *(m./f.) garage owner*
garantie *(f.) guarantee*
garantir *to guarantee*
gazole *diesel (for cars)*
gelé *frozen/very cold*
genre *(m.) type/sort*
gens *(m. pl.) people*
gentil *kind*
givre *(m.) frost*
glacer *to freeze*
goût *(m.) taste*
grandeur *(f.) magnitude*
grandir *to grow*
gratuit *free (not paying)*
grave *grave/serious*
grève *(f.) strike*
griffé *designer-labelled*
gris *grey/overcast*
gros *big/bulky*
grosso modo *roughly speaking*
guerre *(f.) war*

habitable *inhabitable*
habiter *to live/dwell*
habitude *(f.) habit*
hebdomadaire *weekly*
hebdomadaire *(m.) weekly paper*
hectolitre *(m.) hectolitre*
heure *(f.) hour*

hier *yesterday*
historique *historical*
Hollandais *(m.) Dutch (person)*
homologue *(m./f.) counterpart*
horaire *(m.) timetable*
hôte *(m.) host/guest*
hôtesse *(f.) hostess*
humide *damp/wet*
hypermarché *(m.) hypermarket*

ici *here*
idée *(f.) idea*
illégitime *illegitimate*
illettrisme *(m.) illiteracy*
imbuvable *undrinkable*
immatriculer *to register (officially)*
immobilier *estate (agent)*
impasse *(f.) dead end/skipped subject*
implanté *set up/implanted*
importer *to import*
impressionnant *impressive*
impressionner *to impress*
inactif *unemployed/jobless*
inclus *enclosed*
incontestable *unquestionable*
incroyable *incredible*
industrialisé *industrialized*
industrie *(f.) industry*
industriel *industrial*
infraction *(f.) law-breaking activity*
inscription *(f.) inscription/enrolment*
inspecter *to inspect/check*
inspecteur *(m.) inspector*
installer *(refl.) to settle down*
insupportable *unbearable*
intéressant *interesting*
intéressé *(n.) the person concerned*
introduire (introduit) *to introduce/set up*
invité *(n./adj.) guest*
irriter *to irritate/annoy*
ivresse *(f.) drunkenness/inebriation*

jardin *(m.) garden*
jeter *to throw/cast*
jeudi *(m.) Thursday*
jeunesse *(f.) youth*
joindre (joint) *to join*
jouer *to play*
jour *(m.) day*
journal *(m.) newspaper*
journée *(f.) span of a day*
justificatif *(m.) (official) written proof*

là *there*
laisser *to leave (behind)*
langue *(f.) language/tongue*
large *broad/wide*
lavage *(m.) washing (action)*
laver *to wash*
laver *(refl.) to wash (oneself)*
léger *(adj.) light*
législation *(f.) legislation/law*
légitime *legitimate*
légume *(m.) vegetable*
lendemain *(m.) day after (the)*
lentement *slowly*
lettre *(f.) letter*
libraire *(m.) bookseller*
librairie *(f.) bookshop*
libre *free/vacant*
licence *(f.) degree (BA or BSc)*
licencier *to sack*
lié à … *(+ noun phrase) linked to*
lier *to link*
lieu *(m.) location/place*
ligue *(f.) league*
liste *(f.) list*

livraison *(f.) delivery*
livre *(f.) pound*
livre *(m.) book*
livrer *to deliver*
livret *(m.) booklet*
loisir *(m.) leisure*
londonien *from London*
longtemps *long/for a long time*
loubard *(m.) yob/thug*
loyer *(m.) rent*
lundi *(m.) Monday*
lutter *to fight/to struggle*

magasin *(m.) shop/store*
main *(f.) hand*
maintenant *now*
maintenir (maintenu) *to maintain/keep*
maintien *(m.) maintenance*
maison *(f.) house/home*
majuscule *(f.) capital letter*
mal *(m.) evil/ill*
mal tomber *to arrive at a bad moment*
malade *(adj.) ill*
maladie *(f.) illness*
mâle *masculine/male*
malgré *despite*
malheur *(m.) unhappiness*
manche *(f.) sleeve*
Manche, La *(f.) English Channel*
manger *to eat*
manière *(f.) manner/fashion*
manifestation *(f.) demonstration*
marcher *to walk/work (of machine, process)*
marié *married*
marier *(refl.) to get married*
marrant *funny/amusing (slang)*
masculin *male/masculine*
mécontent *unhappy*
meilleur *better/best*
mêler *to mix*
mêler *(refl.) to mingle/mix*
même *same*
menacer *to threaten*
mendiant *(m.) beggar*
mépris *(m.) contempt*
merci *thank you*
mercredi *(m.) Wednesday*
mère *(f.) mother*
mesure *(f.) measure/measurement*
métier *(m.) occupation*
mettre (mis) *to put/place*
midi *(m.) midday*
milieu *(m.) middle*
milliard *(m.) billion (US)*
mineur *(adj.) minor*
mineur *(n.) minor/miner*
misérable *(n./adj.) wretched*
mitraille *(f.) grapeshot/bullets*
modifier *to modify*
moins *less*
mois *(m.) month*
moitié *(f.) half*
mon dieu! *my goodness!*
monde *(m.) world*
mondial *worldwide*
montant *(m.) amount (of a bill)*
monter *to climb/go up*
montre *(f.) watch*
mort *(adj.) dead*
mort *(f.) death*
motiver *to motivate*
mourir (mort) *to die*
mouvement *(m.) movement*
moyen *(adj.) average*
moyen *(m.) means*
moyenne *(f.) average*
musclé *muscular/powerful*

n'importe quoi! *anything/nonsense!*
naissance *(f.) birth*

naître (né) *to be born*
natalité *(f.) birth (rate)*
négatif *negative*
neiger *to snow*
nettoyage *(m.) cleaning (action)*
nettoyer *to clean*
niveau *(m.) level/standard (of living)*
noir *black*
nom *(m.) name/surname*
nombre *(m.) number*
nu *bare/naked*
nuisible *noxious/harmful*
numéraires *(m. pl.) cash*
numéro *(m.) number*

obligatoire *compulsory*
obtenir (obtenu) *to obtain*
obus *(m.) shell (munitions)*
occasion *(f.) occasion/opportunity*
occuper *to occupy*
occuper *(refl.) to busy oneself*
œil *(m.) eye*
offrir (offert) *to offer*
oiseau *(m.) bird*
opérer *to operate/act*
opportunité *(f.) opportunity*
orage *(m.) thunderstorm*
ordinateur *(m.) computer*
ordre *(m.) order*
originaire *(adj.) native*
où *where*
oublier *to forget*
ouest *(m.) west*
ouverture *(f.) opening*
ouvrir (ouvert) *to open*

paiement *(m.) payment*
pain *(m.) bread*
pair *(m. n./adj.) peer/even (numbers)*
panne *(f.) breakdown (mechanical)*
papa *(m.) dad/father*
Pâques *(f. pl.) Easter*
par contre *by contrast*
par rapport à *in relation to*
parapluie *(m.) umbrella*
parent *(m.) parent/relative*
parfaire (parfait) *to perfect*
parfait *perfect*
parfois *sometimes*
parlement *(m.) parliament*
parole *(f.) word/speech*
part *(f.) part/share*
partager *to share*
partenaire *(m./f.) partner*
partir *to go/leave (a place)*
partout *everywhere*
pas du tout *not at all*
pas mal *(fam.) not bad/a few*
passer *to go by/spend/pass*
passionner *to thrill*
pâtisserie *(f.) confectioner's shop*
pâtissier *(m.) confectioner*
payer *to pay*
pays *(m.) country*
paysage *(m.) landscape*
paysan *(m.) peasant/farmer*
peine *(f.) pain*
perdre (perdu) *to lose*
perdre *(refl.) to lose one's way*
père *(m.) father*
perfectionner *to improve/perfect*
périmé *(adj.) out of date/expired*
période *(f.) period*
périr *to perish*
personne *(f.) person*
personnel *(adj.) personal*
personnel *(m.) personnel/ workforce*
persuader *to persuade*
petit *small*
pétrole *(m.) crude oil*
peu *little/not much*

pièce *(f.) piece/document/coin/room*
pied *(m.) foot*
pierre *(f.) stone*
piscine *(f.) swimming pool*
place *(f.) place/spot*
placer *to place/to position*
plage *(f.) beach*
plaindre *(refl.) to complain*
plaire (plu) *to please*
plaisir *(m.) pleasure*
plein *full*
plein *(m.) full complement*
pleurer *to cry*
pleuvoir (plu) *to rain*
pluie *(f.) rain*
plus *more/no more/no longer*
plusieurs *several*
politique *(adj.) political*
politique *(f.) politics*
populaire *popular*
portable *(adj./n.) mobile (phone)/portable*
porter *to carry*
porteur *buoyant (market)*
poser *to pose/put down*
poste *(f.) post office*
poste *(m.) post/occupation*
pour *for*
pourquoi *why*
poursuivre (poursuivi) *to pursue*
pouvoir *(m.) power*
pouvoir (pu) *to be able to/can*
précédent *previous*
préférer *to prefer*
premier *first*
prendre (pris) *to take*
prénom *(m.) first name*
préparatif *(m.) preparatory item*
présenter *(refl.) to introduce oneself*
pressé *in a hurry/pressed*
presser *to press*
pression *(f.) pressure*
prestation *(f.) allowance*
prêter *to lend*
preuve *(f.) proof*
prévenir (prevenu) *to warn*
prier *to pray/beg*
primaire *primary*
primaire *(m.) primary (school)*
principe *(m.) principle*
printemps *(m.) spring*
prix *(m.) price*
prochain *next*
productivité *(f.) productivity*
produire (produit) *to produce*
produit *(m.) product*
professeur *(m.) teacher/professor*
profond *deep/profound*
profondément *deeply*
progrès *(m.) progress*
propre *own/proper/clean*
propriétaire *(m./f.) owner*
propriété *(f.) property/estate*
prospérer *to thrive*
protéger *to protect*
protestation *(f.) protest*
province *(f.) province*
prune *(f.) plum*
puis *then (afterwards)*
puissant *powerful*
punir *to punish*

que *that/which*
quelquefois *sometimes*
qui *who/whom*
quittance *(f.) proof of payment*

quitter *to leave (place/person)*
quoi *what*

racine *(f.) root*
raison *(f.) reason*
raisonnable *reasonable*
ramasser *to pick up/collect*
rapide *quick/fast*
rater *to miss (opportunity)*
rationnel *rational*
rationnellement *rationally*
rayer *to cross out*
récemment *recently*
récent *recent*
recevoir (reçu) *to receive*
réchauffer *to reheat/to warm up*
réchauffer *(refl.) to warm (oneself) up*
recherche *(f.) search/act of seeking*
réclamation *(f.) complaint*
récolter *to harvest/gather*
recommandé *(adj.) sent recorded delivery*
recommander *to recommend*
redoubler *to repeat (e.g. a school year)*
réel *real*
réfléchir *to reflect*
regard *(m.) look*
regarder *to look*
règlement *(m.) regulations/rules*
régler *to settle/pay*
régression *(f.) regression/decline*
régulier *regular*
relever *to increase (salary)*
rembourser *to reimburse/pay back*
remercier *to thank*
remise *(f.) discount*
remords *(m.) remorse*
remplacer *to replace*
remplir (rempli) *to fill in*
rencontrer *to meet*
rendre compte *(refl.) to realize*
renommée *(f.) fame/renown*
renouveler *to renew*
renouvellement *(m.) renewal/renewing*
rénover *to renovate/do up*
renseignement *(m.) information*
rentrer *to go back in/to get home*
repartir *to go back again*
répartir *to spread/distribute*
répéter *to repeat*
replacer *to put back*
reprendre (repris) *to retake/take back*
représentant *(m.) representative*
représentatif *(adj.) representative*
représenter *to represent*
représenter *(refl.) to attend again/to resit (exam)*
requis *requested/required*
réserver *to set aside/reserve*
résoudre *to solve*
respectueux *respectful*
responsable *(n./adj.) responsible/in charge*
reste *(m.) rest/remainder*
rester *to stay/remain*
résultat *(m.) result*
retour *(m.) return*
retraite *(f.) retreat/retirement*
retraité *(adj./n.) retired (person)*
réunion *(f.) meeting/reunion*
réunir *to gather*
réunir *(refl.) to get together/meet*
réussir *to succeed*

revaloriser *to revalue/upgrade*
revenir (revenu) *to come back/to get back*
revenu *(m.) income/salary*
revoir (revu) *to see again*
riche *rich*
richesse *(f.) wealth*
rien *nothing*
ringard *(fam.) old fashioned*
rivière *(f.) river (small)*
rue *(f.) street*

sac *(m.) bag*
sain *healthy*
saisir *to seize*
salaire *(m.) salary*
sale *dirty*
salir *to dirty*
salle *(f.) room*
salle d'eau *(f.) washroom*
sans *without*
sans cesse *continually*
sans doute *doubtless*
sans-travail *(m./adj.) unemployed*
santé *(f.) health*
satisfaire (satisfait) *to satisfy*
sauf *except*
savoir (su) *to know*
scolarité *(f.) schooling*
sec *dry*
secondaire *(adj./n.) secondary*
seconde *(f.) second (division of time)*
secteur *(m.) sector*
sécurité *(f.) security*
sein *(m.) breast/bosom*
séjour *(m.) stay*
selon *according to*
semaine *(f.) week*
sentiment *(m.) feeling*
séparer *to separate*
septembre *(m.) September*
sérieux *serious*
serviette *(f.) briefcase/serviette/towel/napkin*
servir *to serve*
seuil *(m.) threshold*
seulement *only*
si *if/whether/yes (emphatic)*
significatif *significant*
situer *to situate*
société *(f.) society/firm*
soigner *to care for/cure*
soin *(m.) care*
soir *(m.) evening*
sol *(m.) soil/ground*
solliciter *to request/solicit*
somme *(f.) sum/total*
sonner *to ring (of bell)*
sortir *to go out*
souci *(m.) care*
soutien *(m.) support*
souvent *often*
sportif *(adj.) sports*
stage *(m.) placement/stay*
strict *strict/severe*
sucre *(m.) sugar*
sud *(m.) south*
suite à *following*
suivre (suivi) *to follow*
support *(m.) support/assistance*
supportable *bearable*
supporter *to bear/support*
sûreté *(f.) safety*
surface *(f.) area/surface*
surpris *surprised*
susceptible de *likely to*
sympathie *(f.) sympathy*
syndicat *(m.) trade union*

tard *late*
tasse *(f.) cup*
taux *(m.) rate*
taxe *(f.) tax*

temps *(m.) time/weather*
tendre à *to tend to*
tenir (tenu) *to hold/keep (promise)*
tenter *to try/attempt*
terminer *to end/finish*
tertiaire *tertiary*
tête *(f.) head*
timbre *(m.) (postage) stamp*
tomber *to fall*
toujours *always/still*
tout *everything*
traditionnel *traditional*
traduction *(f.) translation*
traîner *to lag behind/drag*
tranquille *calm/quiet*
tranquilliser *to calm (somebody/ something) down*
travail *(m.) work/employment*
travailler *to work*
travailleur *(m.) worker*
trembler *to tremble/shake*
trésor *(m.) treasure*
trop *too*
trouver *to find*
truc *(m. fam.) thingy*
truffe *(f.) truffle*
tuer *to kill*
tuteur *(m.) tutor*
type *(m.) type/sort/bloke/guy (sl.)*

ultérieur *later/ulterior*
un peu *a little*
union *(f.) union*
unique *unique/only (child)*
usine *(f.) factory*
usuel *usual/habitual*
utile *useful*
utilité *(f.) usefulness*

vacances *(f. pl.) holidays*
vacant *unoccupied/empty*
vaguement *vaguely*
valise *(f.) suitcase*
variété *(f.) variety*
vase *(f.) silt/mud*
vase *(m.) vase*
vedette *(f.) celebrity*
vendre (vendu) *to sell*
vendredi *(m.) Friday*
venir (venu) *to come*
vent *(m.) wind*
ventre *(m.) belly/stomach*
verglas *(m.) (black) ice*
vérifier *to check*
vert *green*
veste *(f.) jacket*
veuf, veuve *(adj./n.) widowed*
vie *(f.) life*
vieux *old*
vigne *(f.) vineyard*
villa *(f.) villa/bungalow*
village *(m.) village*
vin *(m.) wine*
visiter *to visit*
vivant *alive/living*
vivre (vécu) *to live*
voir (vu) *to see*
voisin *(n./adj.) neighbour*
volant *(m.) steering wheel*
voler *to fly/steal*
vouloir (voulu) *to want*
vous *you/to you*
vrai *true*

xénophobe *xenophobic*

yeux *(m. pl.) eyes*

Index of language points

Number-only references are to units and sections: '1/3.1', for example, means 'Unit 1, Section 3.1'. 'LLT' stands for 'Language learning tip', so 'LLT 3/2' means 'Unit 3, Language learning tip 2'. 'Act.' stands for 'Activity', so 'Act. 3/11' means 'Unit 3, Activity 11'.

Photo credits

Front cover: FoodCollection/Photolibrary.com

Back cover and pack: © Jakub Semeniuk/iStockphoto.com, © Royalty-Free/Corbis, © agencyby/iStockphoto.com, © Andy Cook/iStockphoto.com, © Christopher Ewing/iStockphoto.com, © zebicho – Fotolia.com, © Geoffrey Holman/iStockphoto.com, © Photodisc/Getty Images, © James C. Pruitt/iStockphoto.com, © Mohamed Saber – Fotolia.com

Pack: © Stockbyte/Getty Images